THE GEMINI PLOT

By the same author

NINETY FEET TO THE SUN
ATLANTIC ENCOUNTER

THE GEMINI PLOT
A Submarine Novel of World War II

Eric J. Collenette

Walker and Company
New York

OZ Edition
Copyright © 1985 Eric J. Collenette

First published in the United States of America in 1986 by the Walker Publishing Company, Inc.

Published simultaneously in Canada by John Wiley & Sons Canada, Limited, Rexdale, Ontario.

Library of Congress Cataloging-in-Publication Data

Collenette, Eric J.
  The Gemini plot.

  Sequel to: Ninety feet to the sun.
  1. World War, 1939–1945—Fiction. 2. Great Britain—History, Naval—20th century—Fiction. I. Collenette, Eric J. Ninety feet to the sun. II. Title.
PR6053.04236G4 1986   823'.914   86-18896

Printed in the United States of America

10 9 8 7 6 5 4 3 2 1
ISBN: 0-8027-0930-3

Under the water it rumbled on
Still louder and more dread:
It reach'd the ship, it split the bay:
The ship went down like lead.
> *Samuel Taylor Coleridge.   1771–1834*
> *The Rime of the Ancient Mariner*

I

The Solent stretches olive-green with flecks of white horses scuffed up by a blustery south wind on this fine June day. I stride towards HMS Dolphin, feeling well satisfied, in keeping with the weather. I have had my survivor's leave, and managed to dissuade the medics from sending me to general service to recover from swallowing half the North Sea, after escaping from a sunken S-boat. They have relented, recommending that I stay in submarines, albeit with a month or so on light duty — nothing could suit me better.

The AB on sentry duty at the gate studies my paybook, raising an eyebrow at the grizzled photograph that stares back at him. He hands it back with a look that says quite plainly, 'Christ! That was taken some time ago!' 'Okay, chief — thanks,' he says, opening the gate for me to walk through.

I square up to him. 'Next time I see you with your cap tally tied over your bloody nose I'll run you in. It doesn't make you "Barnacle Bill", you know. Get it over your left ear, and stop acting like an OD.'

I leave him making faces at my back. What did the doctor say? I am too brittle? So what! Coxswains have brittleness built into them; it's part of their make-up. Why should I be different?

The drafting office is dusty, looking like something out of Charles Dickens. Bored WREN writers mingle with their male counterparts, attending to a procession of matelots who come in to wave draft-chits at them. I am offered a slip of paper, and when I read the order I grit my teeth, then go straight to the end of the counter.

'Someone has made a cock-up, Maisie.'

The Leading WREN's face is blank as she lifts her doleful eyes to focus on mine. She is the nearest human resemblance to a border collie I have ever seen. 'Oh aye.'

'I'm supposed to have a spell on light duty.'

Wearily she fishes out some forms and prods at the wording with a bright red nail. 'That's right: you've got until two o'clock today. Here it is: fourteen hundred hours you report to the tank for your regular DSEA drill. Tomorrow you catch your train for 'Guz' to join HM Submarine *Avon*.'

'No, Maisie: I'm due for some shore time – it's laid down in KRs and AIs, gel. The moment you get your feet wet you're entitled to survivor's leave and a spell ashore. It's bin like that since Moses came down the mountain.'

She looks from my face to the form, and back again. 'I expect they'll send you on leave from there. I heard a buzz that the *Avon*'s in dry-dock.'

'Maisie,' I protest, 'the quack says I'm in need of a break.'

'Sorry, Ben: I only do as I'm told.'

'Wish you'd remember that next time I get you behind the NAAFI.'

She grins and loosens up. 'Just think of all that scrumpy.'

*

Going through the tank is nothing new to me, and I sit through the preliminary lecture without taking too much interest – after all it isn't all that long ago since I was giving the lectures myself. In no time I'm kitted up in swimming trunks and wearing goggles as I strap on the yellow Davies escape gear, before testing the valve on the oxygen cylinder. I'm paired up with another chief, to stand like two sallow-skinned Martians while we wait our turn to enter the mock-up of a conning-tower. I am to be number one, so I climb up to the top of the ladder and bend my head under the upper hatch as I wait for my companion to clamber in after me and shut the lower hatch. There is a moment's pause while he turns the valve to allow water to flood in until it rises to my shoulders and stops, with an air-lock in the top of the tower. Now it is my turn and I reach up to pull down on a small lever, allowing the trapped air to escape, so that the tower can flood up completely. One by one I release the two hatch-clips, and hold on to the ladder as it springs open.

'A perfect drill,' I'm thinking to myself, and swim out to lie on my back, relishing the warm water and the sunlight streaming through the windows. This is as close as they can get to a real escape — and it is pathetic.

'Right, chief. You can fucking-well go back and do it all again. This time make sure your relief valve is open. If you had come out of a real boat at any depth your lungs would be the size of the Graf Zeppelin by now.'

Shamefaced I return to the tower and pair up with a young new-entry who beams at my discomfort, and displays an air of superiority that sets my teeth grinding. He carries out the drill meticulously, and I am relegated to number two position, with my face inches away from his cherubic backside. This time I follow the drill and float out with him.

If he knows my rank he makes no concession as he spits out his mouthpiece and grins at me. 'There you are, mate. Nothin' to it really. Just follow old Soapy and you can't go wrong.'

'Piss off!'

The smile fades and he swims off disconsolately. I drag myself out of the water in a grey mood. What do they know of it? I've been there and won through. I know the numbing cold: the hot feeling of panic, and the animal passion that boils in a man when he competes for survival. There is no drill that can give a man the will to turn back to help his mates, or take his time when every nerve says 'swim away and save yourself'. I hope Soapy never finds out the truth and that innocent grin is changed to a bestial snarl in a fight to win a mad scramble to reach God-given light and air.

*

I decide to trudge along to a small pub just far enough out of Gosport to escape the air-raids. It is run by a buxom blonde called Wendy, who always manages to rustle up a meal of sorts, despite rationing. My usual routine is to gorge myself and snuggle into a corner near the fire, to swop yarns with the locals, most of whom are ex-matelots with memories of the first world war, Spithead reviews, regattas, and a Navy with bright brass-work and bunting — not the sombre, grey fleet of tired ships that creep in and out of Portsmouth now. The talk brings back warm memories, and a man can put up with the watery beer in such company.

The place is cosy, with the smell of polished leather and ale. Wendy greets me with a huge smile and we bandy words as her husband stares at us from a photograph standing on the piano. He is a marine on the KGV: most likely swinging round a buoy in Scapa Flow. I've never met him, but he looks a nice fellow, who wears his uniform in a way that shows it is only for as long as it takes to get the bloody war over, then it will be unceremoniously bundled up and slung into the nearest dustbin. Not like me: my uniform fits like a second skin, and armchairs and fireplaces are just visions of a distant future.

'So they let you out, Ben?' she grins. 'Officially sane then, are you?'

'Somethin' like that. Looks as though I'm going back to the war. I've tried chewing the quack's stethoscope and piddling in his inkwell, but he ain't having any of it. He reckons I'm as sane as the rest of the mad bastards who go to sea in tin cans.'

She laughs and pulls a frothy pint for me. I look at the weak mixture and decide to press my luck. 'Have you anything stronger, Wendy? I've had a terrible shock to the system: a nice drop of the hard stuff will go down nicely.'

The grin fades for a moment, and I feel I have asked too much. Then, without a word, she disappears for a moment through a back door, to return carrying a half bottle of Bells. I gasp, 'Where have you been hiding that?'

'Tell you the truth, Ben,' she says soberly, 'I've been keeping this to celebrate the end of it all, but right now the end seems so far away: each time I look at it I get more despondent. Harry's a long way away now, but you're both fighting the same rotten war, and you've had a hard time − so I reckon you're entitled.'

I look from the bottle to her face. Something in her eyes goes deeper than I've seen before and a surge of warmth floods my innards. I feel a kind of guilt as I taste the fiery liquid, while she watches closely as I knock it back. Without speaking she tops my glass again, and I drink it more slowly this time, savouring every sip. We stand with a secret growing between us − a mutual understanding for the pain we feel. She for the long years that stretch ahead — me for the memory of dead shipmates and the sour stench of a sunken boat.

Later that night when the last local has left, we sit together with the flickering flames etching lines in our faces as we stare into the fire, our conversation soft and domestic. Sometime, with the bottle empty and the door locked, our hands come together. The suffering wells up to fill her eyes as she leans her head on my shoulder. I place an arm about her, and feel the swell of a soft breast against me as I kiss away a salty tear. She turns to me, bringing her lips to mine in a hungry, trembling kiss, and I respond with a devouring hunger of my own.

We clutch at each other, and I search for the moist centre of her: coaxing her into writhing movements until there is nothing but a clumsy struggle to remove the last obstacles that keep us apart. I thrust deep into her as she grips me hard with panting, whimpering undulations, until I groan and sob with the final surge that sucks out my soul.

'Oh, Ben!'

'Yeah — I know.'

'Oh, Ben! I never thought I would,' she sobs.

We pull apart, and turn away to tidy ourselves. There are no words; we've broken the rules, and there is no use feeling guilty or finding excuses. We don't even say goodnight when I go out into the blackout. Stuff the war! It makes animals out of all of us.

*

It is a God-awful journey, with numerous stops at remote stations and sidings, to wait while troop trains and essential goods trains thunder by. The connections at Southampton and Salisbury are all to hell, and it is dark when the train comes to a halt in the middle of nowhere, while Goering's demolition experts bomb the blazes out of Plymouth. When we finally pull into the terminus I heave my stiff bones out of the corner seat and drag my kit out onto the platform before standing for a moment to get my bearings.

A heavy kit-bag hits me right between the shoulders, and I am hurled to the deck. Before I can recover and scramble upright a hammock lands on me, and I am flattened once more.

On the brink of exploding, I sort myself out, and leap up to do battle with the perpetrator of these indignities; to find myself face to face with Soapy.

'Sorry, chief,' he says brightly, 'didn't see you there. 'Ere, I'll give yer a hand.' He reaches for my kitbag.

'Get your hands off that!' I roar. 'Stay away from me.'

Our gear is mixed up, and as I sort out mine I read a label on his, and it says, 'HMS *Avon*, Devonport.' 'You write that?' I ask.

'Yeah,' he says proudly.

'Why didn't you write a personal letter to Hitler and tell him where you were going?'

'Eh?'

'Haven't you heard of careless talk? The government spends thousands painting out signposts and taking down station notices, and you come along with an address on your kit-bag.' I'm enjoying this; it makes up in some way for the escape tank. 'You're gonna buck your ideas up, laddie, if you're going to the *Avon* − I'm your new coxswain. You must learn to think before you act.'

I pick up my gear and start off towards the exit.

''Swain!''

I ignore him and stride on. There's a couple of thirty-hundredweight naval trucks sitting there, and I'm betting that at least one will be going to Devonport.

''Swain!'' He is chasing after me, but I'm not in the mood to bandy words. If he wants to speak to me, he will have to do it on the boat. I am right about the trucks; they are both going to the dockyard, and I pile my gear into the back of one of them. Before I have time to get in beside the driver Soapy is tugging at my sleeve urgently. I am outraged. 'You can use the other truck, lad. You can't go round assaulting CPOs. Watch your step or I'll run you in.'

He is wringing his hands when I drive off. The city is in a mess and we dodge through heaps of smoking rubble, where dark figures are searching for survivors. It has been a small raid; nothing like the ones that came in 1941 to flatten the heart of the shopping centre; but it is enough for me.

The driver takes me right to the dockyard, and I unload my kit. Out of the corner of my eye I see Soapy's truck sweep by. It looks like he has got a lift right to the boat; lucky bastard. I start to gather my gear together for the final haul, and stare at the label on the kitbag. 'S. Opie, HMS *Avon*,' it reads in scrawly writing.

II

These Thames class boats are monsters. Someone had the bright idea that submarines should operate with the Fleet, so they designed a follow-up to the old steam-driven K-boats. Twenty-two knots on the surface with plenty of comfort is all that can be said for them: for they cost half a million to build, and they are too big for the type of job we do. Over two thousand tons and one hundred and forty five feet long, they are slow to dive, and much too easy to spot from the air.

I find the *Avon* in a state of chaos, with every spare inch of space crammed with cargo — even to the extent of laying out false decks in the passages. We are allowed only the minimum steaming gear and told that the rest of our kit will follow on, to be reclaimed at a destination which is still secret. The big submarine is engaged in the one job that suits her bulk — blockade running. My guess is that we are on our way to Malta.

Even as the sky floods red from the east and the sea begins to lose its battleship grey to turn green we nose out of the Sound in company with two destroyers. There is time for but a brief interview with her First Lieutenant: a square, dark, blue-jowled bloke called Murray who apologises for the rush, promising a longer talk when things settle down. Meanwhile he is glad to have me on board, and assures me that my predecessor loaded all the victuals required for the trip.

Once clear of the land the two destroyers flash a fond farewell, squat their backsides down, to go haring off in a welter of foam. I ease the spokes of the bridge wheel to hold a steady course south, while Tubby Fenton, our skipper, casts a last look about the scene before ordering everyone below.

By the time I reach the control-room the crew are at diving-stations, and I take my place at the after hydroplanes. We are to submerge in slow time today without the klaxon. The boat is overloaded, and although Murray has done his sums we will not know for sure how she swims until we have carried out a trim-dive. She has to be turned broadside to a long swell coming in from the south-west, because a stern sea tends to lift our tail, while a head sea will hold the bow up to make diving difficult — even dangerous.

As the diesels choke to a stop and the electric motors take over she begins to roll heavily. I hold on tight to the metal wheel of the after 'planes to keep from falling backwards from the stool, while Petty Officer Briarley, the second coxswain, hisses through his teeth as he does the same. The bridge voice-pipe is cut off and I can hear the clamps going on the upper hatch.

'One clip on,' announces the signalman, looking up the conning-tower. 'Two clips on.'

We are water-tight. The roll becomes even more ridiculous, for the cargo is making nonsense of our stability. A clattering from forward causes Murray to curse, threatening retribution for the person responsible for stowing the crates in the fore-ends. The skipper chooses to ignore our discomfort and floods main ballast in stages until we are wallowing like an ageing hippo. Satisfied, he orders, 'Flood main ballast!'

The ERA on the diving panel reaches to operate the last few levers to destroy our positive buoyancy. He manages only one before a violent roll sends him sprawling across the control-room to crash into the helmsman in a tangled heap of arms and legs.

The bubble in the spirit-level in front of me slides aft as the bows sink and the needles in the shallow-water gauges revolve round the dials. Briarley sucks his teeth as he grips hard on the wheel. He is a sallow-faced man with deep lines etched into his features. I have only spoken briefly to him, but it is enough to realise that he has a chip on his shoulder and resents my presence in the boat. He feels the coxswain's job should have been his when it became vacant.

Now the angle is getting out of hand and I begin to slide forward on my stool. Sweat breaks out on my forehead, although my body feels icy cold. There is a sound in my ears like rushing water and I stare into the blank face of the dial, fascinated by the needles sweeping past the numbers. A hand reaches across my shoulder to shut off the shallow gauge, and I automatically switch my attention to the smaller dial of the deep-water gauge.

My mouth is dry and my fingers grip the brass rim of the wheel to hold it firmly in the 'midships' position. My brain is numb and my stomach knotted. Briarley has spun his 'planes to 'hard rise' and looks to me to follow suit. His eyes burn into me, but I cannot move. The noise is loud in my ears. It fills the air about me and the shiny metal of the instruments flashes cruelly in my eyes.

'Blow main ballast.'

The voice drives into my head and forces away the turbulence. The roar of high-pressure air expanding in the tanks calms me, and I take hold of myself. The angle is off, with the needles sweeping anti-clockwise as we swim towards the surface. The skipper floods up again as we settle on ninety feet, while Murray juggles with the trim tanks. I am automatically adjusting the after 'planes with practised ease, and we go to patrol routine.

The one non-essential item of kit I have brought is a small bottle of neat rum, put by for just such an occasion as this. Keeping my back turned to my colleagues, I drink it dry in one gulp, as my hands shake uncontrollably. It has been a long day, and my body is drained as I accept a plate of supper that tastes like rubber, while I stay on the diving-stations in sombre mood, when we surface for the night.

Later, in my bunk, I will myself to sleep, while the sound of the sea reverberates on the pressure hull, inches from my head. There is a sickness in me that no medicine can cure, and my body is weighed down with a burden I feel unable to bear. I hear every watch change throughout the night, and, after we dive before dawn, I am summoned to the wardroom.

Murray has persuaded the other officers to leave, so that we have the place to ourselves. He invites me to squeeze into the bench opposite, and looks at me keenly, with deep-set eyes that peer from beneath heavy brows. There are creases in his forehead, while his square face registers concern. There is no fight left in me, and I am prepared to swallow everything he can throw at me, without retaliation; just so long as someone else knows what a bloody nightmare it all is. My guts are in a knot, and I no longer trust myself.

'We have a problem, 'swain,' he says calmly, 'and I must admit that I am not sure how best to deal with it.'

'No problem,' I think to myself, 'just pack me off home from Gib. I'm no bloody use here; and a danger to all my shipmates – much better tucked out of the way.' I say nothing, and wait for him to make the running.

'It's been with us for some time, and something must be done, before the whole crew is affected.'

'Too true! – get rid quick – that's the answer. No point in arsing about.'

He leans back and purses his lips. 'I'm no psychologist, and I don't pretend to know much about these things; so I'm looking to you to come up with some bright ideas of your own, if you can.'

I am speechless. I can't believe I am hearing right. Talk about 'physician heal thyself'. I can only sit with my mouth gaping like a hungry goldfish.

'It's difficult, I know,' he goes on, 'but you live amongst the men more than I do, and you must come up against this sort of thing often. The crew is heartily sick of his silence, and his morose behaviour. Newly married or not; he has got to be brought back to the fold. I don't want to launch you into the deep end, Grant; but having read reports of some of your escapades in Norway, I have no doubt you will do the right thing. Oh, and there is one other thing: the captain has asked me to congratulate you on your actions yesterday – it took a lot of nerve, and fore-thought to hold the after 'planes in the horizontal until the stern was well submerged as you did, and your timing was perfect – well done.'

I am drained. I don't know where I am now. 'Thank you, sir,' I mumble, and half rise to leave now that I am obviously dismissed. I can't leave it there though, and I brace up to him. 'Er – there is just one thing, sir.'

He smiles. 'Yes?'

'Who are we talking about?'

The smile freezes. 'Bloody hell, Grant. What the dickens do you think I have been talking about all this time? You led me to believe that you know all about Miller.' His face is a sort of deep purple. 'I've been rambling on and you haven't a clue. I'm not going through it all again; talk to Briarley — Miller is his "dickie" and he must know the score. Honestly, Grant, I don't expect my coxswain to play these sort of games. Away you go; and pull your finger out, for God's sake!'

I slope off to find Briarley who is about as forthcoming as a broody hen. His attitude is that a rating's life is private, and if Miller wants to move about the boat like a zombie and treat his mates like they have leprosy, it's his affair. Provided he carries out his duties, we have no right to interfere.

It isn't as easy as that however. Once the crew find out I am charged with doing something about the situation a small delegation arrives at the chief's mess, and the whole sorry story unfolds in my lap. Miller is twenty years old, an AB and married for only three months. During which time he has become over-domesticated and lost all interest in war and submarines. He does as much as he is required to do with reluctance, and moons about the boat like a moron. Every effort to shake him out of his despondency has failed. He is having a bad effect on his mates, and it falls to me to do something about it. In my own ingenious way, I take the bull by the horns, and make a complete balls of it.

III

Standing on the steel casing I can feel the hot Gibraltar sun burning through my shirt, and a trickle of sweat courses down my spine. Just above my head a torpedo swings on the hook of a dock crane as the torpedomen guide it down until the runners each side of the bellyband rest on the loading rails that lead down through the fore-hatch, into the gloom of the stowage compartment. The TI is replacing two of his charges, standing at my side, staring with a bored expression, having seen it all so many times before. His lads are trained to a degree whereby they have no need of guidance from him, and there is time to gaze round at the massive might of the Fleet lying there. Huge battlewagons, cruisers, and an aircraft carrier line the outer wall of the harbour, while a host of smaller ships crowd the docks and anchorage — grim reminders of the serious situation in the Mediterranean.

'It ain't gonna be Malta this time,' muses the TI, as though he is talking to his torpedo as it is nursed down through the hatch by his minions.

'You don't reckon?'

'Naw,' he states firmly, staring into the distance, 'a couple of the boxes burst open when we were rollin' our guts out off Plymouth, and the bits and pieces that spilled out were tank parts; and they don't want those in Malta. That new stoker Soapy reckons we are off to Tobruk.'

'What's he know about tank parts?'

'His old man works in a factory where they make 'em. Seems he has brought a few samples home.'

'That figures — knowing Soapy. I hope he kept his mouth shut.'

'He will now.' I look at the set features, and feel a certain sympathy for Soapy. 'Anyone else see it?'

'Half the torpedomen; it happened in the fore-ends – you don't keep something like that hidden for long.'

'Bloody hell! and I sent Miller ashore.' I bristle at the thought of the AB spreading talk about what he has seen. Everybody knows that the enemy watches and listens to everything that goes on in this neck of the woods, before passing it to the Spanish mainland. Every movement of every ship is noted, and any loose talk about the possible destination of a submarine will be pounced on eagerly.

'Silly little sod!' growls the TI. 'Trouble with these kids; they get married when they're still wet behind the ears – it's a licence to dip their wicks on a regular basis, and put their feet up on the mantelpiece.'

'You're a cynical bastard.'

'No, I'm not: I went through it all when I was a lad, mate. Got spliced, and shagged me lugs off for a month; then got sent off to the Med for two and a half years – I was amazed when she got put in the spud-line by the insurance man.'

'Think I did right?'

He looks at me and grins. 'You're the coxswain, mate. Me, I'd 'ave let him stew in his own juice, and hope that his mates would sort him out.'

We go silent as the tail of the torpedo disappears, and I try to shrug it off, as we dismantle the rails, so that my own supplies of fruit can be brought aboard. The nagging doubts persist though, and I wonder what a lad in his frame of mind will do. The last look of outrage and anger I received from him didn't reassure me, and I envisage him somewhere on the rock, wandering about like a lost weekend, getting in with all kinds of dubious company. Perhaps he is even looking across to Spain, considering the possibility of getting over the border, free from the clutches of the Navy. As fast as it comes I dismiss the idea. Miller has little imagination, and it is much more likely that he is sat in the corner of a bar wallowing in self-pity.

My thoughts are interrupted by a call to report to Murray, and I descend to find him standing in the fore-ends watching the last torpedo being inserted into its tube. The place looks like a grotto in some weird Wagnerian saga, with gear hanging from the deckhead like stalactites, while gnome-like shapes move about their duties in sweaty silence. The first lieutenant stands to one side of the ladder, looking resigned to the chaos about him and leaving the running of it all to the TI. Now and again the silence is broken by a well-directed torrent of choice phrases to spur them on with insults and obscenities born of a colourful mind.

I stand beside Murray for a moment, watching with him, and wondering if things will ever come back to order. We are due to sail at nightfall and it seems impossible that all will be in order by then. The whole boat is in a state of disruption as electricians lift deckboards to test the density of batteries. Briarley and his men work on a slack periscope wire, and in the engine-room the guts of a ballast pump lie in an oily mess on someone's discarded vest. Deep down I know it will happen; it always does.

There is small chance of holding any sort of conversation in this bustling hive of industry, so by mutual consent we climb out of the hatch into the sunshine and go aft to the gun platform.

'Miller has not returned from shore yet, coxswain,' he says, coming straight to the point.

'No, sir.'

'His leave expired half an hour ago and the boat is under sailing orders. He could be in serious trouble.'

'Yes, sir.' He doesn't have to remind me that overstaying leave when the boat is due to sail is almost as serious as desertion. If the stupid sod doesn't come back soon he will be in it right up to his scrawny neck, and I have a feeling that most of the blame will fall squarely on me.

'I think you had better go on shore and see if you can find him, and bring him back.'

I stare at the mass of buildings climbing away from the harbour. 'I wouldn't know where to start, sir.'

'That is your problem,' he replies coldly. 'After all, you sent him; you must have some idea what you thought he would do.'

'Sir, there's a couple of thousand matelots on each of those battle-wagons alone. It's a big haystack and a very small needle: I won't stand a chance.'

'I don't intend to stand and argue with you, Grant. You have until nineteen hundred hours to get him back. It was a stupid mistake to send him ashore – especially without consulting me.'

'Aye, aye, sir.' Fuming, I set my cap on firmly and stride over the gangway, with no attempt to hide my disgust. My anger stays with me until I am walking through Alemena Gardens. I aim for Main Street, merging with a busy throng of chattering humanity. Shops brim over with colourful souvenirs and goodies for sailors to take back home. It won't occur to most of them that they have convoyed much of it out from the UK just for the pleasure of taking it back again.

My eyes pick out every white-clad figure hoping to recognise the squat shape of Miller, but it is a pretty hopeless task. All I can think to do is visit a small café where the proprietor is an ex-submariner, and where we tend to congregate when on shore. I have doubts in Miller's case though, for this is his first visit to Gibraltar. He is more likely caught up in the centre of activity, far away from this quiet little alley.

The place looks neat and tidy with all the tables set ready for the evening trade. It is familiar ground to me and I go straight to my favourite chair, close to the window, to wait for the owner who comes through a beaded curtain that divides restaurant from kitchen.

This bloke was designed with a compass, for everything about him is circular. Eyes, face, body — they all have a global look about them, and there are always beads of sweat trickling down his face while his pudgy arms and legs pump away busily all the time he attends to his clients needs. His features erupt into a huge grin when he sees me sitting there, and it widens even more when I explain the reason for my run ashore. Soon his mouth is a chasm and his eyes squeezed shut as a gurgling, chortling sound emanates from his nether regions, and his big belly quivers with merriment.

'Aye, lad; I know where he is — and I ain't surprised 'e ain't come back yet. Real baby-faced 'e was, and taken in tow by a big motherly type when she found him sittin' 'ere all forlorn, and looking like a spare prick at a wedding. Poor little sod never 'ad a chance. Last I saw was 'im follering 'er like a little doggy; before 'e knew what time of day it was.'

'Where is he now?'

'I'll show you.' With great effort he waddles to the door. The way his breath wheezes shows that he isn't used to venturing far from his kitchen; and that ties in with the pallid hue of his skin in a place where most people are tanned to the colour of mahogany.

He leads me to the bottom of a steep alleyway that climbs up between blank walls, with an occasional door giving evidence of habitation on the other side.

'Third door on the right,' he gasps. 'Just walk through — everybody does.' He leans closer and leers at me with an evil smile. 'Don't be surprised at what you see.'

With that warning echoing in my brain, I leave him to struggle back to his cafe, and I begin to climb the cobbled steps to a faded, green door. At a touch it swings open, and I go through into a stone-floored room, devoid of any furnishings other than a stone sink fastened to one wall, with an evil-smelling drain beneath. There is another door gaping in front of me, and I enter an inner sanctum that boasts a ragged carpet with the remains of a bullfight showing bleakly through a haze of dirt and frayed weaving. Two religious pictures hang dejectedly on one wall in a vain effort to inject a note of sobriety into the sour surroundings, and a kind of bench seat runs round the perimeter of the room with horsehair showing through splits in the upholstery. It is like the waiting-room of a very seedy doctor's surgery.

A sound leads me through a third door, and I am in a passageway with heavy curtains hanging on either side. Realisation begins to dawn. I have seen establishments like this in Hong Kong, Singapore and Alex, catering for the sexual appetites of sailors, but I had no idea they existed in Gibraltar. Before the war, if you were that way inclined, you went across to La Linea or Algeciras.

I am aware of sounds coming from behind those curtains; it is as though half a dozen all-in wrestlers are going berserk just out of sight. Without thinking I drag aside one of the curtains, and I am rewarded with the repugnant sight of a pale, undulating backside working away between the raised thighs of an amply proportioned female. A big, hairy face glares at me over huge shoulders and I lower the curtain discreetly.

'So!' I exclaim, and stamp through the passage to yet another door. 'Christ! The place is all doors and curtains!'

The room beyond is a kitchen, heavy with the strong smell of frying fish. In one corner, wearing an off-white apron and wielding a large frying-pan, is the object of all my trials and tribulations. He comes close to dropping the pan when he sees me standing there glaring at him, on the verge of exploding.

'Hello, 'swain,' he ventures tentatively, and risks a weak smile that fades abruptly into an anxious frown as I move towards him in a way that causes him to raise the smoking frying pan in front as a shield.

I stop midway; fingers clenching and unclenching as I fight back an overpowering urge to throttle him. 'What the flaming hell do you think you're doing?' I manage to grind out eventually.

His frightened features take on a certain belligerence, and there is a firm set to his jaw as he braces up to me, full of outrage. 'What did you expect?' he challenges defiantly. 'You sent me ashore — what was I supposed to do?''

'What any other matelot would do — get pissed!' I hurl at him, ignoring a chorus of protesting shouts from the working area of the establishment. 'Bloody hell! I didn't even know there were any knocking-shops in Gib; and you find one on your first run ashore! What happened to the love-lorn, ever faithful, newly married husband?'

His eyes blaze with fury. 'Hell! you don't think I've been shaggin', do you?'

'Well, that's what this place is for, isn't it? Or perhaps you thought it was a fish and chip shop!'

He brings the pan down hard on the stove, and it spurts boiling fat all over the place, before sizzling away dangerously as he squares up to me. 'You've got a mind like a sewer, 'swain — just like all the rest. All I've done since I've bin here is fry up some sprats, and drink some wine with the only people who give a damn about me. I didn't know where to go when you sent me away from the boat, until these people found me — bin good to me, they 'ave.'

'You didn't give a thought to going back to the boat then? Do you know what time it is?'

'Yeah.'

'You know you're adrift then – and the boat is under sailing orders.'

'You didn't tell me when my leave expired; I was coming back tonight. You can't 'ave it all ways, 'swain – makin' me come ashore when I didn't want to, and then moanin' because I don't come back on time.'

With great difficulty I bottle up my rage. Ominous noises are coming from the passageway, and I reckon our conversation is distracting the occupants of the curtained cells. The situation could become very nasty if we prolong the argument. I am about to drag him out of the premises, when a large, greasy-looking man enters, and looks from me to Miller, and back again with open hostility.

'What do you want?' he snarls.

'Nothing – you don't have anything to offer me – I'm just here to get this bloke back to his ship before he winds up in serious trouble.'

'Maybe he doesn't want to go.'

'He's got no choice – he's got to go – he's in the bloody Navy, for Christ sake!'

The big man moves easily across the room, to stand between me and the passage door, 'You his boss?'

'That's right.'

'No wonder he don't want to go back.'

'It's not what he wants – it's what he has to do. What has it got to do with you, anyhow?'

'I run this place, and I look after my guests. If he wants to go; fine. If he doesn't; he don't have to.'

'Who says he doesn't?'

A dangerous glint comes into his eyes, 'Who says he does?' He swings on Miller, 'You want to go back to your ship?'

'This is bloody ridiculous!' I burst out. 'He's got no choice. He either comes back with me, or he'll be dragged back with an escort, and he'll be in real trouble – he'll be in a wheelchair by the time he comes out of chokey.'

Miller is looking from the big man to me, and back again in agitation. 'I'd better go,' he says plaintively, 'I'll be in all sorts of trouble if I don't.'

'The Navy don't own you, does it?' He advances on me with

an expression that says he is only looking for an excuse to tear me limb from limb. One glance at his bulging biceps is enough to convince me that if it comes to a brawl, I will be the one to sustain the most damage.

'I — I'd better go with him.' Miller's voice is anxious now, as though he realises at last that he has allowed things to go too far, and is about to witness an attack on his coxswain. Not before time as far as I am concerned. Thank God for small mercies, I'm thinking, as I prepare to lead him through the door. The big man is in no hurry to let me go, however. He is itching to have a go at me, and stands firmly between me and escape. If I am to get out of here, I will have to force my way past his enormous bulk.

Just as things seem about to dissolve into a mêlée of violent conflict a giant flame leaps up from the frying-pan to scorch the ceiling, and scatter everyone to the four corners of the room. The big man lunges across the space to try to grab the handle of the pan, but he slips on the greasy floor. His hands knock the handle of the pan, sending it hurtling to the deck with gouts of flaming fat spraying in all directions. A dishcloth catches fire, and in a moment the whole place is a raging inferno as wooden chairs and tables ignite to crackle away with the fierceness of old, dry timber. Roars of anguish and fear come from the big man as he writhes on the floor with his clothing on fire.

I grab a curtain from behind me and rip it away from its fastenings; disclosing a brief vision of two nude, entwined bodies, grappling inside the space it had covered. I rush over to the squirming man and try to smother the threshing arms and legs. He is in a panic now — a blind, agonised terror as the flames consume his greasy clothes, burning his flesh with greedy appetite. Miller joins me, and between us we manage to overcome his struggles and muffle the flames. Together we drag him through the door as he moans and pleads, flaying about in the midst of the billowing black smoke that follows us along the passage. There are shadowy figures scurrying along with us, semi-clad in most cases, in all sorts of trouble as they finally get the message, and try to escape being burned alive in the midst of their favourite pastime.

One glance is enough to tell me that the fire has taken hold to the extent that only the expert help of the fire-brigade will have any effect. I doubt if even they will prevent the place from being reduced to a ruin. The smoke follows us out into the alley and belches up into the sky, to beckon all the neighbours to come and gawk. They respond with eager, gloating eyes to crowd around and offer advice, but little more. Nothing attracts folk more than a good disaster – especially if there is the added value of agonised, injured human beings to savour, like the big man with his scorched limbs and pitiful groanings.

I drag Miller away, forcing him to follow me through hurrying sightseers until we reach the street below. The quicker we put distance between us and the scene of disaster the happier I'll be. Our blackened appearance causes a certain amount of passing interest when we go along Main Street, but these people are hardened to the quirks of sailors and quickly cover up their curiosity. I look back once more to see a rising pall of smoke lifting into a blue sky. A hefty thrust into the middle of Miller's back sends him staggering forward again and we leave the town behind.

At the dockyard gate two bored policemen come alive and stare with open amusement as we approach. 'Gawd almighty!' says one. 'You bloody matelots don't half get yourselves in a state when you go ashore!'

'Get stuffed,' I blurt out ungraciously, giving Miller a further thrust that almost sends him sprawling.

The whole casing-party stop what they are doing and line up to greet us when we reach the boat. I bark at them in an effort to drive them back to their duties, but they are too interested in two disgusting-looking objects that stagger across the gangway. One look at my expression quells any further remarks however, and we are left to climb through the hatch in silence.

One person I cannot ignore is Murray as he stands on the casing, just forward of the hatch, watching with cold eyes until we are almost out of range before he speaks.

'Coxswain!'

I hesitate. My head just above the hatch. Not wanting to look at him. 'Sir?'

'I'll see you in the wardroom in fifteen minutes.'

'Aye, aye, sir.'

I carry on down into the fore-ends, and come face to face with the TI, who wrinkles his nose in distaste. 'Cor, blimey! Don't you stink!'

I say nothing, and stare back at him with a look that stops him dead. I'm close to breaking point now, and it won't take much to push me over the brink, and become violent — and he knows it.

IV

The sea is a sheet of glass when we slip our moorings and sail
before sun-up, gliding stealthily through the black shadows of
the sleeping fleet. Huge battleships, cruisers and such brood
silently, and hold aloof from this minnow that disturbs the
unblemished sheen of the still water. Somewhere ahead a converted yacht steams toward the open sea, leading us out of the
bay with the lights of Spain twinkling innocently on the fringes
of the dark pool of the outer anchorage.

The first lift of the bow comes when we feel the dying swells of
the Atlantic, as they funnel through the straits and encroach on
the inner sea. The helm is easy in my hands, and the compass
ticks obediently within a point or two of the ordered course.
Even the rumble of the diesels has a comforting sound this
morning as they spray clouds of exhaust into the clean air, to
drive us away from the land. Soon we are on our own, churning
towards the east.

Before sunrise we dive into the warm safety of the ocean and
swim along at ninety feet. Dawn sends shafts of brilliant sunlight piercing into the depths of the blue sea, where we move
through galleries of changing light. The only dark, undeviating
shape amid an ever-changing galaxy of moving entities. We are
blind in a world of beauty — an alien body invading a sphere of
undulation; with our artificial environment of half-light and
trapped air. Inside our metal skin we are alive to every sound,
and wary of every unseen shadow.

The boat goes to patrol routine, with one third of the crew on
watch. By now we are settled to a pattern and there is no need
for more than the occasional quiet command from the officer of
the watch. Those off duty gather in small groups to chat, or
withdraw into little worlds of their own. Remote, even though
they rub shoulders with their messmates.

The chiefs' mess is a select club and rules are strictly observed. Caps are removed, and there is no talk of past exploits, religion or politics. In the claustrophobic world of the submariner the word 'shipmate' means something special, and anyone who threatens disruption soon realises his error. For the first time I feel the cold finger of censure pointed iɴ my direction. Throughout the boat I am treated with reserve: even downright insolence by Briarley and his croneys. In general service I would accept this as part of a coxswain's lot; here it worries me.

Mid-morning the fore-ends are cleared for 'defaulters', and Miller is brought to answer for his crimes before the captain. Fenton dresses him down and lets him off with a caution after I have read the charge. I have the feeling that they would prefer to discipline me and I'm glad when the formalities are over. We are anxious to find out how much talking the AB has done ashore, and cringe when he replies to some of Fenton's questions.

'I didn't tell 'em anyfink they didn't know already, sir,' he protests.

The skipper grits his teeth. 'What do you mean by that?'

'Well, sir. They said they know all about the boxes and what was in 'em. In fact, the bloke said I should keep my mouth shut about what I've seen.' He looks at the skipper's set features. 'He works for the Government, sir. He asked me if I thought anyone knew what was in the crates—' His voice tails off, and a cloud of uncertainty crosses his face.

'You told him about the tank parts,' accuses Murray.

There is no need for an answer. The lad's a picture of misery as the cold truth hits him.

'That's it then,' says Fenton evenly. 'We might as well have sent the enemy a telegram — they'll be watching for us every inch of the way.'

We leave Miller standing dejected in the fore-ends to wallow in his own guilt. Fenton has told him not to dwell on it, for the damage is done and it is a lesson for the future, but Miller's world is collapsing about him and he yearns to be anywhere but in this steel cocoon with shipmates whose lives could be forfeit to his stupidity. He is too distraught to realise that as far as the crew are concerned, most of the blame falls on me.

The captain talks to the crew and tells them officially that our destination is Tobruk, and how desperate the army is for the goods we carry. The town is surrounded and there is a calculated risk in delivering the goods, but that risk is worthwhile. He intends to creep in at night, and remain dived amongst the sunken wrecks during daylight hours until the cargo is offloaded. He says nothing about Miller, but there isn't a man who doesn't know the score.

Having given us the bad news, he tries to cheer us up by explaining that in the summer months it is possible to find layers of different densities in the Mediterranean, caused by cold water from the Atlantic entering the Straits to compensate for evaporation. It is confusing to the enemy's detection equipment, and in any case, we have orders to avoid even the most tempting targets. Add to this the fact that their listening gear is not as good as ours, the vast area of the Mediterranean, and there is every chance we will slip through without interference. If everyone does his job properly we should be in and out within twenty-four hours.

His speech doesn't inspire me with confidence. This is no holiday playground as portrayed by the pre-war brochures, but a violent area where everyone is out to destroy each other. A boat the size of the *Avon* can be spotted at a depth of one hundred feet in the clear water by searching aircraft, and Miller has already given the opposition a trump card.

We have fourteen hundred miles to go, and at economical speed can hope for little more than two hundred and fifty miles every twenty-four hours. Five to six days if all goes well, and anyone who looks at a map will realise that our troubles will begin when we enter the narrow seas between the North African coast and the islands of Sardinia and Sicily; not to mention the little island of Pantelleria that stands guard right in the middle. That area could have been designed to trap the likes of us, and I have no doubt that there will be a host of eager-beaver antisubmarine vessels in position when we arrive.

Our eyes and ears remain on full alert to pick up every sound, and register every speck that might be a ship or aircraft. We have no friends in this part of the world, and every stranger must be considered a predator. Fenton ensures that our best asdic operator is rested in preparation for the critical time, and those with the sharpest eyes are told off for bridge duty as we draw near.

It is Yorky Baker, our best asdic operator, who warns of the approach of our first adversaries when his trained ears pick up the distant sound of propellers. The skipper is called to the control room, and Yorky keeps up a constant stream of reports that show we are closing on a ship somewhere on our port bow. We go to diving stations and ring for silent running – anyone who coughs now will earn himself a lot of enemies. Two, possibly three, ships and Yorky reckons they are small anti-submarine chasers – the size of trawlers – patrolling an area that stretches across our path.

We alter course to starboard and head south towards the coast of Africa, and wait for Yorky to tell us that the two ships are moving away. Not a bit of it! It seems they do not work to a set pattern, and at our slow speed it makes little difference which way we go – unless we do a 'U' turn and head back for Gibraltar. I wouldn't argue with that, but the skipper decides to press on and try to anticipate their next move, so that we might find a gap to slip through.

The next report confirms that there are three ships, and that one is almost stationary while his mates move out on wide sweeps. He is the joker doing all the listening, so that he can tell the others if there is any sign of life down here, and where to plant their depth-charges to good effect. Our stokers carry leather-coated wheel-spanners and every piece of unnecessary machinery is frozen. We stay quiet and sweat as the boat gradually descends to one hundred and fifty feet, to creep through the water stealthily on one screw.

She is difficult to control, and we try not to use more hydroplane than necessary, but Murray is unable to help with the ballast pumps. She starts to porpoise and the skipper sucks his teeth as he sees the bubble moving aft with both 'planes at full rise. He will have to decide if it is worth risking a surge of speed to control her. The time goes slowly and the ships show no sign that they are suspicious. We are almost congratulating ourselves when Yorky spoils it all by reporting another ship approaching from dead ahead. I can sense the skipper would dearly love to have a look, but those boys are just waiting for a periscope to pop up.

At this point the sound of a distant explosion is clearly heard throughout the boat, to be echoed from another bearing. It seems the enemy is trying to discourage the likes of us with indiscriminate depth-charging. It is a favourite trick of the Italians, but not a very wise move on their part, for it causes a lot of disturbance, and drives their hydrophone operators up the wall.

I wonder if everyone's guts are churning like mine, and if their nerves are stretched to breaking point, while each noise, imagined or otherwise, drills into over-sensitive ears. I can see Murray's face reflected in the depth-gauge as he bends to peer over my shoulder to satisfy himself that the 'planes are at maximum. Beads of sweat run down his grim features and I look up longingly at the useless ventlouvre above me. With the fans shut off the temperature is mounting minute by minute and we are already sweltering.

With grim determination we creep on towards what we hope is a gap, but Yorky demolishes all again by reporting the nearest vessel speeding up and coming our way. He has about two thousand yards to cover and there is no more time to arse about. The skipper orders 'full ahead' group up − our fastest under-water speed − and our noisiest. There is an immediate reaction up top and a new sound takes Yorky off guard as a fourth ship starts her engines, working up to full speed, to join in the fray. The bastard must have been waiting for us to make this move and her detectors have us pin-pointed. Now they have us to rights. With four of them to perform the coup-de-grâce there doesn't seem to be much hope for us.

Depth-charges are primitive weapons when all is considered; just canisters filled with explosive, set to explode at the right depth and rolled or thrown from the stern. Nothing very technical; but effective. In a moment they are on to us like a pack of wolves, and the way they go about it suggests they are no novices at this game. We are about to be stalked by methodical, skilled opponents, with everything in their favour. All they need to do is pound us into oblivion, or wait for our air to give out.

Now the ballet begins, with all the participants in their set positions on stage for the macabre, three-dimensional dance of death. It should please anyone with an eye for beauty. Sheer fantasy and alive with ever-changing iridescence. Our own shadowy, phantomlike shape will creep along to the soft whine of our electric motors and the occasional interjection from our ballast pumps. On the surface the forces of destruction will wheel and cavort through the bursting waves to the music of their threshing screws and the wind howling through the rigging. They sway and surge to the whim of the sea, with smoky breath belching from their funnels as the engines work up to full speed for the climax of the show, when the percussion section overpowers all with thunderous detonations. The finale is most spectacular of all. The ocean is torn asunder, and blood and guts boil up in a mixture of glutinous oil, to the delight and applause of an enthusiastic audience.

The artistry is lost to me as I stare into the vacant features of the depth-gauge, watching the spirit level. Alongside me, Briarley is sitting at the fore-'planes with a scowl on his face. We work well in tandem, and can be relied on to anticipate sudden changes of density and weight. Apart from our work, we have nothing in common; burying our mutual dislike under a cloak of efficiency.

Yorky drones on with his monologue; telling of ominous moves going on up top as a pattern begins to form from his interpretation of the sounds he can hear. Our nerves are in tune with his reports, and Fenton forms a mental picture as he voices commands in a low voice. If he gets it right, we'll live on for a few more minutes — if he's wrong; the fishes will have a feast. It doesn't take a practised mind to know that a concerted attack is building up, with the first murdering bastard pounding in towards us. We can hear the thrush — thrush — thrush of his propellers, and the gorge rises into my throat.

'Port thirty!'

The helm goes over as we try to wriggle clear, while everyone grips hard to whatever comes handy in anticipation of the earthquake to follow. For a few vital seconds the enemy will lose contact as he runs over the top, and he must work blind, and by instinct, as the last few yards are swallowed up.

The batteries are working in unison now, pouring out power

to drive us through the water at ten knots, to carry us clear of the canisters of destruction that are even now plunging into the sea, sinking to their depth settings.

A giant hammer hits the boat and the air is filled with cork particles, as she rolls forty-five degrees and a ponderous roar envelops us in a body of sound. Again and again it comes, shattering the mind and isolating each man in his world of lonely terror. Crashing sounds of loose gear falling all over the place comes from the fore-ends, while the second coxswain and I fight with the hydroplanes to gain control and bring her level at the right depth. The motors stay at 'full ahead', while the disturbance hides all other sound and we move as far away from the area as possible. The gauges settle on two hundred feet. There are reports of minor damage and a hatch is leaking.

The first whisperings of our next attacker can be heard now as he swings his bow in our direction to come racing in. On his bucking quarterdeck the crew is setting the depth on their charges as they wrench their disappointed eyes from the empty whirlpools of the first attack; trying to pierce the placid surface above the spot where the noise of our screws can be heard. They are the experts with the right equipment, and our lives are in the hands of one man, as he waits with eyes lifted in an unconscious effort to see the shadowy hull that bears down on us. Skill, practice and steel nerves are required to give a chance of survival. Fenton has them all, but the odds are heavily stacked in favour of the enemy.

The gods are with us on this run however, and they get it all wrong. The screws pass right overhead, but the settings are shallow and we escape with no more than a bad shaking. No time for complacency though; the next set of screws are already coming in from a new angle. This time the boat heaves over violently and I'm sent sprawling from my seat. A long way off men are shouting, as the boat assumes a bow-down angle. Briarley is still recovering from where he has been thrown, so I heave his wheel over to add its influence to mine. She is on her way down: determined to go all the way.

'Blow main ballast!' Fenton is alive to the emergency, and the experienced hands of the ERA flash over the controls. Everyone is holding on as the angle increases. There seems nothing to stop her downward plunge.

Flat out, with the batteries discharging at an alarming rate, the screws drive us towards the bottom, and in this part of the Mediterranean no submarine will reach the bottom intact. We watch the bubble with hypnotic gaze, willing it to slide forward. Our concerted prayers are answered, as the boat begins to level off at three hundred and seventy feet. The needles falter on the depth-gauges, then begin to swing anti-clockwise.

'Flood main ballast!' The last thing the skipper wants is to lose control of her, and find ourselves wallowing on the surface, with happy German gunners pumping shells at us. They must be grateful for the noise we make. Any submariners amongst them will smile knowingly when they think of the drain on our batteries.

A very wet first lieutenant staggers into the control-room, looking like he's had a battle with a soggy sea-monster. 'We can't get the forward escape hatch shut, sir. The men are stuffing hammocks and bedding into it, and we are using the cargo to shore it up. I think we can stop most of the water coming in, but can we use the pumps?'

'Not unless you have to, Number One. I'm flogging the batteries to hell even now.'

'Yes, sir. They have us by the short hairs, haven't they?'

'Not yet they haven't,' states Fenton firmly. He switches on the tannoy, and his voice comes loud and clear through the boat, 'Captain speaking. I think it is about time we took the initiative and gave that lot some of what they have been giving us. It's the opportunity our worthy gun-layer has been waiting for — We'll give those beauties the shock of their lives. Stand by gun action!'

The boat comes alive now, as the gun crew climb into the tower and the lid comes off the magazine. Even as the work goes on Fenton takes time to explain his intentions. 'We will have to put up with one more attack, but I intend to surface in front of the next ship as he starts his run. We should get two, or even three rounds off before they are over their surprise, then we've got six fish to deal with anyone else that gets in the way. I will remind you that we have twenty-two knots under our belt, and I doubt if they can muster more than sixteen. With only an hour to sunset, they won't be able to whistle up aircraft.'

Our luck still holds, and the next attacker is miles off target. The wireless operator reports his radio on the blink, but everyone has more immediate worries. In the fore-ends the TI is getting his tubes ready, and Murray is positively gloating − he seems to relish the idea of surfacing amongst those vengeful bastards − I'm serving with a crowd of nut cases!

The orders are rattling out now and we take the boat up to ninety feet. Fenton vents the quick-diving tank into the boat to build up more pressure, and I gulp hard to re-adjust my eardrums. Yorky's voice is droning on as he gives ranges and bearings for the next attack that is already developing. Four-inch shells are being passed up to the gun crew and the layer and trainer clutch their gunsights as they wait for the whistle to send them out through the hatch. There is just time for a final look round before Fenton gives his last quiet orders to Murray.

'Hold this course at ninety feet, Henry. Blow main ballast when we close to one thousand yards and blow your whistle at fifty feet − we'll all get a soaking, but I want that gun firing before they know what's hit 'em.' He turns to me. 'Abandon your 'planes as soon as you have put them to full rise, coxswain, and then follow me up to the bridge − I want you on the bridge-wheel.'

'Aye, aye, sir,' I reply, amazed that I can still speak through my tightened gullet.

The fore-ends report all tubes ready and the skipper's legs disappear into the tower. Murray calls out to the gunners, 'Target is a small anti-submarine chaser; bearing dead ahead − no deflection − shoot!' That final order gives the gun-layer permission to open fire without waiting for orders from the bridge.

'Range one thousand yards,' raps Yorky.

'Blow main ballast,' orders Murray, and the boat goes light. Briarley spins his hydroplanes to 'full rise', but I hold mine to 'dive' for a few moments to keep her level. The gun crew will have enough problems without having a bow-up angle to cope with. We hold her for a few moments before the buoyancy takes over and she starts for the surface. Nothing will stop her now, and I slide off my seat to mount the ladder behind the signal-man.

'Seven hundred yards', calls Yorky.

'One clip off,' announces the signalman as Fenton prepares to open up.

The whistle shrills, and the hatch flies open to admit a deluge of warm Mediterranean water. The sun is bright as I climb out on to the dripping bridge and connect the wheel: they are doing away with these bridge wheels these days, more's the pity. Fenton is beside me, crouching behind the torpedo-sight as the four-inch barks.

Submarine gunnery is basic open-sighted stuff, with no pretension to sophistication. Just climb out of the hatch, ram a shell up the spout and fire on the upward roll, while the deck is still awash. Done right; the first round should be on its way before the casing drains down. Fourteen rounds a minute when they are on form − today it will be nearer twelve − but a cheer goes up, and I guess they have hit something.

I can't resist a look as the gun fires again, and I see a shell burst right on her bridge. There is brown smoke billowing from her fore-castle, with orange flecks of flame. She is finished as a fighting unit and we have to swerve to avoid her as she swings helplessly out of control.

Fenton is mouthing orders into the voicepipe − the master at work, bringing our bows to line up with the only obstacle that stands in our way of escape. One lone vessel, stationary in the water as she listens with her detectors. She has no time to retaliate as she sees her sister ship devastated, and her detection gear is useless for the hunted has become the hunter, bearing down with all tubes ready, with spray pouring from the diesel exhausts. A surge of white foam spreads from her stern as she tries to get under way, but it is much too late to overcome the inertia before the first torpedo explodes under her bow with a deafening roar. That one would have been enough, but we have fired a salvo of three, and the second one breaks her in half, so that we plough through a mess of rubble as our speed builds up to twenty knots.

Badly aimed missiles are splashing nearby, and the remaining two ships are swinging in our direction, but they haven't a hope of catching us now. If the Luftwaffe has the message, it is much too late for them to react as we slip away into the sunset. Fenton straightens up to lean over the front of the bridge and congratulate the gunners. They are kicking spent cartridges over the side, and unshipping the gunsights before training their weapon fore and aft. He has turned defeat into victory; but you would never know it to look at him, as he searches the horizon with his binoculars, then gives the orders that sends the boat to 'patrol routine', so that we can have a meal, charge the batteries, and build up our reserves of compressed air. The day dies quietly, as a cloak of velvet darkness conceals us from those who would do us harm as we press eastwards.

We disconnect the bridge wheel, and return to control-room steering, making me redundant. I go below, and Murray is waiting to do the rounds with me, so that he can give a complete report to the skipper. There is minor damage in all compartments, but the main problems are the leaking escape hatch and the wrecked radio equipment. We find that the hatch has jumped its lugs, but the engine-room department somehow contrive to force it back with a little gentle persuasion from a crowbar to make us watertight once more. The radio is another matter; the telegraphists will work on it, but it is a mess, and we must remain incommunicado until we reach Tobruk.

The rest of the evening meal is cleared away as we settle to night routine. I roll into my bunk to lie awake in the glow of a blue police light; hoping for a few pleasant thoughts before sleep overcomes me. My head aches slightly and my stomach is unsettled as I listen to the diesels sucking air into the boat. We are travelling fast through a boisterous sea. The boat judders and rolls as waves burst over the hull, sounding like someone shovelling gravel on to stretched canvas.

Close to my upturned eyes airpipes join in a complicated mass, with tentacles snaking off in all directions. I am fascinated; unable to look away as they begin to undulate. A sick feeling sours my innards while sweat runs down my face as I begin to shake. Entrails of putrid flesh reach out to me and I feel my body lifting to meet them. My mind searches for an escape, but weird visions of waving arms and skulls with empty sockets revolve in a nightmarish kaleidoscope.

There is the vile stench of corruption in my nostrils and worms feed on me, searching for my pulsating organs. My mouth is filled with acrid gorge as I try to scream for help but find no sound. My throat is clamped, so that I cannot force air into my dry mouth. I try to push myself out of the bunk, but my limbs are frozen and the deckhead presses down on me with crushing force. Every nerve is screaming; but I am alone in a world of silence.

Suddenly it stops, my brain has registered an outside noise that forces through my delirium and I breathe heavily in a welter of sound, as bodies rise from their bunks, trying to decipher what new manifestation has invaded their slumber. The atmosphere seethes about me, while my brain battles with an enigma. I am balanced between imagination and reality.

'Coxswain!' The urgent voice wrenches me out of my bunk, and I find myself staring into eyes that have seen horrors beyond those conjured up in my own mind. I follow Soapy to the seamen's mess to find a body arched back across the table with the top of its skull missing; exposing what is left of a brain. The rest decorates the bulkheads.

Strangely enough, the face is unblemished, although the back of the head has disappeared. A row of Lee Enfield rifles are lodged in a rack with a chain through the trigger-guards. Miller has levered a round of .303 ammunition up the spout of one. Placed his mouth over the nuzzle, and thumbed the trigger. One jerk, and it is left to his messmates to clean up the gory mess. What final torment cracked his addled brain we will never know; but deep down I have the feeling I have something to do with it.

I chase the ghouls out of the mess as Murray arrives. Between us we stretch the body out on the table for the TI to lay out − he seems to have a knack for this sort of thing, and he will get no argument from me.

Despite the crater in the skull, he manages to make him look pretty. Murray goes off to give the news to the skipper. We drag out Miller's two hammocks to be made up into his shroud by Briarley, who has produced a sailmaker's needle and thread. I suggest that we use one of the empty tubes for the body and Murray agrees. So the AB takes the place of number one torpedo. It will keep him out of sight, and if we are unable to give him a burial on shore quickly, the watertight door will keep the atmosphere sweet – not to mention a convenient method of burial at sea if the need arises. Contrary to the impression given by war movies we do like to give our dead marked graves.

Things stay quiet as we progress eastwards, and on the morning of the last day before we are due to arrive at Tobruk we go deep to avoid sharp-eyed reconnaissance aircraft, with the coast of Cyrenaica closing in to starboard. Fenton is suspicious of the lack of activity, and prepared for a reception committee when we get in to the approaches of the harbour. No one has much appetite except for rum, and even that is served without the usual banter. I come face to face with Briarley several times and he makes no attempt to conceal his contempt for me, or to hide the blame he attaches to me for Miller's suicide.

The skipper risks a couple of trips up to periscope depth to get bearings on the coastline, which he passes on to the navigator to pinpoint our position on the chart. One glance shows me that we are creeping in at a speed that will bring us to our destination well after dark. We have had no radio contact for two days or more, and have no idea of the situation ashore – except that it is a safe bet that the coastline on our starboard beam is enemy-held, and will be until we arrive at the vicinity of the anchorage itself. The last we heard, the British held about fifteen miles of coastline and anything could have happened since then.

Sometime during the afternoon when most of those off watch are having their siesta, the TI coaxes me up to the tubespace, and we solemnly tie a black ribbon to the door of Miller's crypt. It is all done in silence, but when I turn to move off he stops me and pulls the tubespace door shut.

'You can't go on blaming yourself, you know,' he says, peering deep into my face.

'I know it,' I grunt without conviction, 'but there are a lot of blokes that think I made a complete balls of it.'

'Only those that don't matter; you can't dwell on it, or it will get your guts in a knot.' He watches my reaction and knows I am on the defensive. 'We are getting too old for this game, Ben. We think too bloody much, mate. Trouble is, they need us older blokes to keep order, and hold a rein on hot-headed youngsters.

We should have to be zombies not to take some things to heart, and it helps to have a mate when things get on top of you.' He looks embarrassed now, as though he regrets having started on this tack, but he perseveres. 'What I'm saying, Ben, is that you are not alone, and if you want somebody to unload it on — er — well you know what I mean — you can tell me to get stuffed if you like.'

He's really struggling now, and it has cost him a lot to say the things he has said. I look at his scraggy features, ingrained with the grime of the past few hours, etching the lines round his grey eyes. His battered old cap, with the cracked peak folds down over his ears like it is part of him, along with the black finger-nails that rasp on his beard when he strokes his chin.

'TI,' I say quietly.

'Yeah?'

'Get stuffed!'

He grins shapeless teeth at me. 'I knew you'd fuckin' say that — It'll cost you a tot, mate.'

V

I am a romantic at heart. The Sahara conjures up pictures of legionnaires chasing Arabs across endless dunes of unblemished sand. Visits to squalid parts of North African ports have not dampened these visions, and I am convinced that just over the horizon a world of Hollywood-style desert waits to be discovered.

Tonight my imagination will be stretched to the limits, and beyond. We smell Tobruk long before Fenton and the navigator are able to identify the marks on the headland that mark the entrance to the harbour. It reminds me of the stench that comes from a very large rubbish tip where someone is burning old tyres. The night is bitter cold, and the stars seem close enough to touch. On the bridge everyone speaks quietly, as we listen to the sounds, trying to form pictures of what is happening ashore. The arms of the rocky coast close in on either side as we creep in on our electric motors. It is midnight on 19/20th of June 1942, and if we knew the situation developing on the outskirts of the town, we would be going astern as fast as the propellers could take us.

On the perimeter of this arena, grim-faced men are staring out into the night, as they hear the sound of tank engines, watching the shadows for the first sign of an advancing enemy. Rommel is poised with his panzers to drive out this stubborn garrison of tired, war-weary men. They come from all parts of the British Commonwealth, and speak in many languages, with one thing in common; they are veterans of a long struggle and have their backs to the sea. All about them the wreckage of war defiles the parched earth, and the stink of cordite and sweat mixes with the sickly stench of putrefying flesh. The night has a strange quiet as they wait for all hell to break loose. Just the occasional crunch of an explosion, or the nervous staccato of an automatic weapon. The crouching soldiers tense and grip their rifles, determined to be first to pull the trigger when the enemy comes.

Ignorant of all this we glide through the black water, watching the distant explosions and the glow of fires until the masts and funnel of a sunken ship mark the beginning of the anchorage. Fenton and the navigator peer anxiously at the chart with the aid of a shaded light, trying to recognise marks from the silhouette of buildings cutting into the skyline to starboard. It would be disaster if we ran aground now, and we are trimmed down so that if we do touch bottom we can blow ballast and lift clear. The skipper trains the sight of the compass to bring the azimuth mirror on to bearings that will tell him when to signal Briarley to let go the anchor. At last the cable rattles out and we bring up to the hook, swinging in the dark pool that is the centre of a simmering cauldron.

No one seems aware of our arrival, and with no boats to take anyone ashore to investigate, we can only guess at the situation in the town. Fenton has no intention of using even the small walkie-talkie to contact anyone, in case it is picked up by the wrong people. Meantime, he decides that there is enough noise going on to hide the sound of our diesels, and orders the batteries charged. The exhausts choke into life, throwing gouts of smoke and water into the night. I am pleased to hear their throaty roar, for in emergency they will take us out of here much quicker than the motors. I have a feeling that something is terribly wrong in the harbour. Fenton must feel the same way too, for he orders the gun crew closed up, while the rest of us stay on the alert.

An hour goes by without anyone coming out to investigate. The uncertainty increase with each passing minute. We search the sea front with binoculars for signs of movement and see a couple of trucks picking their way through the piles of debris. A motor-cyclist roars along the coast road, but it is impossible to recognise his uniform — he could be friend or foe. The signalman reports movement in the harbour and two dark shapes move slowly by on a course that should take them out of the anchorage towards the open sea. Small merchantmen, with half-submerged propellers beating the water as they go at slow speed. They ignore us, determined to escape the confines of the beleaguered port, attracting as little attention as possible. Their silhouettes merge with the night as we stare at the empty blackness they leave behind, wishing we were going with them.

Suddenly the sharp crack of an eighty-eight barks out and all eyes swivel to focus on a spot near the entrance of the harbour. Several flashes split the night, filling the void with the yellow burst of exploding shells, to show the ships naked and vulnerable for a moment. On both shores more guns open up, but the ships are at full speed now; their engineers forcing their charges to efforts beyond that for which they were designed. They escape to the open sea while the guns go silent. One thing is certain; we may have got in all right, but it looks as though the enemy has closed the door. Those gunners are just waiting for someone like us to come within range. For us to attempt to run the gauntlet would be suicidal, and as a further precaution, Fenton stops the charge to reduce noise.

The sounds of conflict are growing now. A continuous thunder of gunfire comes from the surrounding desert while the sky glows with numerous fires. This is no place for a submarine, so we lift the 'hook' to shift berth, snugging in close to an abandoned tanker that has remained afloat even after her cargo has burned away, her superstructure charred to a ruined skeleton of twisted girders. We moor alongside, hoping to merge with her and remain unseen. Fenton sends for Murray.

'I want you too, coxswain,' he adds before I've got time to disappear below.

Murray climbs out of the tower and we stand in a small group, remote from our fellows, to talk in low voices. The skipper is anxious to learn what goes on ashore, and I find myself volunteering to swim with the first lieutenant to a small jetty in an attempt to make contact with a small naval detachment who should be somewhere in the town. It should be an easy swim, especially if we use two exposed wrecks as stepping-stones. We are to take clothing wrapped in canvas bags strapped to our backs.

Without further ado we climb down on to the ballast tanks before launching our naked bodies into the sea. The water is comparatively warm, and we have no difficulty finding our way from wreck to wreck as flares arc into the sky from the south, and hang suspended on their parachutes to bathe the area in a golden glow.

A crumbling jetty emerges from the glow, and we clamber onto the gritty stone to dress hurriedly. I am amazed to see that Murray has even brought his cap, and I wonder if he is going to produce a collar and tie for the occasion. He settles for a blue jumper under a battledress blouse, but still makes me look a tramp in white submarine sweater and oil-stained trousers. 'I'd have put on my number ones if I'd known we were out to impress the natives,' I muse: then I realise my socks are missing and have to pull hard boots on to my tender feet.

Buildings huddle round us as we move into the town and go by deserted shops and houses. The place stinks to high heaven, with traces of smoke filtering from piles of rubbish. Timber smoulders inside gaping holes, and as we turn a corner a huge wall crumples in slow motion to add its rubble to the pile.

In front of an open doorway is an ambulance, parked with its engine ticking over. We enter the building to find sprawling shapes of wounded men in every corner. Busy medical staff move amongst them, sorting out the injuries and working on them with words of comfort mingled with rough commands for silence and patience. No one has time for us, so we go out again into the street.

At last we find a place that has the appearance of a headquarters of some sort. Inside, men with dirty faces and tired eyes crouch over radios, making urgent calls to squaddies deep in the desert, where the ogre of an advancing army closes in, and the metallic might of a steel wall of tanks bears down out of the night. A rich Australian voice answers our queries and directs us back to the sea-front.

'You'll see a wrecked three-tonner with its bonnet dug into the side of a warehouse; your mates are using the office there — or they were when we last heard of them.'

He turns away as a fresh piece of disastrous news comes through.

Our luck is in, and we find the place, to be welcomed by a group of incredulous colleagues, who marvel at our story, and tell us that Tobruk is under siege — in case we had any doubt.

The garrison is prepared for a final stand, but is under no illusion that it can hold out for long. We should return to our boat as soon as possible, to get out while we can.

'We would like to go with you, if you've no objection,' says a two-ringer. 'You'll find us house-trained, despite appearance. The only people to benefit if you land your cargo now will be the enemy, and there's nothing more for us to do here.'

'Hold it a minute!' warns a voice, and we cock our ears to the tune of aircraft droning overhead. The drone develops into the sour scream of diving Stukas, and bombs crunch somewhere to the south.

'Poor bastards!' breathes someone, and I get a mental picture of men cringing in trenches, while the earth is torn apart around them. The telegraphist turns away from his portable radio. 'They're bombing the minefields to let their troops through,' he says. 'The lads in front are pulling back to new positions.'

'Alright, Sparks. Leave it — it's none of our business now,' says the lieutenant in a sad voice. 'There is no more time now; come on, I know where there is a boat.'

Murray nods agreement, and we go out to where the first shreds of a growing dawn are unveiling the scenes of devastation. We chug out across the bay as the air reverberates to the detonation of many guns. Once on board, a hasty report puts Fenton in the picture, and he decides we would not last five minutes if we tried to run in daylight with those eighty-eights waiting with their ugly snouts trained out across the exit. The Luftwaffe is about too, so he orders everyone below, and we settle under the shadow of the tanker, with just enough water to cover the bridge.

A conference is held in the wardroom, while I go forward to the chiefs' mess, where the remains of an early breakfast still litters the table. I scuttle aft to the galley to see if I can scrounge some grub for my hungry belly. The chef is tidying up, and grumbles when I demand nutrition. With great reluctance he produces two ageing strips of bacon to make a sandwich — it is like asking for blood.

The whole crew is awake, and eager to know what is going on, but I keep my mouth shut; leaving it to Fenton to demolish their hopes and aspirations. In fact, I go aft to the engine-room sooner than face the questions from the lads up forward. There's fewer people down this end of the boat, and most of them are too busy to notice me.

The diesels slumber in oily silence, as the chief ERA and the engineer officer examine them, and talk in monotones about things mechanical. I would have liked to have a chat with the chief, but move aft to the motor-room. A mouth-watering aroma of bacon and eggs pervades the atmosphere here, drawing me further aft to the steering compartment. There, crouched like a monkey in a cave, sits Soapy, nursing a plate, filled to capacity with at least four eggs, a pile of fried bread, and a stack of bacon.

'What the hell's that!' I explode.

He looks at me with his mouth drooling with half demolished food, 'It's me breakfast.'

'There's enough for five normal blokes there,' I protest.

He grins happily, 'Oh, well, you know, 'swain. The chef cooked too much grub, and some blokes went ashore, I think. I said I'd eat the extra if no one wanted it — he was only gonna put it in the oven to go dry.'

Realisation dawns. 'That's my breakfast, you bloody wart! I've bin risking my flaming neck on shore with Jimmy, and you're eating my fucking breakfast!'

His chumping jaws come to a stop, and he looks from my infused features to the congealing remains on his plate. 'You can have some of this, 'swain.' He offers it to me, and I recoil in disgust. 'I'll get another plate if you like.'

'I'm warning you, Opie,' I fume, choking as I wave a finger in his face, 'Don't come the old soldier with me!'

I leave him staring after me, with a hurt expression, and stump forward to the control-room where the signalman tells me I'm wanted in the wardroom. Still seething, I join the officers round the table, to learn what new exploits are in the offing.

'I don't have to tell you that we are in a mess, 'swain,' says Fenton; straight to the point, as always. 'We are bottled in, and it won't be long before some Jerry or Itie comes nosing by, and we are discovered. If we are to escape, we have to act quickly.

We have devised a plan, but I must stress, it could prove hazardous. So, after I have explained what I have in mind, and the part you will have to play, it will be up to you. I promise no one will blame you if you refuse to take part.'

'I understand, sir,' I find myself saying. 'But I'd like to know more before I start volunteering.'

'Of course. Well, it's this way. The first lieutenant has put forward an idea to get us out of here.'

I listen quietly as the plan unfolds with a sick feeling gathering in my stomach. It seems the major snag to just steaming straight out of this hole is that we are virtually blind and dare not risk using the periscope. The harbour is shallow, so for the first part of the journey we must bump along the sea-bed on the sand, to stay out of sight until we reach deep water. To succeed, Fenton has to navigate through a mass of sunken vessels. All they want me to do is put on a DSEA set and go out through the gun-hatch with Murray, each of us carrying a spare set. Once we are out we will scout a route to the open sea. That is where the best bit comes: I am then supposed to return to the boat, and come back inboard through one of the torpedo-tubes with the necessary instructions – leaving Murray to signal course changes by tapping on the hull with a wheelspanner. No need for him to explain why I cannot come back the way I go: the gun-hatch can be used only once – for it cannot be drained down.

I sit and stare into space. 'Take your time, coxswain,' advises Fenton. 'Don't be ashamed to say no; nothing will be held against you. You have been chosen because you are the most experienced in this sort of thing, and the last to go through the tank, so the drill should be fresh in your mind.'

I can see it all. The full, perilous connotations swim in front of my eyes, turning my guts to water. Every phase of such an operation is fraught with unpredictables. A thousand things can go wrong, and no man should be asked to do what they are asking me to do. I have every right to refuse, tell them to go to hell, and put their stupid plan where it belongs – in the pages of a boys' adventure comic.

'I'll give it a go, sir.' What am I doing it for; medals? I don't want their stinking medals. I'm certainly not doing it to ingratiate myself with anyone: perhaps I'm just insane!

Fenton comes to wish us luck as we get our gear together, and broadcasts the news to everybody. I receive pats on the back from some, plus a look from Briarley that says quite plainly, 'More bloody heroics!'

As though to emphasise the insanity of it all, the boat shudders as a bomb explodes some way off. I shut my mind to a picture of what I'll look like if one of those beauties lands somewhere near me when I'm in the water. 'Concentrate on your drill, and how to stay alive — that's the answer,' I tell myself. 'If the worst comes, you can always swim ashore. If you hold your hands up high enough, some nice German will come along to take you prisoner, and you'll spend the rest of the war safely tucked away in a concentration camp' — it's a tempting thought.

VI

Returning to the chiefs' mess I find a pair of decrepit shorts amongst my gear, and decide to wear them for the escapade; if only for modesty's sake. There is plenty of advice and good wishes coming in my direction from well-meaning friends, but on this occasion it will be up to the two of us to make up our own rules as we go along. No handbook has been written setting out a drill for such a mad scheme. I undress, and stack my gear on my bunk. As I do I notice the cluster of pipes and the memory of the nightmare comes back. There was a time when I would have been caught up in the excitement of an enterprise like this, with the adrenalin flowing inside me. My mind is filled with evil thoughts today and paints pictures designed to cool my ardour, and tie my guts in a knot. Can it be that I will mess things up by going into a blue funk? Or will I forget part of the drill? Should I go to the skipper and admit that I am not up to the job before I balls things up for everybody?

I get into my shorts with my brain in turmoil. How do I go about telling Murray I'm not going because I'll be more a liability than an asset. I stand with him in the wardroom, with the lower gun-hatch gaping down at us as we sort out the escape sets and strap them on. Sweat is seeping out of my pores, and my hair and beard are soaked with it. A thought comes suddenly – a legitimate way out. I cannot understand why I didn't think of it before. The question is: how do I explain it without making it look as though I am chickening out? There isn't much time now, and it would mean putting someone else's life in danger. Mention it casually – that's the answer – as though it is an afterthought.

'I'm surprised you didn't think of Selby for this, sir.'

He looks sharply at me. 'Because he's a qualified diver, you mean?'

'That's right, sir.'

He purses his lips as though a big doubt has crossed his mind. 'Selby's a stoker PO, Grant. This is a job for a seaman with some knowledge of navigation. We haven't much time left now,' he warns, in a tone that says quite plainly, If you're going to welsh, do it now; before you are out there, messing things up for me. 'If you have any queries, you had better be quick about it.'

I look into his dark eyes, and see a mixture of disgust and contempt. With anger boiling inside me, there is no way I'll admit to him that I'm not up to it. 'No queries, sir – just wondered, that's all.'

His face hardens, 'Get on with it then – we have got to get out while things are still in turmoil on shore.'

In silence we finish strapping on and testing the gear. Fenton wishes us luck before we clamber up into the tower. I'm number one this time, placing myself on the top rungs of the ladder, to wait for Murray to come in after me. There is a cold anger in me now; mostly directed at myself; for I know I haven't fooled the first lieutenant one little bit with my casual mention of Selby. More than that, it is the knowledge that I had been quite willing to subject another man to the hazards of a job I have no stomach for. I have never shirked my responsibilities, and a hot sense of shame floods through me as I carry out the drill mechanically. I jerk off one clip as water floods up from below, to cover my shoulders. Automatically I reach up and pull down the vent lever. I have no feelings now, and release the second clip with a detached sense of resignation. I can accept things as they are, with no lurid visions colouring my mind.

The hatch springs open, and brilliant light shimmers through the clear, shallow water. I'm shocked to see how close we are to the surface. Fish are swimming through the handrails on the gun deck, and I can see the tops of the periscope's standards are only inches beneath the sea. A hard tap on my shoulder draws my attention to Murray, who jerks a thumb upwards. I let go the rail, to allow myself to float up. We are unprepared for the dissonant welter of violent noise that hits us when we break surface. The sky is filled with the black bursts of anti-aircraft shells, while shrapnel rains down about us. Columns of black smoke rise hundreds of feet into the sky from ammunition dumps and store-piles, as they are destroyed by the garrison before the enemy can capture them. The air resounds with the detonations of shells and bombs as unopposed German and Italian aircraft scream from the sky, to pound the defenders into submission.

'Come on!' growls Murray, after he has spat out his mouthpiece. 'We'll climb on to the tanker to get bearings.'

I follow obediently, cursing my tender feet, and the rusty steel deck with its many snags that rip my soles into a bleeding mess. From up in the remains of her bridge we can see the masts and funnels of several sunken ships, but it looks as though there is a clear passage in line with the edge of a large building rising above the rest to the north of the town. We can use that as a bearing, and hope to find an open way to sea, once past the bows of a wooden schooner that lies with her bowsprit pointed to the sky. I can see why it is not possible to use the periscope − only a human eye can look down through the depths to pick out a passage in this mess.

We take our goggles, but leave our sets behind on the tanker, before we swim out together, peering down at the smooth sand with undulating patterns of light playing on it. It stays that way, with the water so clear it is possible to see anchor cables running along the sea-bed. If enemy aircraft were not distracted by what goes on ashore they could not fail to see *Avon*'s shape nestling there. It emphasises the need for haste as we paddle towards the schooner.

We reach it without any problems, and take a rest while Murray points out different landmarks he has memorised from the chart. 'When the boat reaches this point,' he says, 'just beyond the bowsprit, I will give five raps on the hull. That will be the signal for a forty-five degree turn to starboard. I reckon that's near enough the way we came in − look, there's the first wreck we saw when we entered.'

Right enough. I can recognise a blue star on her funnel showing through the wartime grey that has peeled away. The passage looks good all the way to the gate, and I guess the distance is something like two miles to open water. We must assume that the coast on either side is held by the enemy, once clear of the town itself.

'We'll swim in that direction until there is enough depth to use the periscope,' he says; and once more we take to the water. I hope it isn't too far: my swimming is not up to olympic standards and we are going to run out of handy wrecks to hang on to shortly. I needn't have worried though, for the bottom shelves to fall away sharply after fifty yards or so. The submarine should find plenty of depth from now on. To my relief he seems satisfied. We hold on to a wooden marker buoy, while he studies the area for a moment, before coming to a decision.

'See those ships over there?' he asks, and I follow his pointed finger to where two small ships lie close together, overlapping, to hide a stretch of coast for some five hundred yards from this angle. I nod, and he goes on, 'We are a good half mile from the south shore, and those ships will hide us from the north while we poke the upper hatch up to get me back inboard. After that, we can use the periscope.'

Without waiting for a reply he swims off towards the tanker, leaving me to tag on after him. We cross the area without incident, to climb back to the rusty old bridge. He is about to speak when I spot a shape in the sky, and push him into the shelter of an overhanging steel plate, as the Junkers 88 howls overhead, so low I can see the rivets in her skin and the bombs still hung up in the open bay. She is lifting in a long, curving climb, as though she has made a dummy run over us. We watch as she circles the bay, dropping a wing to wheel in our direction again. Her nose seems to be aimed straight at me, as she screams in at sea level.

'She's seen us!' I shout, but Murray is watching her with half-closed eyes, saying nothing. Her shadow crosses over us as her front gunner opens up, and we whirl to see a small dhow receiving a stream of tracer, as the three-man crew dive overboard. The Junkers roars away to find targets more worthy of her bombs. I am shaking, and gripping the metal so hard, my knuckles are white.

'Coxswain!'

I stare into angry eyes as he grabs my shoulders to shake me back to reality. I blink and take hold of myself.

'You all right?' he asks irritably.

'Yes, sir.'

'Right then.' His eyes are clouded with doubt. 'This is the drill.' He hesitates to make certain I am grasping what he says. He is treating me like an idiot again, and the old anger comes back.

'I'm listening, sir. That plane deafened me for a moment.'

'Good. You must go back into the boat now. Tell the captain I will be on the bridge, tucked in under the forward windbreak. Tell him to stay on the same course until I bang five times; then turn forty-five degrees to starboard. Allow about three minutes before risking the periscope. He should then be in position to pick me up. The total distance is about six hundred yards – say about ten minutes at the sort of speed that won't make things difficult for me. These sets give about twenty minutes of air, so if you use your spare set and leave me the rest I'll have plenty of time.'

'Yes, sir.'

'I will allow enough time for you to get into the boat and make your report to the captain; then I will signal with five raps on the hull. If there is no response I'll assume all is not ready and try again after a short interval. Remember: no raps – no go. Otherwise it is all fives. Five to go and five to alter course; that way no one gets confused. All other signals will be standard 'rule-of-the-road'. One starboard, two port, three astern, and so on – understand?'

'Yes, sir.' He's a cool bastard; you've got to give him that. Cool as yesterday's custard – I just hope I can match him.

'Right. That's all then. No questions?'

We look at each other for a moment. His face tells me that he depends on me entirely. In a few minutes he will be out there alone, and if I make a cock-up; there he'll stay.

'No questions, sir,' I say firmly.

He offers me a hand. I'm taken off-guard for a second before gripping it hard.

He watches me strap on my gear and I check him out in return. I close my mouth over the mouthpiece, breathing a couple of times to make sure it is okay, then I go down into the water.

Now I am on my own; pulling my body along the casing hand over hand towards the bow. Small eddies surge through the holes in the deck as I go past the square gap that gives access to the fore-hatch. Just below there the TI and his minions are waiting for me and the thought gives me a lot of comfort. Here are the fore-'planes already rigged out, with the anchor just forward of them in its housing. A stream of bubbles rises as I breathe on my airbag, and I recall vague warnings of staying too long on oxygen, but it is too complicated to ponder on and I am at the bow. I work my feet round to stand upright so that I can push down towards the tubes. The visibility is perfect, with small shoals of inquisitive fish coming to see what strange invader disturbs their peaceful world.

I'm in front of the tubes now, sliding down slowly past the bowcaps until I reach the gaping mouth of the one I am to use. It looks small, and there seems little room to spare as I prepare to enter. I force myself to think calmly and methodically. I must go in head first with my arms extended in front of me, holding my spanner so that I can signal the TI that I am here, desperate to be let in. It seems a long while since I left the surface, and all this time is being added to Murray's reckonings. I can't afford to hurry though. One slip and the whole thing goes to pot. Carefully I ease my torso into the tube, using my feet to propel me towards the inner door. There is no room to move and the smooth metal closes in on me as my body settles to the bottom of the tube. I touch the steel concave of the inner door and give it three loud bangs with the spanner, then slump down to wait.

The TI is on the ball. The outer door swings shut, leaving me in total darkness, terribly alone. My ears are aching and I am lying on the airbag of my escape set, but there is no way I can lift off it. A surge of panic threatens to take hold and the water goes icy cold as it envelops me. I try to ease a cramp coming into my leg, but the tube holds me fast, and the movement shifts my mouthpiece to allow water to enter my mouth. I try to stop choking as it trickles into my throat, causing me to gasp. The mouthpiece flies out to fall away into the blackness. I cannot bring my arms back to retrieve it, and I hold my breath while the nightmare comes with its writhing entrails swirling inside my head.

Where are they? What are they doing for Christ's sake! My lungs are bursting and there is no sign of the tube draining. The water enters my lungs, choking me as I begin to struggle. I am like that when the tube drains down to leave me spewing my innards out. I try to scream again as a spasm seizes me, sapping my strength, so that I lie sobbing in the tube as the inner door swings open and hands reach in to pull me out.

They drag me into the light and warmth of the fore-ends, placing me on a bunk while I retch sea-water and vomit. My head is splitting as I try to gulp air into my lungs. Everything swims about me and it takes a long time to get things into focus. I feel no gratitude for being alive; no shame for having broken. No one will ever get me into that situation again — never — never.

'Grant!'

I focus on Fenton's face and control my breathing until it is possible to talk. Step by step he takes me through it, noting every phase, and making me repeat it if he isn't sure. I have to be coaxed every bit of the way, for I have no will to make an effort, but at last it is done, and he goes aft to wait for Murray's signal. I doubt if it will come though; it must be hours since I started out and he has long since drowned, or gone ashore to give himself up. In fact it has been eight minutes from the time I left the tanker's bridge, and it is another five before Murray's signal comes.

*

I am supposed to remain in my bunk to recover from the ordeal, but they know nothing of the delirious visions that infiltrate my brain the moment I lie still and try to sleep. Out comes that faithful old medicine bottle with its answer to all my problems, and with its fire burning in my belly I go aft to the control-room. Fenton's face is a picture when he sees me take my place at the after-'planes. He is not to know that I cannot bear to be alone, needing to be kept active so that my mind stays clear of monsters with waving arms that threaten to take away my reason. The men in the control-room stare at me with something like admiration, and even Briarley seems to have a grudging respect for me as I sit beside him. My silent acceptance of it all only serves to convince them of my stoic determination to do my part.

The five knocks come loud, and Fenton bleeds air into the tanks until we feel her rock upright. All Briarley and I can do is keep the 'planes amidships for now. It is up to the skipper to keep her down by using the trim tanks. He must use the screws to steer with for the rudder is useless at the speed we'll be doing. I can imagine Murray peering through one of the glass ports in the fore end of the bridge, as the sea-bed slides by beneath us. We trust in him completely as our keel cuts the occasional furrow in the soft sand. I glance at the clock, with the hands moving up to ten o'clock – mid morning; if all goes well we will be at sea for tot-time. I must be feeling the influence of the rum I've already drunk to have those thoughts, for the world is beginning to look a little brighter.

No one speaks as the motors whine to push us gently along as though we are on rails, while the minute hand moves towards ten past the hour. Five hefty bangs come, and the starboard screw is put into reverse to swing us unto our new course. I'm the only one who can visualise the scene up top, and I can imagine the bowsprit of that old schooner sliding by with our bows pointed towards the open sea. On each side the long arms of the creek stretch out with their enemy guns poised ready to blast us out of the water. Murray will see no further than twenty-five yards, even in these clear waters, and I pray that we missed no projecting rocks or chunks of wreckage when we carried out our survey.

I jump as Fenton snaps his fingers and the after periscope swishes up from its well. He crouches to rise with it, still squatting when he signals to the operator to hold it there, as daylight reflects in his eyes. He is using the small 'attack' 'scope, with its thin stem to make a quick circuit before standing back to wave it down again. 'Smack on!' he says with relish. 'We will take her up easy. Stand by number two and four, chief. I don't want to show more than the standards and top of the bridge if possible. Get up the ladder, Bunts. Take one clip off.'

The signalman clatters up into the tower while the needles on the gauges swing towards zero. We all hear Murray's wheel-spanner beat a staccato on the upper hatch. 'Open up!' Fenton yells.

A cheer goes up from the men in the control-room as Murray

comes down the ladder in his wet shorts, carrying the escape sets. Fenton dives the boat again, ordering 'half ahead – group down' to nose out towards the sea at a more respectable speed. He finds time to pat his first lieutenant on the back. 'Well done, Henry – well done both of you,' he adds, and his hand comes down on my shoulder while I concentrate hard on my instruments. The hydroplanes are having effect now as we go down to forty feet.

It is a straightforward navigating job now, with occasional sightings with the periscope to keep us on course. Those army gunners are not looking for submarines, and don't see the 'feather' left by our periscope as it moves through the water. Soon we are out of the creek, in our own element.

'All right, coxswain. I think it is time to issue the rum.' He lifts the tannoy 'mike' to his lips. 'Watch diving! White watch to patrol routine!'

We are clear now, with everybody relaxing to speculate on runs ashore in Alex or some other den of iniquity. The talk grows louder as the rum loosens tongues and the tensions of Tobruk crumble away: laughter and banter in full swing when the tannoy crackles. Everyone goes quiet, to absorb the good news.

'This is the captain. Now that Tobruk is out you will be wondering where next – and I've no doubt there are some attractive speculations on offer. Our orders are to proceed to our alternative destination to discharge our cargo. We have managed to repair the radio, so there is no reason why we cannot carry out these orders. Tomorrow we will rendezvous with a destroyer to be escorted into Malta, where they have a desperate need for some of the goods we carry. I don't need to tell you that the island is cut off and under continuous air attack. Therefore, the sooner we are in and out the better. However, the engineer has certain repairs to make following the depth-charge damage, so I have agreed to a lay-over of one day. The repairs can be carried out dived, or under cover of smoke screens, then we should be on our way to Alex for a break – thank you.'

There is a long pause before anyone speaks. Then the subjects steer clear of runs ashore. We sail westward, to stay deep until nightfall when we surface. Several small ships are sighted, but we are under orders to ignore them. Fenton decides to take Miller's body to Malta, where there are people better fitted than we are, for the gruesome task of transferring the body ashore. It is touch and go whether he should be buried at sea, after the time he has spent in the tube in the heat of the Med, but it goes against the grain to fire him like a torpedo.

VII

Malta is a familiar haunt of mine, having spent many months there in pre-war days when the full pomp of a peacetime Navy filled the harbour, and the narrow streets were thronged with spotlessly whiteclad matelots. Now, in contrast, war has transformed it into a drab, rubble-strewn mass of sand-stone with people dashing along between air-raids, intent on getting what has to be done over with before the next load of bombs comes screaming out of the sky. Naked, blatant death has been laid bare in the streets and hunger gnaws away the spirit of everybody. People live like moles underground while the days reverberate to the raucous cacophony of war.

The *Avon* has to be repaired before going to sea again. We are brought ashore into the barracks on Manoel Island, leaving only a skeleton crew on board to shift berth and dive the boat. I have requested permission to go to the Naval Hospital at Bighi on the pretext of receiving attention to a wisdom tooth, hoping to find someone who will have the answer to the recurring nightmares that will not let me sleep.

I hire a dghaisa to take me across to the Valletta side of the creek, where I can climb the steep hill to the town itself, straddled high above the harbour. From there it is an easy descent to the steps at Customs House on the Grand Harbour side of the chunk of land separating the two main creeks. The hospital lies on the other side of the harbour, and with luck I should be able to catch the pinnace manned by a Maltese crew that regularly makes the crossing.

The sun is hot on my back as I walk along the road that follows the edge of the creek, with my thoughts far away from the war and submarines. A buoyant sense of freedom lifts me away from it all as I stride purposefully along the dusty footpath; that feeling known only to a sailor on shore, after a spell at sea. Rounding the head of the creek I glance back to see *Avon* being warped away from her berth, to another part of the harbour. Half a dozen seamen move lazily about her casing, tending the hawsers, and I wonder where the hell she will be when I return for duty.

I shrug the thought away as easily as it comes however, for this is no time for morbid contemplation, and my eye has caught a glint of flashing sunlight high in the sky, where nothing should blemish the clear blue. Even as I blink away the grim reality of what I've seen; wailing sirens lift their baleful voices in nerve-racking chorus. Three twin-engined aircraft come roaring in from seaward — straight towards the submarine, as she swings unprotected in the centre of the open area — wide open to their attack.

I cringe back into the shelter of a small shrine, carved out of the cliff face at the side of the road, and watch the leader come howling in towards me. I see the bombs leave the belly of the 'plane, and they seem to hang suspended in the air for a long time, before arcing down towards their target. The peace is torn apart by a bedlam of hellish noise as guns open up from ships and shore. Dust and smoke fill the air, and bursting shells pockmark the sky.

The bombs explode with thunderous detonations, sending great gouts of dirty water high, to hang with small rainbows glinting in the vapour, before showering down again.

The submarine is hidden by a curtain of climbing water, but I see orange flashes through the spray and know that she is being hit. The shadows of the bombers pass across the roadway as they climb away from a perfect attack. They have caught the island unawares. When the boat comes into view again I can see she is mortally wounded and going down by the bow. No one moves on her casing.

Numbed by it all, and sickened by the loss of the men who had been working there so recently, I stand in utter dejection, unaware that fingers are pulling at my sleeve until a faint voice urges me to take notice. I look down to stare bewildered into the wide, anxious eyes of a brown-faced girl, wearing a thin black dress that emphasises the darkness of her skin. Her eyes are glazed with panic. I see that she is driven to distraction by the exploding bombs and the fury of the guns. She must have lived through many such attacks, as every Maltese has, but the breaking point has come. Her quaking body can take no more.

There is little room for me, let alone the two of us, so I lead her out into the sunlight, keeping close to the shelter of the cliff wall, trying to shield her with my body. All goes well until a bomb hits the water nearby with such violence that we are thrown into a heap on the ground; and I thought the raid was over.

My ears ring and acrid dust fills my nostrils and throat as I haul myself upright. She is clinging to my legs, convulsing to the sound of the bombs and gunfire. I'm all she has now as terror blots out all reason and her brain refuses to function. I search round frantically for somewhere to take her for shelter. A few yards further on I can see a pile of rubble, half filling the entrance to what has once been a wine shop, where men sat to discuss topics of the day over glasses of potent Maltese wine.

She allows herself to be led into it, stumbling after me, muttering incoherent sounds from trembling lips. I half push, half carry her over the rubble and into the gloomy interior of this sanctuary. It is like a cell, though vague outlines of murals on the walls still strive to colour the drabness. The rubble closes most of the entrance to shut out some of the sound, and there is an air of relative peace in these sombre surroundings.

We settle together at the bottom of the heap of wreckage. Self-consciously I take her in my arms to quell the shuddering that shakes her small frame. Her fingers clutch at me with a strength far beyond what I expect from such tiny hands, and she buries her face in my shirt-front, to cuddle up tight against me in a way that makes me wonder if I'll ever prise her loose again.

I mutter vague terms of endearment and comfort to try to calm her down a bit. The shuddering begins to subside. Soon we are holding each other while the madness of the world crashes and bangs outside. Her warm body is beginning to mould into my thinly-clad torso with an effect far removed from pure sympathy. The thin clothing she wears does little to conceal the shape of her body, and I can feel the roundness of her breasts pressed tight against me. I bury my beard in the mass of black hair while her convulsions ease a little. Soon she is gently sobbing into my chest, but she still clings with that same desperate panic, as though I am the only thing between her and insanity. I caress her back with my hand, running fingers softly up and down her spine.

Eventually, she raises her head so that her warm cheek moves up over my face until our heads are together. My body is churning with all the pent-up emotion that has lain dormant since Portsmouth. She knows full well the effect she is having on me, because a new kind of urgency has taken over now, and she is pressing her thigh against me in a way that leaves no doubt in my mind that she feels the same way.

Her head comes up until her lips are searching mine, to respond to my hungry kiss with a wild eagerness that fills me with an agonising need for everything she has to offer. I find the soft swell of her breast, and caress it as her lips move busily over mine and we are lifted together on a surging wave of lust. Groping frantically beneath her thin dress my fingers probe the hot, moist secrets of her; feeling the answering movement of her loins as she moans in my ear.

I am seized with an almost wild panic now, lest I lose it all in my impatient clumsiness. Stripping away the last remnants of clothing that shields her from me, and struggling with my own obstinate buttons, we come together on the harsh slope of the rubble in a savage, gasping turmoil. I force myself into her. Filled with a cruel madness, overpowering all my other senses in the semi-darkness, until I groan with the agony of it — driving into her with one final thrust, to stay deep inside her while she cries great wrenching sobs, and clings hard to me.

For a long time we stay together like that as her sobs die away. Reluctantly we realise it is all over and must pull apart. The sounds from that other world outside invade our sanctuary once more, and we become aware of our surroundings. The long, steady wail of the all-clear punctuates the episode, and we must gather ourselves together, to leave the cool shadow of our haven and go out into the brazen sunshine.

I watch her go, walking uncertainly through fresh piles of debris, which is still smoking and reeking of high explosive. She looks back just once, as though to make sure it all happened, before turning a corner, leaving me staring into the settling dust of the empty street. A black mongrel shambles by me, sniffing round a demolished building with an anxious whining. A pathetic array of furniture stands open to view through a gaping hole, and the dog's interest is centred on a ruin of stone and wood in one corner. His tail wags excitedly, while his nose digs into the shadowed gaps between the timbers as he scratches at the dust with an urgent paw. Two men arrive, moving in to find out what excites him so much. Me – I don't want to know what lies under that mess, and leave to attend to my own affairs.

I walk back along the way I came; the scars of the raid plainly show amongst the ruins of previous bombings. The sandstone is newly cracked and sharp-edged, spilling out across the road. To walk all round the creeks would take hours, so I search along the shore to find a dghaisa or some kind of water transport to ferry me across the narrow creek. Already a few people are going about their business with an air of apathy as they take in the new destruction with dull eyes. It is day to day living here now, and providing it is not your home that is reduced to a pile of debris the most important thing is where to obtain the basic ingredients required to stay alive.

Something catches my eye, and I see a boat driven up on to the beach close by. It is a destroyer's motor cutter – but as I approach I can see it is a wreck, and one of the crew appears to be trying to bite his way through the engine. His gaping jaws are clenched on the hot metal, with congealed blood cooking steadily in the heat of the sun. Sightless eyes stare across the cylinder head at the dark water slopping in the bilges. I fancy he winks at me as I look. 'Just watch me,' he is saying, 'I'll get my own back on the bloody Navy – I'll eat one of their flaming engines.'

I can look at the scene with cool detachment. It is as though death has become so repetitious now that it is like staring into a butcher's window, to see the corpses of virile men lying in attitudes that can only be achieved when the body is lifeless. Surprising what contortions the body will adopt when it is thrown about by explosives.

Looking towards *Avon*, I can see her stern sticking out of the water, with the fore-hatch already under, and I reckon her bow must be dug into the seabed. A bustling throng of sailors swarms over her, clambering amongst her torn metalwork, hauling things over the rim of the bridge. A vague sense of guilt grows in the back of my mind, taking me to task for not being on board when the tragedy occurred. In circumstances like this, the coxswain should always be there, materialising like magic out of the woodwork, when everyone else is numbed by the situation. I've seen it so many times when things go radically wrong — it might be necessary to search for some people; but never the coxswain — he is always about.

From nowhere, the inevitable dghaisa appears, its owner pushing it along with his oars crossed in front of his body with that timeless stroke that is the hall-mark of these Maltese boatmen. They lean into the stroke, allowing the weight of their bodies to do all the work as they face forward, swaying to and fro with the rhythm of a lifetime's practice. I sometimes think these blokes could row their craft to China and back if the price was right.

The paintwork of the vessel is brilliant, reflecting the scolloped water as it noses in towards me in response to my wave. It is a day for wordless communication, for the brain has had more than enough to cope with without trying to sustain conversation. We cross the expanse of the creek with nothing said; but an exchanged look when we pass close to the stricken submarine is enough. He has seen it all before, and life for him has become a trial of shortages, violent bombings, and quick burials. He will support his family by legal or unlawful means, waiting year after year for the interminable misery to pass by, and for peace to return to the island. As far as he is concerned I am only a fare; another chunk of the grim machinery of war — a means to an end.

We pass close to the boat. I can recognise some of the men who are working on her deck. There is not much sign of damage to be seen, and only the sharp incline of her hull indicates how water-logged she is. Most of her bridge is still above water and I reckon the conning-tower hatch must be clear. I begin to hope optimistically that there may not be too many casualties. Slipping a shilling into the boatman's hand I stride over the baking stone towards a landing-stage, where a group of people stand round a couple of ambulances that are backed up to the jetty.

They are mostly strangers, but there are a few familiar figures amongst them, and I go to join the group with the intention of finding out the score. At this moment a launch swings in towards the jetty. I can see shrouded bodies stretched across the thwarts and a slumped shape sitting in the stern-sheets draped in a blanket, nursing an arm wrapped in a bloodstained bandage. It is one of the casing-party, and his face is grey as he stares into the distance with painfilled eyes.

'You going back to the boat?' I ask the coxswain of the launch. He nods, so I drop down into it as the bodies are being lifted out, to be placed on stretchers and carried to the waiting ambulances.

It takes no time at all to cross the short distance. I climb up to the sloping casing and go aft towards the bridge. Briarley is there, watching me as I approach, with a sour expression on his sallow face.

'Miss the fun, did you?' he sneers, with a mirthless smile. 'Must have had a grandstand view of this lot.'

'How many?' I ask coldly.

'Eight dead – five wounded. There is a hole the size of an Austin seven in the fore-ends. You certainly know when to go missing.'

I ignore his insinuations. 'She doesn't seem to be settling any more.'

'The bulkhead's holding, I reckon. Murray's down there now, making it safe with shoring. We're dry aft of the torpedo-stowage compartment. It is gonna be a dockyard job though.'

I look at the slouching body with distaste. 'What are you doing up here when there's still work to be done?'

His face goes hard. 'I'm havin' a break, swain. I helped get most of the bodies and the wounded out, and now I'm havin' a loaf. If it's all the same to you.' He is spitting the words out now, full of venom and hate, 'I was told to have a stand easy, because I have been floggin' me guts out, while you've been gallivanting on shore.'

'That's enough, Briarley.'

'Truth hurts, does it, 'swain?' he squares up to me. 'You don't fool me – I've seen men scared before, and, boy, you were shittin' yourself the other day on the 'planes.'

Others are taking notice now, and pausing in their work. I must put a stop to it. 'Stow that sort of talk — I'll see you later; when you come to your senses — until then, keep that big mouth of yours shut.'

I leave him then; yelling down to tell those below that I'm on my way down the ladder. A couple of men stand back to wait for the tower to clear as I hit the deck. I can read nothing in their expressions, and leave them clutching bundles of clothing, waiting for their turn to go out into the sunshine. There is a steep slope to the deck, and I stare about to get my bearings. All the action seems to be going on forward, so I move to the door leading into the passage that runs by the messes, toward the distant door, holding back the water in the fore-ends; and stop dead. Memories of another time when I looked towards a similar door in a submarine with her nose sloping down to the sea-bed fill my head. For a moment I see a white arm waving pathetically, while tons of encroaching sea press against it, pouring over the sill, to advance towards me as I struggle back with my lifeless burden; the dead man that I have dragged the whole length of the passage for no purpose. I see desperate men clambering back up the slope, with filthy faces and staring eyes, while the water rises up the sides of the door. The arm continues to wave, accusing us of leaving it behind to save our own skins.

It takes an effort to step over the sill and go forward through the bulkhead, to sidle past a procession of men carrying their personal gear aft. Murray and Fenton are right forward at the bulkhead, talking together as they examine the door. I stand for a moment until they notice me.

'Ah, coxswain!' says the captain. 'We are getting all our personal stuff out; leaving her to the dockyard. It has to be done quickly, before some more enemy aircraft come back to complete the job.' He turns to Murray. 'I'll go ashore and see if I can arrange a smokescreen or something. Do your best, Henry, but don't risk any more lives. It's not worth it.'

'Yes, sir.'

We watch the skipper struggle aft against the slope of the deck, then Murray swings on me. 'Where the hell have you been, 'swain? I could have had ten teeth pulled in the time. Your place is here; not wandering round Valletta.'

I'm struck dumb; I thought I had a legitimate reason for being held up on shore, but when I recall what I was doing while all this was taking place I choke back my protest. 'I was taking shelter, sir.'

'Were you indeed,' he growls. 'Well, I would have thought you could have made it back in one of the lulls.'

'What lull?' I'm thinking, but I keep my mouth shut and wait for him to make the running. It seems he has shot his bolt for now though, for with a curt order to, 'Get on with it, and pull your finger out!' he dismisses me.

I get my gear together, and chivy the crew along until the last boat-load crosses to the jetty, where arrangements are made to put them all up in the NAAFI while Murray and I sort out accommodation in Phoenicia Barracks. The stores issue clothing to those who need it; and most of us do, for we have only our steaming kit, which has taken quite a thrashing since leaving Plymouth. Once these arrangements are made I'm left to get together with the chief ERA to make sure the crew are settled in. With that done, everyone is given the rest of the day to get organised, and told to fall in on the parade-ground at 0900 tomorrow, when the skipper will tell what our future is.

Briarley's accusations, and Murray's comments about my lack of dedication come back to me later, so I decide to get the hell out of it for a spell. I cross the causeway and turn right towards Sliema. I've had many runs ashore on this waterfront, where the lights and music from the bars invited in the crews of a peacetime fleet to sample the goods, encouraged by grinning youngsters with shouts of 'Inside Navy! – Come on, Jack! – Steak, eggs and chips! – Lots of girls; all virgins!' The air filled with raucous banter and lewd responses, while bottles of 'Blue Label' beer washed down thirsty gullets at a prodigious rate; and this was nothing compared to 'The Gut'. Otherwise known as Strait Street, in Valletta, where the narrow, sloping alley became a concentrated avenue of debauchery every pay-day, with running fights between ships' companies, or with the Maltese police who liked nothing better than to crack open a couple of sailors' heads. Drunken orgies, obscene cabarets, and frequent forays by naval patrols all went to make up the scene, accepted as part of everyday life by the locals.

Now I seek out a small café to sit on my own, nursing a glass of cloudy, colourless liquid, designed to rot a man's stomach or tear out his gullet. It takes a couple of drinks to get acclimatised to the stuff, but once the initial damage has been done it is plain sailing. So I get down to emptying the bottle. No one disturbs me, and I am oblivious to all goings-on elsewhere while I indulge in some serious drinking. The proprietor is only too willing to ensure I do not go dry. Replacing the empty bottle with alacrity after relieving me of what he considers the right price in these hard times. At last he has to admit that I can take no more, and pushes me out into the night.

Everything is black out here. The harbour whirls about me as I try to take my bearings, only to find that everything looks the same to my unco-operative eyes. In fact, I've never seen such a mess. The houses seem to be falling in on each other, and the ships are rolling on a flat calm sea. I fall into the gutter a couple of times, having hell's own job regaining my feet, but no one seems to take notice, so I am able to stagger along with the help of the occasional wall until I fall into a dark alley that leads off to the left, away from the harbour, where I stumble along between two high walls that are about to fall in on me. The whirlpool inside my brain is building up revs and I have an urgent need to rid myself of some of the cause of all this. I hold on to the corner of a wall, spewing out a repugnant mess unto the pavement.

There isn't much fight left in me now. I'm finding it an effort to put one foot in front of the other, even if I knew which way to go. After two or three futile attempts to cross the road I am forced to resign, sliding slowly down to lie in my own mess, to wait for the world to stop revolving.

I come to sitting under a shower which is turned full on, hitting my head with a force that threatens to split my skull. I am wearing my clothes, and as my brain begins to function I realise someone has just thrown me there, to let me fight my own way back to consciousness. I struggle to rise, fighting back nausea and an urge to vomit. My head thumps and my mouth is a cesspit. As I drag my body upright to stand with that beautiful, cold water pouring over me I hear a sound, and get my eyes into focus. The TI and Soapy are watching me from a safe distance, keeping well clear of my splashing with wide grins on their faces.

'Oh Christ!' I groan, holding my head, surprised to find it is still the same size, and not blown up to the dimensions of a barrage-balloon.

'You certainly hung one on last night, Ben,' drawls the TI. 'Good job Soapy got to you first. If the police had found you in the state you were in, you would be runnin' rahned in a little rahned 'at and a square collar next week.'

I stumble out of the shower as Soapy turns off the water. I'm shaking all over and my head will not stop going round. I've never felt so ill in my life. 'What time is it?'

'O six double O – you've got a couple of hours or so to get yourself cleaned up, and back to the land of the living. I take it you've got whatever it was out of your system?'

'Uh! Oh yeah – guess so.' I am beginning to wake up. 'You say young Soapy found me?'

'That's right; and he had the good sense to get hold of me before anyone found you. We had a hell of a job gettin' you back. It's lucky I knew the PO on the gate; and that he is a mate of mine – you owe him half a tot.'

I focus on Soapy with great difficulty. 'Good thinking, lad: thanks

A wide grin splits his face. 'That's okay, 'swain. Makes up for that breakfast though, don't it?'

A brief vision of congealing bacon and eggs threatens to disrupt my innards again, 'Don't mention food please, lad. You'll only ruin it all, and undo all the good you've done.'

'I've brought you this,' says the TI; offering a glass with nothing in it.

'Thanks!' I say sarcastically. 'That will do me the world of good.'

'Don't be a prick!' he growls. 'I'm gonna make one of my specials; a Bombay Oyster.'

'Oh?' I mutter suspiciously.

'Hold the glass, Soapy; he's shakin' like a leaf.'

I watch him break an egg into the glass with a flourish, adding a drop of vinegar, with salt and pepper, before shaking it up to a yellow mess that turns my stomach as I look at it.

'What am I to do with that?'

'Drink it down in one gulp,' he says proudly. 'I'll guarantee it'll put you right.'

'What!'

'Go on — don't be such a bloody coward — get it down. Do I have to hold your nose?'

I take it in a shaking hand and gulp it down in one go, then hold hard to my reeling senses as I wait for the inevitable. Nothing happens. It doesn't seem to do any good, but on the other hand, it doesn't do any harm either, so I suppose it is a success. He stands back with a confident look on his face, and I haven't the guts to disillusion him.

'Thanks,' I manage to squeeze out of a strangled throat, and he is satisfied that he has saved my life.

'Ready?' he asks.

'I think so.'

'Right. Let's go then. Okay, Soapy; you've played your part okay, we can manage from now on — remember; not a word to anyone about this, or I'll have your guts for garters.'

'Okay, chief.'

There are a few funny looks when I enter the mess, but a warning glare from the TI stops any comment, and I am able to change into a presentable rig in time to take charge of the crew when they fall in at nine o'clock.

*

As I walk along the outside of the old fort, I can look out across Lazaretto Creek to see poor old *Avon* with her arse in the air, surrounded by tugs and other craft. She is out of our hands now, swarming with dockyard mateys and salvage experts. I go through the archway into Fort Manoel itself, where the crew is lined up in three untidy rows, with Briarley and the TI sorting them out. As I take over, to bring them to order, I have the feeling that this will be the last time we will be together as a unit. The effects of the night before are slow to wear off, and the hot sun doesn't help. When I call them to attention I try not to wince as my own voice drives into my sore head; or to look too sick when I report them to Murray.

When the skipper turns up, we have stood there for almost

twenty minutes, and with the high walls of the fort cutting off any breeze that might have made things easier we sweat and boil together as he outlines our future. A fast mine-laying cruiser — one of those beauties with about forty-five knots to play with, has got through to the island, and we are to take passage on her when she sails for Gibraltar. Once there, we will be allocated to different boats, or returned home to make up the crews of new boats as they come into commission. He thanks us all, and wishes us luck before going off to attend to his own affairs.

Murray dismisses the crew after giving details of the routine for embarking on the cruiser. He warns that discipline in the big ship will be much more strict than we are used to, but feels sure we will not let him down. Finally, almost casually, he mentions that some of us might be required to remain for an enquiry into the cause of Miller's tragic death, but that everything is being done to get it over with before the cruiser is due to sail. In the meantime written statements from myself and several other chief witnesses will be required.

I get on with the job as soon as we disperse, and write a plain, factual report of my part in it all. When I read it back, it seems to have no bearing on the real reasons for the AB's problems. The cold, callous script makes him sound like a lump of meat that has gone bad, but I'm no Charlie Dickens, and the facts are there as I saw them. When I present it to Murray in the afternoon, he reads it through, and suggests a couple of corrections before placing it on a pile, with several other versions, submitted by other budding authors.

'I've got this as well, sir.' I hand him the little, buff-coloured request form, and watch him study it for a moment without comment. After the silence stretches beyond endurance, I have to add, 'I've given it some thought, sir. I think now that the doctors were right; I could do with a spell in general service. I've done well over my five-year stint on boats now, and there's been times lately when I've felt I'm not up to the job.'

He looks at the form, tapping a pencil on the desk-top while he considers what I'm telling him. There is no hurrying this bloke. I'm fidgeting uncomfortably as the silence drags on, 'It's got nothing to do with that, sir,' I persist, pointing to my statement on Miller. 'Things seem to have caught up with me, that's all.'

'Shut up for a minute, Grant,' he says impatiently. 'I'm trying to think.'

'Yes, sir.'

The thinking time ticks by slowly, and I concentrate on a cockroach, who is setting out to cross the vast white spaces of the windowsill, while the sound of marching men comes from outside. He's doing it on purpose, I'm sure. He's enjoying keeping me standing here with my nerves jumping, and my blown-up brain throbbing.

'I would like you to give this more thought before I take it to the captain,' he says at last; and looks up into my face with an intent expression. 'You have every right to make this request, and it will most likely be granted, but I am not convinced that you are in the right frame of mind at the moment. We all have doubts about ourselves from time to time; as well you know, coxswain: and I'm saying this is a hasty decision. There is no hurry. I suggest that you sleep on it for a couple of nights.'

He goes silent again, and seems to be considering whether or not to add something extra — something that I might not be entitled to know. 'Leave it with me for now, Grant. I promise I won't hold it up if you finally decide that is what you want. In the meantime, keep yourself available — I have something up my sleeve that may be the answer. Away you go, coxswain. Don't fret too much, and I'll try not to keep you on tenterhooks.'

Obviously dismissed, I go out into the baking heat, with nothing settled, but a sense of relief for having admitted to authority that I have had a gut-full. Murray seems to be sympathetic enough to take my request in its right spirit, although that little rider about 'having something in mind' niggles a bit. The hangover is still pounding my head, and my stomach is in a turmoil — so much for the TI's miracle cure. I reckon it will stay with me until tot-time. Now I'll take advantage of my rank, and skive off to some place of refuge, to nurse my ailing body.

I turn a corner, and step into the cool shade of an alleyway leading between two blocks of messes; and who should be coming towards me, wearing that same old evil grin, but Briarley. It is impossible to pass each other without some kind of acknowledgement; even though it sticks in the gullet, so I prepare to grunt an abstract word in passing.

He has other ideas however, as I soon realise when he slows down to a stop, standing astride the narrow passageway, completely blocking it with his heavy frame. He knows full well where I have come from, but he misinterprets the sick look I have about me, and its an opportunity too good to miss.

'Copped an earful, 'ave you?' he taunts, relishing the moment to the full. Deep down I know I should push on by, and ignore him if I had any sense. But I am in no frame of mind to back down to anyone — least of all him.

'Who the hell do you think you're talking to?' I grind through clenched teeth.

His thick lips broaden into an even wider grin as he gloats on what he assumes is my discomfort, allowing his eyes to wander up and down my body, as though I am a sick beast. I know that on this day, in this place, I am going to do something stupid that I will regret for a very long time, yet I am unable to pull back from it, and I allow myself to be goaded into a situation that can only lead to disaster.

'Abaht time yer was given a tongue-lashin', yer pompous bastard. I ain't fooled by yer fuckin' medal, or the stories that's bin put abaht. A lot of good matelots 'ave died because of yer pig-'eadedness, and yer goes rahnd lordin' it over everybody else like a little tin god.' He pokes a finger into my chest with every word as he goes on 'Sod you, Grant. I've waited a long time ter get yer on yer own, and now we're 'ere I'm gonna knock seven bells aht of yer.'

Without further ado he hauls back and launches a punch designed to send me flying to the other end of Malta. Instead, because I am no longer there it sails over my head, and his knuckles smash into the masonry. He must have done a hell of a lot of damage to his fist, because he is unable to hold back a yell of anguish as he clutches his hand, nursing it with harsh groans forcing their way past his tight mouth.

That would have finished most blokes; but not him. It would take more than that to stop him now he has got going. Blind fury transforms his face into a demonic mask of total rage. He gives up all idea of finesse as he bends forward to charge at me like a mad bull. His thick skull hits me in the midriff so that I jack-knife with all the wind blasted out of me. Coloured lights flash and I strive to refill my lungs, but it like trying to force air into a deflated balloon. I am so engrossed in trying to breathe that I hardly feel the flaying fists and boots that he hammers on me. He has one good fist and two feet in good repair; using them all to good effect as he comes in at me like a wounded buffalo.

With half-filled lungs I fight back desperately with nothing in mind but an urgent need to stop the crazy onslaught. I get a great sense of satisfaction when I land a hefty blow on the side of his face that sends him reeling back to hit his head against the opposite wall. It's a God-sent chance to take a couple of deep breaths, to make my lungs begin to function once more.

When he comes back at me now I am more than ready for him. I am in no mood for Queensberry rules either. We scrap like two maniacs, with arms, legs, heads, knees – anything that will bruise, hurt or break. We are oblivious to all about us as we roll in the dry dust. Gone is the hangover; along with all sanity, as I give vent to my pent-up emotions, and pound into the sweating body of the bastard who has been riding me since I joined *Avon*. We scuffle in the shadows of the two high walls; bouncing off the stonework; grunting our rage like two wild boars. Blood is coming from his mouth and forehead, and I can taste my own as I grapple with him; determined to smash the sneer from his face.

He has met more than he can cope with. His rage has been with him a long time now, and he has made no effort to bury it, but I have bottled mine inside me until it boils with restricted energy. Now the cork has blown, it is uncontrollable. There is no thought in my mind other than the need to hurt, and he falls back under the insane fury of my attack. His face is a bloody mask. There is fear in his eyes. He has no use in his right arm, and would like to turn and run, but I don't allow that. I have him cornered in a doorway, where he can only stand and absorb the punishment I am dishing out. I do not even realise that he is unconscious when he slumps down into a crumpled heap on the step. I am still pummelling him when strong arms grab me from behind.

'Well, you've done it now, Grant,' says a cold voice, and I look into Murray's angry features. My madness dissolves, to leave me empty of any feelings. For a chief petty officer to be caught fighting is enough to finish his career. Men are picking up the bloodsoaked mess that is Briarley, while bubbles of frothy blood fill my mouth, and runnels of the stuff dribbles down over my chin, to stain my uniform.

'You will report to my cabin as soon as you have cleaned yourself up,' Murray says coldly.

I can't speak, and I slump off disconsolately, past wide-eyed sailors; towards the chiefs' mess. Sick with shame, I go to stand under the shower, to allow the gore to wash into the plug-hole — I only wish the whole stupid episode could wash down with it.

VIII

I am in limbo for a couple of days, waiting for the repercussions
of my fight with Briarley. The crew have been divided into
working parties while we wait for the cruiser to make ready to
sail. Some are even working on *Avon* now that she has been
brought up to the surface, and towed round to the dockyard.
They are stripping her of everything that is not a fixture.
Torpedoes, ammunition, stores; all have to be off-loaded before
the dockyard can get on with the business of repairing the
bomb-damage. It comes as a relief, therefore, when I am
summoned to Ricasoli Barracks on the southern promontory,
overlooking the entrance to Grand Harbour. I know the place
well. The ghost of a 'White lady' is supposed to haunt the battle-
ments at midnight. The legend says she leapt to her death to
escape the ravagings of invading Moors, and judging by the
comments of the present-day occupants, she would have to give
a repeat performance if they get within clutching distance.

The petty officer on the gate directs me to a long balustrade
that shades a row of offices. The one I want is half-way along the
row, with a faded notice telling me to 'knock and enter'. When I
do, I find myself in a dingy outer office furnished with a shabby
old desk that supports the elbows of a Maltese leading writer, as
he watches over a tray with the makings of half a dozen cups of
tea laid out. He doesn't wait for me to introduce myself, but
merely inclines his head in the direction of an inner door, leaving me to rap on the woodwork.

'Come in!' calls Murray's voice, and I go in to find three
officers waiting for me. Murray stands to the left of a large desk,
and a commander is sitting behind it, with his brass-hat resting
in front of him. He beckons me to take a seat and as I move to
take a chair up to the desk, my attention is caught by the other
officer with two criss-cross rings of the Royal Naval Reserve on

his cuffs. Something about him makes me hesitate with my backside inches above the seat. It isn't only the disreputable way he wears his uniform, or the position of his cap with the peak over his left ear. It isn't even the large expanse of belly showing above his grubby shorts, or the buttons missing from his shirt: although all this, and his slovenly manner, would cause anyone to do a double-take. No: I recognise a figure from my distant past, when I made up a fifth of the crew of his old dredger working at Plymouth.

He slouches there, wearing an enormous grin, with gaps in a row of yellow teeth that look like tombstones. He has tufts of hair growing on his cheekbones, and purple lines of twisted veins showing through the dark tan of his round face. Splay-legged, he waddles towards me.

'Christ, Ben! You look like you've seen a ghost!'

'Bloody hell! What are you doing here – sir?' 'Sir', to a bloke who spent most of his prewar days in filthy overalls, chewing tobacco, and spitting with deadly accuracy through the wheel-house windows; so that his crew learned to take a precautionary look before passing. How the hell he fits into the refined atmosphere of a wardroom beats me – we always insisted that he exercised his prerogative as skipper and ate alone. One experience of eating a meal with him is enough for anyone with a delicate constitution. He monopolises the conversation, and explodes with roars of raucous laughter at his own jokes; spraying everybody with half-chewed food in the process. He consumes grub in roughly the same fashion as the jaws of the bucket on the dredger.

The commander allows this altercation to run its length, and seems to enjoy it to the full, before reminding me that I was in the act of sitting down. The others drag chairs up, and the three of them focus their eyes on me while I try not to look too disconcerted. It's a queer confrontation – and I cannot believe it has anything to do with me knocking seven bells out of the second coxswain.

'I had better introduce myself, Grant,' he says with a smile. 'You know everyone else. My name is Brigginshaw, and I am the "Special Submarine Operations" section. I don't know what you know of our function, but, briefly, we devise means of penetrating the defences of enemy harbours — usually with human torpedoes and midget submarines. On this occasion, however, I have devised a new scheme; and that is where you and Lieutenant Linklaker come in.'

'Linklaker', that's his name. I've always known him as Half-Shackle; a nickname from God knows where; but one that fits him well.

'Perhaps you would like to explain, lieutenant?' invites Brigginshaw.

'Nah, it's your idea — best you tell him.' He beams at me. 'It's the craziest scheme you've ever heard of, Ben. Just listen to what this "Burke" has to say!'

I gasp at becoming involved in calling a full commander a 'Burke', but it seems Brigginshaw is used to it, and takes it all in his stride. He opens a large, buff envelope, and pulls out several photographs, before handing one to me.

'What do you make of that?'

'It's our old dredger, sir,' I say, without hesitation.

'Look again — closer this time.'

Raising an eyebrow, I lift the glossy plate, and stare at it. Sure enough, it's the old bucket herself, with the jib of her grab-crane draped over the side. If this was a moving picture, we would see her rolling with every swing of that jib, to the amusement of other harbour-craft crews, because she rolls like a barrel in the calmest of water, until her hold fills enough to give stability.

'That's her — I would recognise her anywhere — there's no mistaking that rusty old crate; there isn't two like her.'

Brigginshaw grins, and Half-Shackle chortles. Another photograph is shown to me. It is the dredger again; only this time I can see it is part of a larger picture; blown up to show more detail, and I can see fittings that were not on our vessel. This is another of the same type.

'Well I'm damned!'

They are like a pair of kids with a secret, not to be revealed until every ounce has been milked out of the situation.

'Now, just one more.'

Yet another photo is handed to me, and they study my face eagerly. I'm flattered by all the attention I'm getting from three

officers, but I can't make sense out of anything. The picture
shows the same dredger, but this time working in a setting far
removed from Plymouth, or any harbour I'm familiar with. I
look up, puzzled.

'That is as far as we go until we know if you decide to go along
with us,' he says quietly. 'Over to you, Murray.'

I switch my eyes to the First Lieutenant, and he leans forward
on the desk. 'We have been presented with a situation that is
little short of incredible, Grant. If we can utilise it properly, the
effect on the war in the Mediterranean will be considerable. It's
risky, and involves a certain amount of cloak and dagger stuff,
with only a fifty-fifty chance of succeeding, so we only require
volunteers. I might add that if you do decide to come along,
nothing more will be said about your little episide with
Briarley.'

They wait while I absorb everything. I'm tempted to tell them
I won't be blackmailed, but I've done similar things in the past
to unsuspecting would-be volunteers, and there is a certain
amount of fire in my belly, urging me to leap into it without
further thought. Murray can't have forgotten the way I came to
him with my request-form. This must be what he meant when
he said he might have the answer. Whatever it is, it can't be
worse than slinking back to general service, and I don't feel my
nerves will stand the long periods of boredom and tension that
goes with normal patrols.

'I'd like to go along, sir.'

'Fine!' he says cheerfully, 'then I'll tell you more about it. The
idea is to adapt a small submarine so that her conning-tower fits
in the open bottom of the dredger, so that she can be secured
and taken in tandem through submarine nets. We are banking
on no one taking notice of a rusty old dredger. If things go true
to form, she will be treated as part of the furniture so long as she
continues her work as normal. The scheme would need a great
deal of work to make it feasible, but there is an urgent target
lying in a secluded bay in southern Greece. That photograph
you have just studied was taken by reconnaissance aircraft of the
Fleet Air Arm. It shows the dredger clearing the bottom of a
second entrance into the bay: opening up the way into a creek
where she will be completely safe from attack. We reckon it will

take three weeks to do the job. An H-boat is already on her way to Alex, and there are several of that type of dredger operating in Port Said and the Suez Canal. We'll borrow one of those to practise with, and with several other modifications we will be on our way.'

Half-Shackle did say it was a crazy scheme, but he seems determined to go along with it, so I assume there is a lot more detail buried under Brigginshaw's brief explanation: but I have to throw in a dampener.

'It can't be done, sir.'

'Why not?' The commander's voice is cold and unfriendly.

'Because there are two thumping great girders straddling the hold that will prevent the H-boat's bridge from rising into it.'

He's exasperated. 'Don't you think we have given thought to that? There is oxy-acetylene equipment there, and ERA Hargreaves is to go with you to cut away those cross-members – he'll have all day to carry out the job according to the plan.'

There seems nothing more to object about.

'What's the target, sir?'

They exchange glances. No one seems eager to divulge this top-secret piece of information, Brigginshaw nods to Murray, who turns to me to explain in a very confidential tone.

'The Germans have been working on a new method of propulsion for their U-boats. It is a very volatile mixture of peroxide and hydrogen. Dangerous to use, but once fully developed, it can drive a submerged boat at speeds estimated at twenty five to thirty knots; independent of outside atmosphere. They have installed one such power unit on a standard VIIc boat, and she is now in that bay with her mother-ship. I don't have to spell out the mayhem she will cause in the Mediterranean if she is turned loose. She can outrun our escorts, overtake convoys, and carry out high-speed attacks without bothering to surface. It would be suicide to try to destroy her with bombers, because she is tucked in under cliffs that bristle with AA guns. We have to move quickly before the dredger opens up the new entrance, or miss the opportunity altogether, for once she is tucked away inside the creek she will be protected on both sides by rocky outcrops – it is a natural submarine pen.

'We have explored all possibilities, and the only way to get her and her parent ship is by penetrating the bay with a submarine. There is plenty of water there, and all we have to do is take that old H-boat through the boom — a thousand yards — no more. Once inside, their hydrophones may pick up the sound of our engines, but all they'll see is the familiar shape of the dredger going about her normal duties. It should be simple enough to line up the boat for a torpedo attack. She will be a sitting target at point-blank range; it couldn't be simpler. It should cause such a rumpus that we should be able to creep out again while they are chasing their own tails.'

He stops, watching my reaction. I have a moment of doubt before throwing caution to the wind. This is right up my alley; there should be no time for those damned nightmares while I'm charging about with this lot, and the Navy wouldn't sanction any scheme without a lot of consideration. I look at Murray when I say:

'Sounds all right, sir, I'll go along with it.'

He gives a reassuring nod, and I know my confessions will stay safe with him. I can even feel a surge of mounting enthusiasm welling up inside.

I can't get very worked up about Brigginshaw though. After the meeting breaks up I find out he has earned a reputation in the island for being a bloody nuisance. Since he arrived with Half-Shackle, having cadged a lift on an aircraft which is now a charred wreck on the airfield, he has been demanding equipment and supplies from a garrison so short of materials, it has to ration its own guns. He came because he wished to be close to his target, and managed to persuade the RAF to carry out a reconnaissance to obtain photographs of the bay — the aircraft did not return.

To him nothing exists but the need to destroy that submarine, and he frets impatiently over the eight days it is taking the H-boat to make the journey from the UK to Alex; even though the crew are risking their lives by travelling on the surface day and night. The sinking of *Avon* provides him with a source from which to recruit his 'volunteers', and when Half-Shackle reads my name on the crew-list, it seems fate has given him a sign.

He has another piece of good luck when he finds out that a

party of VIPs are flying to Egypt, with half a dozen spare seats in the rear of their Dakota. Before dawn on the day after my interview, I am bumping along the dusty Maltese roads to Luqa airfield. We are told to take the back seats, and stay as unobtrusive as possible.

We take off and fly out into the darkness to go to meet the rising sun while I take stock of my companions. Brigginshaw sits with Murray, opposite two aides; forming a barrier between us peasants and the gold braid.

I sit with Half-Shackle across the aisle from the last two members of the group. ERA Hargreaves has motives for volunteering far removed from any patriotic considerations. Two bigamously married 'wives' are closing in on him from various parts of the UK, and this enterprise will ensure that his whereabouts are kept secret to allow breathing space before he gets down to sorting out his domestic problems later — *much* later, if he has anything to do with it. Now he sits with his long, mournful face staring at the vibrating headrest of the seat in front without saying a word to anyone. We will discover that he is a prophet of doom and can be relied upon to spread pessimism and despondency wherever he goes; but it is a facade, and in truth he will be one of the mainstays of our group, keeping us level-headed when all seems to be falling apart.

The remaining participant beams back at me from the window seat beside the ERA, and I should have anticipated that he would turn up to haunt me. Soapy has been chosen by Hargreaves to help with the engine and the cutting equipment; not because he has any special talents, but because the old lecher has seen a photograph of the youngster's voluptuous mother. Whatever the reason I'm glad he is here, although I would not admit it, not for a thousand years.

It is not by accident that I'm sat next to Half-Shackle. I am determined to have a go at him and find out what I have got myself into, without the embellishment of patriotic verve that comes from Murray and the commander. The drone of the two engines keeps our conversation private, and the dredger skipper is quite willing to talk without any inhibitions.

Shortly after the war began he had persuaded an overworked recruiting officer that as 'captain' of a dredger he was every bit as worthy of an RNR commission as any trawler skipper. The commander found him in charge of a boom defence vessel guarding the entrance to a Scottish loch. Flattered by the attentions he was receiving from a full-blown three-ringer with scrambled eggs on his cap, Half-Shackle took little persuading to come into the scheme, and received a second ring to his sleeve to encourage him.

He joined with the commander in the long process of persuading sceptical senior officers to go along with the idea, until they were heartily sick of them both, and only Brigginshaw's influential background prevented the authorities from packing him off to some remote corner where he could do no harm. He chose to ignore the snags until they stood up and hit him in the face, and even then he would assume a knowing look, and pretend he had it all figured out anyway.

Despite this optimism however, the whole enterprise seemed doomed until Intelligence came up with the news of the U-boat. Sceptics were accused of having cold feet by more professional officers who weighed up the lives of a few adventurers against the disaster that loomed in North Africa and gave the go-ahead for the scheme. From then on there was no stopping Brigginshaw, while Half-Shackle was borne along by the impetus, hardly able to catch his breath, or weigh up the full implications.

'You don't inspire me with confidence, Half-Shackle,' I comment.

He looks at me a bit old-fashioned. 'I told you it is a mad scheme, and that he is a berk — trouble is, you won't listen.'

'What are you doing it for, if it's so flaming stupid?'

'I'm after a medal,' he says flatly.

'Jesus!'

'Oh it's all right for you — you haven't spent half your life with a father that wallowed in the last war and the medal he got at Jutland: only because there was nowhere for him to run to. He thrived on it, and took the piss out of me for being a dredger skipper until I was utterly sick of it. Well, if I get a medal out of this I will have earned the bloody thing. I'll take it to the silly old sod, and in front of all his croneys at the old folks home, I'm gonna wave it under his boozy nose before he packs up and dies.'

'If you live to get it.'

'Ah yes,' he says, with a knowing look. 'Old Brigginshaw might be a berk; but I know the Navy, especially the submarine Navy. You blokes will make it work — I've got no doubt about that.'

'Do you reckon it's feasible?'

'Christ knows! We'll find out in Egypt, I suppose.'

It is hard work holding a conversation in this noise, so we leave it there and settle back to sleep away the long flight. The sun warms the Dakota, and we are given sandwiches and beer to sustain us. Far below the Mediterranean gleams and sparkles as the sun comes up to pierce the depths with its rays. I search the transparent fathoms for the shadow of a submarine, but the sea is empty, and remains so until we pick up the North African coast. We touch down on a dust-bowl with an emergency runway spread across it, waiting while a lot of bowing and scraping goes on as the VIPs disembark. The plane gets unbearably hot, and we sweat buckets until we are allowed out to board a three-ton lorry that takes us away from civilisation into a deserted area of scrub on the perimeter of a wide, sweeping bay. Three buildings squat on the barren sand, two nissen huts and an old fort, and we can see luscious green vegetation not too far away that serves to emphasise the spartan conditions of our billet. We take up residence in one of the huts and eat a meal of corned beef, dehydrated spuds, and sandy vegetables.

Next morning I am told by Murray to get the others out of their bunks, have breakfast, and fall in on the rock-strewn expanse of arid dust that is the parade-ground. Five minutes later three men arrive. Their appearance takes away any doubt I might still have about the unorthodox nature of my new role. Brigginshaw is the 'Big White Hunter' from his bush hat with its leopard-skin band, to his jungle boots and low-slung holster. He strides purposefully to take up position in front of us, accepting a somewhat hesitant salute from Murray, who is not sure how best to greet this outlandish figure, until he notices epaulettes with gold stripes on the jungle-green shirt that he can recognise as something close to a unfirm.

After greeting us with a gleaming set of molars, Brigginshaw introduces his two companions. A smiling Greek with curly, black hair escaping from a woollen hat, and Mediterranean eyes that light up at the least excuse. He is to be our guide and liaison with the local partisans. His name is secret, because he has relatives still living in Greece; so we know him under a code name, 'Felix', and grow to like his cheerful, carefree nature.

The other man stands respectfully in the background. 'This is Sergeant Bullock from the marines,' says the commander. 'I have persuaded the powers-that-be to arrange a toughening-up course while we wait for the submarine to arrive. We will receive four or five days' weapon and commando training with a squad of marines. Sergeant Bullock will be in charge.'

'Oh goody, goody, fucking gumdrops!' says Soapy, in what he considers an undertone; though I notice a sharp look from the sergeant — he is not amused.

There is something familiar about the bronzed features that I vaguely recognise, and I try to recall where I might have seen him. It comes as a shock when I realise the last time I saw him he wasn't wearing battledress, but full uniform, with a peaked cap shadowing a pale, young face; quite different to the hard, mature features of this bloke. Nevertheless, it is the same man, and on that occasion he was staring down at me from a photograph on a piano, while I made love to his missus. He's grown up since then, and there is a lethal quality about him now as he looks us over as though we are a malignant growth.

Brigginshaw finishes his little speech, and goes off with Murray and Half-Shackle. Bullock waits until the sound of their small truck fades before taking stance in front of Soapy with a grim smile. 'I've got a week to knock you into shape, laddy, and you'll find I have little time for dabtoe comedians; so you had best keep your stupid remarks to yourself.' He takes a step back to address us all. 'I don't like this set-up any more than you do. I'm used to drilling marines, not over-weight, under-exercised matelots playing soldiers. You will draw weapons from the store in that nissen hut, sign for them, and take them to your quarters. You will then clean them for inspection at fourteen hundred hours, when you will fall in with my squad, fully belted and gaitered. *Fall out!*'

He sucks his teeth as we shamble off like an undisciplined mob, to go into the store where we are provided with sten guns

and .38 service revolvers, along with packs, webbing, water
bottles, field dressings and gawd knows what. Back in the hut I
spread my new acquisitions out on my bunk, trying to think
where to begin. A corporal turns up before I give up on it, to
give us a lightning session on how to dismember the guns and
bring them up to the required standard. He leaves it to our
imagination to find stowage for the rest of the gear.

'Christ!' blurts Hargreaves, 'I wonder where they keep the
'orses?'

I work at my sten with dedicated enthusiasm, until it is a
gleaming example of surgical cleanliness. I have wiped, oiled
and dismantled each part meticulously; convinced that it is a
prime example of what an automatic weapon should look like.
So, I am full of proud confidence when I fall in with the rest for
inspection. The same corporal who gave us instructions for
cleaning the guns places us at the end of, and apart from, the
three ranks of marines, so that we do not besmirch their
soldierly appearance. Satisfied, he reports us to Bullock.

We are called to attention by the sergeant in a voice that
rocks the foundations of the old fort nearby, and he begins
inspection. One by one my colleagues are slated for their
slovenly appearance, reviled for the state of their equipment,
and ordered to parade after hours with their weapons
properly cleaned. I smugly await his congratulations when he
peers down the barrel of my sten. He takes out a spotlessly
white handkerchief to probe a screwed up corner into a
remote part of the breech mechanism. He holds it an inch
away from my eyes, and I can see a minute spot of oil clinging
to the point.

'What is that filth doing there?' he screams. 'What the hell
have you bin doing with this automatic? Diggin' trenches?'

I am aghast. 'I spent a long time cleaning it, sergeant.' I out-
rank him in true terms and I do not intend to be browbeaten in
front of my associates.

'Rubbish! Don't try to "old soldier" me, chief. This weapon is
dirtier than it was when it was issued to you.' He peers into my
eyes. 'I would expect you to set an example, chief.'

'Yes, sergeant,' is all I can think to say. I am choked with
indignation, having seen the other lazy buggers idling their way

through the morning while I dismembered my sten, cleaning it and replacing the parts with studied deliberation.

He looks with disgust at the protuberance of my round belly and the quaking limbs that support it. 'I have bin given the job of making you fit for whatever games you are playing, chief. While you are under my command you have no rank, and that goes for your officers too. It is the only way I can do the job, and Commander Brigginshaw has agreed. So when I shout "Jump"; you will jump, just like the others, and perhaps I will be able to sweat some of that blubber off you.'

He stands back to survey us with an eye that says we are an affront to his world of soldiering, and I wonder whatever happened to that nice bloke that smiled out of the photograph on the piano.

The afternoon is spent on the firing range with targets popping up for us to shoot at. They remain remarkably unscathed while Bullock screams at us to use short bursts and aim low. The officers have turned up for this, and I notice that our worthy sergeant tones down his vocabulary, despite his brave talk. Even when Soapy decides to break loose and spray a full magazine across the whole range, Bullock's voice is controlled as he gives the stoker extra drill at five a.m. next morning. As the afternoon wears on we improve to the extent that we receive grudging approval, and march back to our quarters feeling reasonably self-assured. Before he dismisses us Bullock takes delight in telling us that early next morning our toughening-up process will begin.

The Arabs must have wondered for centuries about the purpose of the old, ruined fort, set in the middle of nowhere. Now they marvel at the foresight of bygone builders as the true purpose becomes obvious and we entertain them with wild acrobatics over its walls and buttresses. Scruffy urchins stand on a small hillock nearby, watching our antics in open amazement, long after their elders have tired of the performance and gone off to their own affairs.

The building keeps us occupied all morning, and my limbs protest painfully at the treatment they are receiving. Half-Shackle has joined us now that the morning pantomime and weapon inspection is over. He is excused the indignities of that little episode, and in any case his gear is cleaned by lesser mortals.

With sadistic anticipation I settle to watch him come to grief on the ruins. He disappoints me however, and it is soon obvious that the blubber conceals a stamina equal, if not superior, to our own. It is as though he has a motor hidden away under that round physic to keep him going when other men falter, and eventually I am too concerned about my own discomfort to take any further interest in him.

Noon arrives, and we return to civilisation for a cooked meal served from the back of an army truck. The quality of the food makes me appreciate how lucky I am to be a submariner, but vigorous exercise makes for gigantic appetites, and we all go back for second helpings. It does little to prepare us for the tortures of the afternoon session.

At a time when every native hides from the heat of the sun we are marched out across the broiling desert like something out of *Beau Geste*. Not too far away the green pastures of the delta stretch, with shady trees and running water, but we leave all that behind to trudge like lost legionnaires across sand dunes until we stand on a high cliff, staring down into the sparkling Mediterranean. Like schoolboys we chatter excitedly at the prospect of a swim. Bullock soon shatters that illusion.

'Nah,' he roars with a sadistic glint in his eyes, 'we are gonna do a bit of rock climin'. If you do what you are told, you'll survive. If you don't listen to me, you'll wind up in hospital — is that clear?'

We descend to a small beach below the highest part of the cliff. Two young marines are ordered up with ropes and climbing gear, making it look effortless and simple, and in no time ropes are snaking down to us lesser mortals. Satisfied with their efforts they look down at us from the top of the daunting rock face, waiting to see what a hash we will make of it.

'Nah!' snarls Bullock with relish. 'You lot will do exactly as I do. I'll go up first, then wave you up one at a time. There's nothing to worry about if you do as you are told.'

We cannot fail to be impressed by the way he climbs that cliff. His hands haul him up in great, surging lifts, while he plants his heavy boots firmly against the rock in big jumping strides. It looks as easy as falling off a log.

From the top he waves down to us, yelling encouragement when we waver. He has forgotten to give us numbers, or any order of ascent, so I feel it is my duty to take the lead. I spit determinedly on my hands, before gripping the rope. For about ten feet all goes well; my boots find firm footholds, and my arms hoist my body up with satisfying surges.

'Don't take such bloody great strides!' shouts Bullock. 'You'll never make it to the top.'

'Get knotted!' I grind through clenched teeth. 'I'll do it my own way, or not at all.'

My arms are beginning to feel the strain now, and my boots have developed a tendency to slide on the loose shale. I glance downwards, expecting to see the distant figures of my mates leaning back to peer up at me from far below; only to find that with little effort, I could reach out and touch Half-Shackle's head. The whole thing is bloody depressing, but I am supposed to set an example, so I persevere for a few more feet with grim determination.

For a while I think things are going well for me. True, I am bathed in sweat, and my hands are slipping on the rope, while my arms are agonised limbs of torture, but I am definitely moving upward. It is short-lived; soon my progress is reduced to inch by excruciating inch, with the sergeant yelling at me to do this and do that, but I can't do more than hang on like grim death, and try to force one hand above the other in a series of back-breaking efforts. The top of the cliff is no nearer to my way of thinking, and my feet are scrabbling all over the place, spraying showers of rubble on to the watchers below. Shouts of encouragement come from all directions to no avail. I am at the point where my hands refuse to raise their grip on the rope, so I decide to take a breather.

'Don't stop!' screams my torturer − as though I have any choice.

'Balls!'

'Yer won't get going again if you do!'

'So what!'

'Get on with it! Come on! Only a few more feet to go!'

I've heard it all before; in fact I am a past expert at this sort of false encouragement. Many's the time I've yelled at struggling cutters' crews in pulling races. Telling them the winning post is almost reached, when in fact you need a telescope to see it. It is the oldest trick in the world. That kind of thing isn't going to work for me. If I am to succeed, it must be through my own effort.

Even at this stage there is a spark of pride left in me. I don't want to give in in front of my 'oppos'. So, with superhuman effort I grit my teeth once more, take a deep breath, and make a grab for the rope. My feet slide on the rock, and I'm scrambling madly for a hold, my hob-nails sparking on the dry stone, and the whole thing is deteriorating into an untidy mess of flaying arms and legs. My hands are slipping on the rope, and my toes hammer into crevases. Soon I am upside down, with the rope tangled about my legs, and my helmet dangling from its chin-strap.

Ammunition, sten-gun, along with all manner of accoutrement join in a cascade of rubble falling down to the beach. I am hanging like an animated pendulum as the world revolves in inverted chaos. All that remains now is to be unceremoniously hauled to the top, praying all the way that my feet will remain entangled in the rope. Once there I lie spreadeagled on the ground, oblivious to everything about me as I strive to regain my breath and composure. The blood is pumping through my veins, and the landscape is out of focus; but most of all I am humiliated.

"Ave a rest, then we'll 'ave another go,' says the sergeant with supreme confidence. 'You'll do it next time, you'll see. By the end of the week you'll take it in your stride.'

I cannot answer him, even if I wanted to. For one thing the gorge in rising in my throat, and my breathing apparatus is not functioning too well. Shadows swim about me in a shapeless whirl, and all I want to do is lie perfectly still while the agonies fade. No chance of that however, for the raucous voice of Sergeant Bullock penetrates my shield of self-preservation, to knife into my brain.

'Come on now, chief! On your feet! You're lettin' the Royal Navy down.'

'Sod the Navy!'

'That's better. That sounds more like you. Up you get now —
let's 'ave you.'

A massive hand grabs me under the armpit to heave at my
reluctant body. Protesting all the way, I allow myself to be
dragged upright. Oddly enough, my knuckles are not touching
the ground at the end of five foot arms, and my feet are still
turned the right way round.

Another hand claps me on the back, to remind me that I am a
mass of bruises. 'That's more like it. Nah, then, let's get the
others up. Come on, chief. I need you to give your mates some
encouragement.'

Regaining my senses to some degree, I am able to focus on the
men who have made the climb and see that all the marines are
there, having shinned up the second rope in the same time it has
taken me to reach the top. They have lost all interest in the
Navy, squatting with their corporal, prepared to take it easy
while my incompetent colleagues struggle to the top.

'Let's have a look, chief,' plagues Bullock, 'or it'll be too dark
before we get 'em up here.'

Dumbly, I follow him to the brink, and look at the sheer
drop, shuddering at the recollection of how I have dangled
there, head down, above those jagged rocks. The beach is completely deserted, and I exchange puzzled looks with the bewildered sergeant. All I can see is a straggled row of footprints
leading off to disappear beyond a small headland. Without
speaking, we haul up the remaining rope to trudge back to the
marines, who gather up the gear, and form up to march back to
base. I notice we stick close to the top of the cliff this time, and
within fifteen minutes the fort comes into view — we must have
made a hell of a detour when we marched out here.

As we approach, we are greeted with ribald comments from
members of my group who were supposed to follow me up the
cliff. They all look clean and refreshed, with not the slightest
sign of any ordeal showing on clothing or body. Their broad
grins widen as I stagger in with the remains of my equipment
hanging dejectedly from my tired limbs.

'What the bloody hell!' grunts the sergeant.

'What's taken you so long?' demands the impudent voice of

Soapy, grinning like a moron. 'The two ringer brought us back, and he says we ain't gonna do any more cliff climbing.'

'Does he now!' snarls Bullock ominously.

'We've bin swimmin',' goes on our tormentor. ''Ad a quick dip on the way back.'

'Shut your mouth!' barks Bullock, and we leave them with Soapy still grinning after us as we go into the hut, where we sink into chairs with steaming hot cups of tea. The sergeant sits in brooding silence for some time before coming to a decision.

'Come on, chief,' he says, 'you had better come with me. I'm gonna see what this is all about. Someone is playin' silly buggers, and it aint on.'

'You're making an idiot of yourself, Bullock,' I warn him. 'You can't take a gang of blokes that's been cooped up in submarines for months and expect them to suddenly turn into expert rock climbers.'

His face is furious. 'I've bin given a job ter do and I'm gonna do it despite you slovenly bastards.'

Reluctantly I follow him out, crossing the compound to the officers mess-tent. A peel of hearty laughter from inside does nothing to improve his state of mind. He would like a wooden door to hammer on, but has to make do with waggling the flap of the canvas, until someone gets the message and invites us in.

Half-Shackle and Murray are there, enjoying a much stronger brew than we've just had.

'Ah! I was about to send for you, chief,' exclaims Murray. 'Sit down.' He switches his attention to Bullock. 'What can I do for you, sergeant?'

'I wish to protest, sir.'

'Thought you might,' says Murray obtusely. 'Don't concern yourself, sergeant. There's been a change of plan. The field training is cancelled.'

'Cancelled!'

'That's right — your services are no longer required.'

Bullock is about to burst a blood vessel. 'I protest strongly, sir.'

'Yes, well there are proper channels for that, so away you go. You are dismissed.'

One last look at the set features is enough to convince Bullock he is lost. He snaps to attention, salutes, and bows out through the tent flap.

'Now, 'swain,' says Murray. 'I'm sure you'll be glad to learn that all that nonsense is over with. Lieutenant Linklaker considers it is more important to avoid injury than try to turn you all into Commandos, especially after watching your antics on the cliff-face.'

I heave a heavy sigh of relief, 'I couldn't agree more, sir. Does the commander go along with that?'

They exchange looks before Murray goes on, 'There is a change there too, Grant. Commander Brigginshaw has had an accident while arranging a night exercise for us — seems he was setting up a sort of wire pulley which we were supposed to use to cross over a ravine when he fell and broke an ankle.'

'I'm sorry to hear that, sir.'

'I can see that, Grant,' he says drily. 'The operation is still on, so now it is up to us to make it a success. The dredger is on its way from Port Said and the H-boat should arrive within three days. Felix has made an excellent model of the bay, and tomorrow we start training in earnest. How's that sound?'

I look from him to Half-Shackle, who wears a broad grin on his battered old features.

'Fine, sir — just fine.'

IX

The old dredger comes plodding round the headland early next morning, escorted by a small tug; for this is the longest sea trip she has ever made and no one on board is capable of navigating beyond the entrance to Port Said. After her Egyptian crew is paid off with a special bonus to keep them happy until they get their ship back, they go off on the tug with satisfied smiles on their faces. We go on board to pick our way through a jungle of rubbish and hardened silt covering her upper deck. Years of cloying Suez Canal mud has built up in every corner, caking every piece of machinery so that she resembles a mobile sand pit. Her wheelhouse and cabins need fumigating before we can use them, and she is a refuge for every insect native to the area.

We close our ears to the profanity that emanates from the open engineroom hatch when ERA Hargreaves discovers the heap of rusty junk he is supposed to coax into action. Soapy emerges with a wide grin. 'You've never seen anything like it, 'swain — you can't move for cockroaches, and there's cobwebs all over the place.'

I shrug my shoulders; it's no less than I expected. Moving down to join Murray and Half-Shackle at the brink of the gaping hold I can see the sludge of recent dredgings lying in a glutinous mess solidifying all over the bottom.

'Let's have her opened up,' says Half-Shackle, moving across to the winch that sleeps in the shadow of the raised fore-castle. Heavy duty wires stretch from the drums, through pulleys, and into the hold. The doors themselves are large slabs of steel, hinged to twin keels that run the length of the ship. Hefty metal clamps hold them in position when shut, and the wires are used only for closing them after the cargo is dropped. The advantage, as far as we are concerned, is that the doors swing free when they are open and will slide down over the bulge of the

H-boat's hull when she pushes her bridge up through the gap. That gap is thirty feet long by twelve feet wide; more than enough to take the twenty-one by nine of the stripped-down bridge. With the windbreak removed the height of the bridge is only fifteen feet – well below the level of the dredger's deck: so far so good. Hargreaves and Soapy will cut away the two steel girders that span the hold to give it added strength, after which the positioning of hawsers to lock both ships together can be worked out, so that the fittings can be welded to the submarine's hull.

For the benefit of interested parties watching from shore we go through the motions of dredging dressed in scruffy gear, trying not to look like servicemen. It looks as though we are clearing a berth near the jetty for the H-boat when she arrives. Any enemy agent must have his interest dulled by the monotonous daily routine, and it should tie in quite nicely with the activity that will take place when the submarine finally gets here.

Felix has been busy producing a creditable model of the bay so that we can study the layout and plan our campaign. I examine it closely to fix every detail in my mind, asking the Greek a lot of questions about the countryside and landmarks. On the map it lies just north of Pilos, shaped like a pear, with a small town where the stem would be on the southern shore. It has a long Greek name, but we call it 'Limos'. Two long jetties stretch out from the town. An old one used for centuries by fishing boats, and a new concrete one built by the Germans using slave labour, where the patrolboats berth. Under the high cliffs that overshadow the north part of the small harbour is a quay with cranes and warehouses. This is where the dredger moors when she is not working, according to Felix, and it is restricted to all but military personnel – except for the dredger's crew. A square pill-box guards the entrance, with a couple of sentries on duty twenty-four hours a day.

Felix looks round at our faces, pointing to a spot on the north shore of the bay where the cliffs are highest. 'That's where the U-boat is now; but here is where she will be in two or three weeks time.' He jabs at a small creek that makes the entrance to a river emptying into the sea through a gap between the cliffs and the northern end of a long island closing part of the bay.

'Once they dredge that channel clear the U-boat will be able to berth in the creek, and will be safe.'

He switches attention to the main entrance to the bay south of the island. 'A heavy boom closes the gate, but it opens each day to allow the dredger to go in and out. Over the years a ridge of silt and rubble has built up across the mouth of the river. That is what the dredger is working on.'

It is enough to be going on with, and we emerge into the sunshine just as a small army lorry jolts to a halt in a swirl of dust, close to the jetty. Brigginshaw sits in the passenger seat with a plaster cast on his right leg and a furious expression on his face. Behind him sits Sergeant Bullock, who scrambles out to assist the commander as he climbs out awkwardly, setting himself up on two crutches before struggling in our direction. Until then we have managed to maintain a low profile, but this performance attracts a curious crowd of onlookers who stand and watch as an angry scene develops.

'I'd like to know what you think you are doing, Murray!' snaps Brigginshaw. 'The sergeant tells me you have abandoned the special training.'

'That's right, sir,' says Murray calmly. 'I believed it was doing more harm than good.'

'That is for me to decide, not you!' explodes the commander.

'You were not available. After the report I had from Lieutenant Linklaker I thought I'd better put a stop to it. These men have been cooped up in their submarines for months; they are not up to performing the antics Bullock wants them to do. Time is too short to get them fit for that sort of thing – even the corporal says they have not been properly prepared for it.'

'That's right,' interrupts Half-Shackle. 'It's a bloody pantomime; all he wants to do is take the piss out of our lads in front of his own. After I saw what happened to Grant, I decided enough was enough.'

'They're sailors – they are supposed to be able to climb ropes,' protests Bullock.

'They can climb ropes all right!' I exclaim, 'but they're not bloody mountaineers!'

'All right, Grant,' soothes Murray, trying to take things off the boil, 'leave it to me.'

He turns to Brigginshaw to go on calmly. 'I think we should concentrate on the main business, sir; and that has nothing to do with Sergeant Bullock.'

The Commander is almost spluttering with rage. 'There would be no need for this if you obeyed orders, Murray. If it was not for the limited amount of time available, I'd have you replaced.'

'May I suggest we continue this in private, sir? We are entertaining the natives.'

Without reply, Brigginshaw struggles with his two crutches – waving aside offers of assistance as they go into the wheelhouse. We are left in the hot sun while an animated argument takes place between the three officers.

'They're like a lot of bloody ODs,' grumbles Hargreaves as he peers over the rim of the stokehold hatch. 'I'm goin' dahn ter my engines – come on, yer loafin' bastard,' he roars at Soapy, and they disappear below.

Now I'm left with Sergeant Bullock. There seems nothing left to say, so I move to go on board, but before I reach the short gangplank he stops me. 'What's it all about, chief? Nobody tells me anything. If I knew what was going on, perhaps I'd know what's expected of me.'

'If Brigginshaw won't tell you – I'm bloody sure I can't,' I reply gruffly.

'We are on the same side, you know.'

I look away. I remember only too well a similar statement made by a sad-eyed woman as she offered me a bottle of Bells, and I keep my eyes averted. 'It's up to the officers to bring you in if they want to.' I deliberately stride aft and pretend to coil up a couple of mooring ropes. I hate his guts for humiliating me, for being a marine, and for making me feel guilty.

Summoned by Murray I return to the wheelhouse to find that a compromise has been reached. Sergeant Bullock is now to accompany us when we go ashore at Limos, so that we will have the benefit of his training and experience when we are dealing with the partisans.

A note of warning sounds in my brain, 'In what capacity, sir?' I ask; this is something that must be sorted out right here and now. When I look at the make-up of the group there seems to be a lot of chiefs, but very few indians; consisting as it does of one lieutenant, two chief petty officers, a leading partisan, and Soapy. Now they are talking about another NCO – poor old Soapy!

'That's the reason we called you in first, chief. We don't want any friction,' says Murray. 'Rank will have to go by the board on this occasion. Sergeant Bullock will help Felix to lead the party while you are on shore, but once you are on the dredger it will be up to you to take charge. Lieutenant Linklaker is quite agreeable to this; in fact he suggested you take command, while he attends to the running of the dredger – he feels he would be lost when it comes to the technical side of operating with the submarine.'

It isn't what I would have liked, but there isn't a lot I can do or say, since they appear to have made up their minds. I have to admit that I haven't much idea of guerrilla warfare, and it would not be right to put the lives of the landing party in the hands of the Greeks entirely. So, on the face of it, Bullock is the obvious answer.

I try to look enthusiastic, knowing only too well that this is Murray's concession to Brigginshaw in an effort to bring harmony back to the group. Bullock comes in to listen carefully while the scheme is explained. He absorbs it all without comment or expression. While I watch him for some kind of reaction, there is none – not a glimmer to show that he approves or disapproves until Brigginshaw finishes. Then he pulls himself upright.

'Permission to speak, sir.'

Surprised by this sudden outburst of protocol, the commander nods. 'Carry on, sergeant.'

'How long before the submarine gets here?'

'Two days at least.'

'Right, sir.' The sergeant wears a 'no-nonsense' expression now. 'These blokes won't last five minutes when they get ashore amongst the professional soldiers, and the whole thing will fall flat on its face before it gets off the ground. I want two full days to iron out some of the wrinkles, teach them to use their weapons, move about without being seen, and kill with or without arms. It ain't much, but at least I won't be working with a bunch of complete amateurs. I'll guarantee nothing, sir. Put alongside a party of marines they'll be like a bunch of boy scouts, but at least they'll have some idea, and we won't be putting those Greek partisans in too much peril.'

Brigginshaw and Murray exchange glances. 'I'll go along with that,' says Murray. 'Now you are going with us, sergeant, you will be able to form the landing party into some sort of fighting unit, I'm sure.'

'Yes, sir.' Bullock gives me a look that says quite plainly, 'Now, you bastard, just try any more nonsense and see what happens!'

The next two days are crammed with drills and exercises. The sergeant badgers us from dawn to dusk and into the night. He teaches us to burrow in the dust, hide in doorways, and creep up on unsuspecting foes. We learn how to kill efficiently, and without noise. He drives us until our bones ache, and we yearn for rest, but by the time the submarine comes round the headland we are reacting almost like real soldiers, with a new respect for this uncompromising Marine Sergeant.

The H-boat looks a sad, denuded submarine, with her bridge trimmed down to the height of the upper hatch. A canvas windbreaker has been rigged in the same fashion as the old first world war subs, but it only makes her look even more pathetic. The journey out from the UK is quite an accomplishment for a tiny boat, designed to operate in home waters, as a short range submarine; and although she has extra fuel capacity to extend her range from sixteen hundred miles to twenty five hundred, it has been necessary to rendezvous with a T-boat to refuel. Her normal complement of twenty-two is pared to fifteen − just enough to operate her without watch changes on a short trip. Every man has been specially selected for his experience and reliability, but mainly for his ability to work without supervision.

We begin to prepare her for her new duties by replacing the marker-buoy that is normally used only when the boat is in trouble with a piece of inconspicuous flotsam that will be ignored by anyone who finds it floating on the surface. There is a telephone concealed inside the metal canister amongst the flotsam with the cable running down the mooringwire to the fore-ends. Four large ring-bolts have been welded to the hull to match up with corners of the dredger's hold. These will take the heavy mooring wires to keep her in position. Fore and aft, two horizontal cradles are fitted to the casing with slots to take the twin keels of the dredger. They are padded with matting, and will help to keep the two vessels lined up. The submarine will protrude several feet at each end, but her stern slopes away quite sharply a few feet aft of the bridge, so the dredger's screw and rudder will be well clear. It only remains to put the whole set-up to the test.

All these preparations take place during the day, while the dredger calmly goes about her work as though she has no tie-up with the new arrival. The strange appearance of the H-boat must rouse curiosity ashore, but I defy anyone to work out the purpose of all this paraphernalia from what they can see. Down below, the torpedoes are being withdrawn from their tubes to be serviced. Balance chambers, motors, giros, and all the other delicate refinements of these intricate missiles are checked to ensure that they run true.

The dredger appears to be working at random, but in fact she is moving to prearranged positions to give Half-Shackle experience at picking up markers and taking bearings. A party of strange, bandit-like types move about the scenery like rock-apes, setting up these markers, and taking them down again, to the bewilderment of watching goatherds. Aboukir Bay hasn't seen this much activity since Nelson sailed in to knock seven bells out of Admiral Bruey and his anchored French Fleet in 1799.

At last they seem to put it together to Murray's satisfaction. He gives his approval as the diesels rumble into life to pour life into the batteries. For these practice runs I will be in the submarine, so that we can discuss any snags that might arise when we begin to carry out the vital part of the drill. Late afternoon we cast off to take the H-boat out to sea. This is the first opportunity we have of working with the full crew. Without exception they are the best in their field. Not one of them has less than two years' service in boats, and the quiet competence with which they go about their duties shows this. Together we take the old boat through her paces; to discover that she has capabilities that belie her age. Although built in 1917, she is easy to handle, and behaves like a lady. The crew talk about her with a certain affection that is easy to understand as she performs all the tricks Murray puts her through, so that he can get the feel of her and her crew.

When darkness comes the evolutions are complete, and we push on across a black ocean with the exhausts throwing up showers of phosphorescent spray. By the early hours of the morning we are creeping in towards the shore at slow speed. Standing on the bridge with Murray, I peer across the long, slim bow, watching eruptions of bursting spray sweeping over the casing. The diesels shut down, giving way to the soft whine of the motors pushing us quietly through dark, mysterious waters.

I try to pierce the darkness for the first glimpse of the shore, and eventually I pick up the loom of craggy cliffs. A light flashes, so briefly that I wonder if I've imagined it. It comes again and I take note of the horn of land that rises above the spot, showing black against the deep purple sky.

'Did you see the light, coxswain?' asks Murray quietly, before I have time to report it to him.

'Yes, sir.'

'We'll steer towards it – have you got a bearing?'

'Yes, sir.'

He bends to give the order to the helmsman before turning to me. 'We will see it only once more.'

He is trying to catch me out; I can almost hear him chuckling smugly. But I've got the bastard this time. 'I noticed the position, sir.'

'I should hope so – that's why you were chosen for the job. Where do you make it?'

That's what I like – trust! 'Just below the headland, sir. In line with that rock shaped like a man's head.'

'Very good.'

I glance at him to find him staring stolidly ahead; his features set firm in silhouette. He is concentrating on the shore, and I can see his jaw moving in a chewing movement – so that's what he does when he is brooding – I have a tendency to stick out my tongue. It's nice to know he's human.

The land is beginning to grow out in a long arm, stretching

down our starboard side. I can see tresses of surf breaking on the rocks at the base.

'Stand by to dive!'

I react immediately, without thinking; dropping through the small hatch on to the shoulders of the signalman, who yells as I tread on his fingers — that'll teach him to keep them on the side of the ladder. I am a passenger, so I squeeze into the rear of the control-room, watching the boat's coxswain with professional interest as he settles her level at twenty-eight feet.

'Slow ahead — group down!'

The soft tone of the motors fades to a lower octave, and they have to use more 'plane to keep her swimming along nicely. Swirls of eddying water course through the casing above my head as tension builds in the boat. It may be only an exercise, but with another vessel aiming to plant herself over the top of us, no one wants to make any mistakes. Murray has made it plain to everyone that we can't afford a lot of practice runs, in case someone watching us puts two and two together. Ideally we must get it right at the first attempt, but that seems too much to hope for. There is not a man aboard who isn't convinced that he can make it happen though: it won't be their fault if it doesn't come off first time.

Murray signals for the periscope, rising with it as the eyepiece emerges from the well. He takes a quick look round, then snaps his fingers to send it sliding down; waiting several minutes before bringing it up again. This time to focus on a bearing while the signalman reads off the numbers from the back of the 'scope. Afterwards he stands for a moment, head bent, thinking.

'I'll have to use the attack 'scope, and it'll have to stay up while I get a fix. Hold her steady on this course, helmsman. Bunts! you will put me on green seven oh — hold me there.'

'Aye aye, sir.'

'Stand by to bottom. Up 'scope!'

I'm holding my breath as he waits for the marker to come in view, and line up with the cross-wire.

'Slow ahead together — stop both! Flood Q.'

I brace up as the boat hangs suspended for a moment, until she begins to settle towards the sea-bed. Everyone braces up ready for the crunch when we hit the bottom, but we need not have worried for we go down easy, to sit on the sand with hardly any list; the gauges showing thirty feet – it couldn't be better.

On the day she will have to remain dived like this until late afternoon, when the dredger will be ready to return to her moorings. Now, however, we are anxious to get in as much practice as possible, so the exercise starts at daybreak. Already the boat is warming up as the sun lifts out of the east to glare down on the sea. The trick is to stay quiet, with minimum movement, to conserve air and keep as cool as possible while we wait for Half-Shackle to locate the marker.

'I can hear her, sir,' announces the hydrophone operator. 'She's coming up from astern.'

Soon we can all hear the pulsating rhythm of the propeller, and I can imagine the skipper peering squint-eyed through the wheelhouse window while his jaws champ on a quid of tobacco, as he brings her to sit right over the top of us. Murray takes the hand-set from a rating, gaining contact with the dredger as we come to the most crucial part of the whole business.

With only one screw it will be difficult for Half-Shackle to hold his position. If the wind takes hold of her before she is located on the special cradles he may have to go through the whole thing again, and if someone is watching her juggling about from an enemy shore it will be bound to rouse suspicion. So we must get it right first time.

They should be picking up the special wire from the marker-buoy, which is attached to the bull-ring on the fore-part of the casing, and this should help to hold her steady. Murray orders me up into the tower with two seamen to open the hatch when it breaks surface. The most urgent task is to get those mooring hawsers secured. I hear air hissing into the ballast tanks, and a shudder comes as we lift clear of the bottom. Now is the moment when Brigginshaw's theory will be put to the test.

Below me I hear the signalman calling out the depth. Murray must be in the tower already, waiting for me to open up to scramble out with my two companions. A lot of noise is coming from all sides now, and I can imagine the big metal doors sliding down over the pressure-hull.

'Open up!' yells Murray.

I lift the last clip, and the hatch flies back to slam into its locking clamp. Then I climb out into the sunshine to find the bridge well and truly socketed into the muddy hold. No time for gazing about: the other men are pushing me clear, anxious to get at the mooring wires. I clamber down with them, unclipping the fast-release clamps that hold the coiled hawsers in position. A heaving-line hits me on the head, and I pass it through the eye, before it is wrenched out of my hands by some over-eager body on the dredger's deck. The winches are revolving, taking up slack to lock both ships in a firm grip. I take another look round; amazed that all has gone so smoothly. I hate to think what would happen in a gale force wind or a strong current, but there is little tide in the Mediterranean, and it is June; so I suppose it isn't unreasonable to expect conditions to be right on the day.

There is no time to pause, for we are swinging together to the whim of the steady breeze that blows in from the sea. It has been decided to use the dredger's engine for the next part of the operation, and the first turns of her propeller thrusts her forward against the pull of the hawsers. Immediately the boat is pulled askew – not much – but enough to make it impossible to steer a good course. We delay everything until more slack is taken up on the winches, and the wires made fast once more.

It soon becomes obvious that it is not going to be anything like as straightforward as the commander predicted. His theories are going all to hell as we try again, with the wires straining, and weird sounds coming from the cradles. It takes a full five minutes before there is any movement at all. In the meantime we are drifting in a wide circle towards an outcrop of jagged rocks.

Optimists lean over the side, watching for signs of progress through the water. Murray barks angrily at them, and they slope off to hide in corners, peering out anxiously as things begin to deteriorate.

In the dredger's wheelhouse Half-Shackle is heaving the helm about desperately, trying to steer a course that will keep us clear of those rocks. He is failing miserably, for the screw is having little effect, and both vessels drift aimlessly; out of control. I go to stand by the door, ready to relay any messages to Murray, who bends over the boat's voicepipe – no doubt warning those below to be prepared to take emergency action if things get completely out of hand. By the look of things, he won't have long to wait.

I stare into an enraged face, glaring back at me in between struggles with the huge wheel. Sweat runs down Half-Shackle's features in streams, and his big, black eyebrows bounce up and down over his blazing eyes. Finally, in desperation, he swings on me furiously, leaving the wheel spinning on its own.

'Well! For Christ sake do something! – you stupid bastard! Don't just stand there!'

'What do you want me to do, you big prick!' I yell back.

This is hardly the altercation one expects between officer and rating, so Murray decides to take a hand in proceedings. 'We'll try using both helms together. You will have to relay the orders to me, coxswain.'

'Aye aye, sir,' I'm willing to try anything to get us out of this mess, but the way the old dredger skipper is sulking is not very encouraging. However, he goes back to the wheel, heaving it hard over to port, then stands there, waiting for something to happen. All I can do is watch what he does, then pass instructions across to Murray. Both vessels show utter contempt for our efforts, continuing their swing to starboard.

'Oh well!' I think to myself, 'the whole things a bloody farce anyway. Perhaps we can scrub it all, then go back to our normal jobs.'

Murray shouts across to stop engines. 'We'll use the submarine's motors to steer with. Keep your engine going at half speed, and hold the wheel amidships!'

This time there is a measure of success with the dredger riding on the submarine's back. We move through the water, leaving the rocks astern as the concerted efforts of three propellers drive us out across the bay.

Murray is not convinced that it isn't all a fluke, so we are told to prepare for another run. This time the exercise is to be extended to include a dummy torpedo run on a large rock that represents the U-boat.

There was some discussion yesterday about whether or not to separate the submarine from the dredger once inside the bay to allow more manoeuverability, but Brigginshaw came down on this like a ton of bricks, insisting on doing the whole thing in tandem. He reckons we can get closer, and take more time to line up with the target, reducing the risk of failure. I must admit it makes sense to me. But Murray disagrees – he would like to take the boat in on her own. He's the skipper, but Brigginshaw has the gold braid, so we do it his way.

These arguments are forgotten by most of us as the second operation goes off without a flaw. We are able to build up to a respectable speed of something like six knots using the three screws. Murray lines the tubes up with the target at point-blank range; with four fish, I don't see how we can miss. Satisfied, we take a wide sweep out of the bay, to give the impression that we are returning from patrol when we come back to our moorings.

'How do we get out again afterwards, sir?' I ask Murray, as we stand together for the final approach.

'The harbour is likely to erupt after the attack, Grant. In the confusion I hope to have time to find a spot to sit on the bottom, before they have worked out the truth. From then on it will be a case of playing it by ear. We might even have to abandon the boat, and try to steal a fishing boat or something, but I think we can do what Günther Prien did with his U-boat at Scapa Flow – slip out while the enemy is chasing about like a lot of blue-arsed flies. Don't worry, coxswain, arrangements have been made to take you off too.'

'Yes, sir,' I comment drily. 'Just one thing, sir.'

'Well?'

'Where do I go to join the Foreign Legion?'

He has no sense of humour. 'I'll be obliged if you go about your duties, coxswain, and not bother me with trivialities.'

X

No sooner are we tied up than there is a great deal of disruption in the fore-ends as Brigginshaw is helped through the loading hatch; his plaster cast bumping on various bits of protruding submarine. It would be much easier to invite all concerned to the dredger, or his own quarters; but the commander is a man for gestures. No chance is missed to display his unique individuality. At last, drenched with sweat, but smiling benignly, he holds court in the wardroom, and the main participants, including me, are squeezed uncomfortably round the table. We listen as he congratulates everyone on the success of the exercise, although there is a great deal of 'I told you so' mixed in as he rumbles on.

Just as we are beginning to yawn his oration comes to an end, and he gets down to the nitty gritty. There is no time for further drills, or rehearsals. The Greek dredger is clearing the entrance to the creek much quicker than expected, so we must get under way as soon as possible. He estimates that we should arrive off Limos in the early hours of the fourth day, provided we leave at midnight. Felix will explain the arrangements for getting the landing-party ashore when we are at sea.

'I only wish I could go with you, gentlemen,' he says despondently. 'To see my scheme come to fruition would be quite something, but there's no room for passengers on this trip.'

'Thank Gawd for that!' I think to myself.

'The code name for the operation is "Gemini", you'll be interested to hear. Lieutenant Murray thinks we should have a name for the submarine too, and suggests *Hobo*, which I think is appropriate.'

'What about the dredger?' interrupts Half-Shackle, unmoved by all the theatricals.

'Ah, yes — the dredger,' smiles Brigginshaw, patronisingly. 'We didn't consider her to be part of the "Fleet"; being on loan so to speak. But, if you can think of something, why not?'

Half-Shackle doesn't even look at him. 'Narh! Forget it; She's only a gash-barge really — a number will do.'

'Stuff that!' I'm thinking, as I look at Brigginshaw's condescending face. 'I think she should have a name, sir. Otherwise, we might find it confusing.'

'We haven't got time for all this nonsense,' growls the commander. 'If I had known it would develop into such a charade, I would never have suggested names in the first place.'

Murray comes in to support me. 'It was my suggestion, sir, and I'm inclined to agree with Grant. What about a Greek name — *Cyclops* for instance?'

"Oo's 'e?' asks Hargreaves.

"E's a one-eyed Greek who sells bicycles,' states Soapy.

'I reckon *'ector*'s a better name,' argues the ERA. "E didn't give a sod for anyone.'

"E got clobbered by Achilles,' protests Soapy, obviously an authority on Greek mythology.

'That's the bloke with the 'eel, ain't it?'

'Shut up, you two!' growls Murray, aware that Brigginshaw's face is turning scarlet. 'It's not a bad idea though, sir. Gives a certain character to the dredger.'

'All right, all right! If you must!'

'You've had your bloody turn, Murray,' grumbles Half-Shackle. 'Give someone else a chance; after all, she is my command.'

'Well, for God's sake hurry up!' grinds Brigginshaw. He is almost dancing with rage now.

'I don't want a Greek name for my ship,' says the old skipper solemnly. 'I think she should be called something that means something.'

'We're waiting,' breathes the commander heavily.

'We'll call her *Groveller*. It'll remind me of some of those I've had to work with lately.' He looks meaningfully at Bullock. 'Anyway it fits in with her job.'

'All right, all right, all right!' rants Brigginshaw, at the end of his tether. 'Now; perhaps we can get down to details — your latest report, Felix, if you don't mind.'

The Greek stretches his hands across the table, as though to draw us to him. In perfect English he outlines the situation in the bay at the time of the last piece of information to come from agents watching from shore. 'There are two V-boats in the harbour — these are converted trawlers which the enemy uses for picket duties; they call them *Vorpostenbooten*. They have depth charges, light armament, and hydrophones. There is also an R-boat (you call them E-boats) which they use to patrol the fishing fleet when they are at sea. She can also be used as a sub chaser, and has a dual-purpose, quick-firing gun mounted on her forecastle, with various other weapons scattered about. She is the fastest of them all. They all tie up alongside the new concrete jetty. In addition to these, a couple of small launches carry out harbour patrols, constantly dropping small charges to discourage frogmen.'

'Any questions?' asks Brigginshaw, looking round at the blank faces. 'Right, well, I'll close the meeting then.' He is disgruntled now, having failed to inflame us with his fighting spirit. I have a feeling that we do not match up to the type of fire-eating heroes he had in mind when he dreamed up this scheme. Not for him the humdrum monotony of war — I reckon he read too many comics when he was small.

By midnight we are on our way, churning through a moderate sea on a northerly course, with lookouts and officer-of-the-watch getting a real soaking on the open bridge. The canvas 'dodger' is next to useless in this weather. The watchkeepers come down the ladder soaked to the skin, with their arms aching from hanging on grimly to anything that prevents them being washed overboard, and it gets even worse when we alter course to the west to go straight into it. Even the control-room is receiving its share of sea, so Murray orders the 'bird-bath' to be rigged. This is a canvas contraption that fits over the base of the conning-tower to prevent water from slushing all over the deck, but it makes access to the tower difficult.

The boat is stacked with an assortment of warlike implements, and we have to search hard for places to stow the few personal items we have brought with us. Felix has dragged a huge kitbag on board against all advice; getting up everyone's nose when he begins stowing it away in every odd corner. It consists mainly of things unobtainable in occupied Greece, and we sympathise with him to a degree, but goodwill is stretched to the limit when the electricians find tins of spam lying on top of the batteries.

Sometime during the night there is a roar from the officers' heads, and Half-Shackle comes staggering out covered with what he was trying to get rid of. It falls to me to explain the mechanics of using a submarine's toilet. He watches with a bewildered expression while I go through the various operations with valves and levers, making sure that I build up an air pressure ten pounds more than the outside before putting the lever to 'discharge'; blowing the contents out to sea. Afterwards he decides he will remain constipated until he gets back to civilisation.

Bullock turns pale green before retiring to a bunk to vomit throughout the first forty-eight hours, while gloating anti-bootneck matelots come to offer advice and streaky bacon sandwiches.

It all helps to take our minds away from the fact that we are steaming in broad daylight on a sunlit sea where a vengeful enemy scours the ocean for just such a juicy target as we present. In fact, we go through the whole day with nothing but a glimpse of a distant aircraft to get concerned about. From now on we will be diving during daylight hours as we press on to more hostile areas.

Next day Murray calls for a further conference in the wardroom. The boat is dived; swimming along quietly at periscope depth, with the rest of the crew closed up or resting. Sitting opposite Half-Shackle I notice his fingers fumbling and intertwining nervously. His features are sallow, with glazed eyes, and loose, trembling lips. I've seen this sort of thing before. He's trying to suppress a growing fear in this strange environment. It worries me, for it is completely out of character, and more than just claustrophobia. He catches me studying him, and immediately looks away with an effort to cover up. There is something weighing on him that he can't cope with on his own.

I shove the thoughts away as Felix goes into details about the way we are to get ashore. The Greeks fish in groups now, with German guards on some of the bigger boats, and the R-boat paying occasional visits to make sure all is well. It is an arrangement that has become lax with usage. The enemy realises there is little point in fishermen absconding, for they have families depending on them, and care little for the outside world. So the relationship between the two sides is a grudging acceptance of the status quo. One day peace will return; until then the war goes on about them, but fishing is their life, dominating all else.

There are those who find it hard to conceal a burning hatred for the grey hordes that have over-run their homeland, laying down alien laws that must be obeyed under threat of death. The resentment nurtures inside like a cancerous growth, gnawing away at a man until he needs to fight back by whatever means possible. Some, like Felix and his friends, take to the hills to fight a stealthy battle in the midst of the enemy. Others are less obvious; and probably more dangerous: for they are the thinkers, gathering information, and watching constantly for signs of what the enemy is about, then passing it on to where it will do most good. One such is the skipper of a fishing caique, respected by those who know him, and others who only think they do. He walks through the village with head held high; eyes centred straight ahead, acknowledged by both Greek and German, who accept him for being withdrawn, honest, and unbending.

His boat is the cleanest, the fastest, and finds the most fish, so others follow him, yet he is never in the lead. He is surrounded, but never in the centre. Always alone at sea, and even the Germans learn to accept this; so long as his brown sails can be seen, they do not bother him. The local garrison know he is head-man of the village. They treat him with respect, though he shows them no favour. His Greek blood stems from generations of proud ancestors, and he would be angry if he knew his only son was being called 'Felix' by foreigners, for he is proud of his offspring, or he would not have agreed to breaking his rules, placing his boat where he knows there is small chance of finding a catch, to wait for strangers to come from the depths.

In two days' time a friend will come to him, telling him the time is come. Nothing will keep him from that rendezvous, for he has made a promise to his son; and now that son is sitting in the wardroom of an H-boat, telling us we will be met in broad daylight by a Greek fishing-boat, and we find it hard to believe – but then, we do not know this fisherman.

A bond is growing between the members of the landing-party now, for we are men apart, cleaning weapons, talking tactics and studying maps. Bullock comes back to life when the boat dives into the calmer depths and the rolling stops. He is eager for companionship, talking of home and a woman we cannot begin to know, who waits patiently for his return, regarding other men as mere customers, to be served with beer, kept at arms' length, and tolerated for their crude suggestions.

It is difficult to find isolation in a submarine, but Half-Shackle manages to get me alone in the galley, on the pretext of making himself a drink, 'I'll need your help in this operation, Ben,' he says in a soft voice. 'Up until yesterday, I was okay. Now, I'm feeling sick. I don't know if I'm too old for this lark, but I do know that I'm terrified at this moment.'

He looks at me with pleading eyes. 'I'm certain I will be okay when I get ashore – it's the bloody submarine that's getting me down. I can't breathe in this damned steel tube. I'm sure,' he pauses for a moment, 'at least, I'm almost sure, I can last out until we get there – but I'll need your back-up, Ben.'

'Have you told Murray?'

He looks uncomfortable. 'No – I will if I think it gets bad enough, but I thought you might help me to get over it.'

For a moment I am tempted to tear him apart for trying to lumber me with his problems when I have enough of my own. I think better of it though. Maybe he is right. Perhaps he will be all right on the day, and we need him desperately on the dredger. I know that without him I will be the only one with any knowledge of the old bucket, and I do not want to be saddled with the full responsibility. So, I agree to keep his secret.

Over the next couple of days I begin to relax, and the anxiety I feel over Half-Shackle simmers down somewhat. He is by no means his usual cheerful self, but none of us are under these circumstances. True, he moves about the boat in a quiet, withdrawn way, speaking to no one, and wearing a haunted expression, but I make it my business to speak to him now and again, without laying it on too thick. There isn't a hell of a lot more I can do.

The sea on the third night is still lifting to a strong westerly wind, tumbling the boat about as we crawl along the surface in the deep purple of a warm night. I am up with the lookouts staring at the shadows that grow out of the darkness. To the north is the island of Crete, hiding part of the sky as we creep by. We are warned to watch for a T-boat, for we are passing through her patrol area. She knows about us, but it is a dodgy business meeting another boat at night in hostile waters. The signalman has recognition signals firmly lodged in his brain, but I know Murray wishes to avoid contact with any other ship, friend or foe. So I'm betting he will dive the boat if we spot her on the surface and keep well clear.

It is a few minutes past midnight when one of the lookouts sights a solid chunk of substance that doesn't dissolve into nothingness as we approach. Murray is called and arrives in seconds, still dragging on oilskins. He stares through night glasses while we all wait impatiently for his verdict.

'Clear the bridge!'

His voice acts like a spring, sending as tumbling down through the hatch in a tangle of arms and legs. Even as I touch the deck of the control-room the klaxon blares out its strident message and the diesels choke to a stop. I strive to get out of the way of hurrying sailors as they rush to their diving stations. I have no part in that now, and must take a back seat when the boat's crew is closing up for action. It is a nail-biting experience, for I have never before stood aside to watch other men carrying out their duties in this sort of situation, without taking a leading role.

I am loath to leave the control-room, so try to make my presence as unobtrusive as possible. A difficult business in such a small boat, and only the fact that we are undermanned by normal standards allows me to do so. The gauges are showing twenty-eight feet as Murray drops down through the lower hatch, to stand at the periscope, waiting for the boat to settle on an even keel at the ordered depth.

The coxswain and his mate soon have her level, and everything is ready for a look at whatever is lurking up top. As always Murray takes a quick look round in a full circle before steadying up on the object that sent us scurrying below. He stands back. 'Down 'scope!'

He talks to us all, 'It is a submarine all right, but it's no T-boat, of that I am certain. In fact, I'd lay a pound to a penny that she is one of those big Italian jobs – "Brin" class; with a bridge like the side of a house.'

Everyone who can is watching him as he snaps his fingers for one more look. It is enough to confirm what he thought. 'That is all we need,' he says grimly.

I know his problem. Somewhere, not too far away, an unsuspecting T-boat is churning along, with her lookouts expecting to sight another friendly submarine. It is going to be all too easy to mistake the Itie for us; especially if they see her from an angle that makes her bridge look similar to ours in the darkness. The T-boat will flash recognition signals, and receive a full salvo of torpedoes in return. If we do anything to distract the Italian, we could foul up the whole mission. I'm glad it is his worry, and not mine.

'Can you hear anything?' he asks the hydrophone operator.

'Only her diesels, sir.'

'Well, listen carefully. Tell me the moment you pick up another sound. It's possible that she is miles away, but we can't be too careful.'

'Aye aye, sir.'

'They should be keeping a watch for something like this, sir,' reassures the navigator.

We all look at his pale face sympathetically. Everyone knows how difficult it is to recognise a submarine on the surface at night, with the sea running as it is. Eyes often see what they expect to see. All aces are with that Italian, for she knows that there are no other of her own kind in the area. She can fire first, and ask questions after.

As we wait in suspense I am aware of another man standing by me, and turn to find Half-Shackle there, staring with wide-eyed anxiety at Murray. The strain is etched into his face, emphasized by the pale light, so that he looks ghastly. I can smell the fear in him, and it sickens me.

'New HE bearing red four five — fast diesel!' The voice cuts through the atmosphere like a knife, and we all know what its owner is listening to. Here comes the other boat, all unsuspecting, right into the trap.

'Can you hear the Italian boat?'

'Yes, sir. She's holding her course. I reckon—' he hesitates, 'her diesels have stopped, sir. I think she's dived.'

'Christ!'

There is absolutely nothing we can do now. That 'Brin' boat has the other British submarine in her sights. Running down towards her with all tubes ready primed. Even if we were stupid enough to do something to attract her attention it would do no good now. We can only wait, and pray for a miracle.

A choked sob comes from beside me, and I sense the quaking shape of Half-Shackle as he tries to cope with the panic that grips his guts. He cannot possibly know half of what is going on in this strange environment, and his imagination paints all kinds of vivid pictures. I have a moment to feel sorry for the poor old duffer before my attention is dragged back to the man on the hydrophones.

'I can hear the Italian boat now, sir; crossing from right to left. She'll be between us and the other boat in a moment.'

She is working herself into a perfect firing position — there is not a hope for that T-boat. It's all too much for Murray. The agony of standing by while a full crew of fellow submariners get annihilated breaks him.

'Stand by all tubes!'

His voice is hard. There is no way he can stand back and watch it happen. It might be a futile gesture; firing a spread of torpedoes at a mass of sound, but it can't be worse than doing nothing. He is about to give orders to line up the target when the matter is taken out of his hands.

'Torpedoes running, sir!' How the operator manages to keep his voice steady is beyond me.

Everyone freezes now, as the seconds tick by while the enemy fish run in towards their target. Only too clearly we hear the first one hit; closely followed by another.

'Secure the tubes!' There is a catch in Murray's voice, 'It's too late now.'

'Breaking up sounds, sir!' The voice is thick, echoing the sadness that grips us all.

'What's happened?' ask a weak voice by my side.

I turn to Half-Shackle, devoid of all sympathy for him, 'About sixty blokes have just gone down in their boat — that's what's happened.' I snarl, moving forward to leave him to his own miseries.

The boat sinks into an air of despondency that is difficult to shake off. Most of us launch into preparations for the landing in an effort to shake off what has happened; but the gloom hangs over everything like a shadow. If I was not so busy, perhaps I would notice Half-Shackle deteriorating until he moves about the boat in a daze, with his shoulders slumped, jostled and bumped by the crew as they go on with their tasks.

As fast as he finds a corner to hide in, someone shifts him, and he is constantly moving from one hiding place to the next — unnoticed, and all alone. All the time fear gnaws at him with relentless cruelty. The weight of it presses down on his tired old body like the tons of water, outside the boat, until all spirit has gone, and the shattered body is left with no driving force to keep it going — just a mass of skin and bone. By this time he is beyond the help of anyone.

The preparations go on throughout the next day, and everyone is becoming more and more keyed-up for the operation as we draw ever closer to the area. The torpedomen haul their charges out of the tubes for the umpteenth time to give them a final check-up. We spend a lot of time sorting out our equipment in readiness for the big event, with Bullock hovering over us offering advice.

Felix is the one least affected by the tragedy, hardly able to disguise his exuberance as we get nearer to his homeland. I have never seen a man so worked up about anything in my life. He talks to anyone who will listen to him — and many who won't — full of enthusiasm for the task ahead. In other circumstances he might have inspired us all, but today he finds it impossible to break through the barrier of our sadness. I bless the fact that he is coming with us, however, for I can appreciate the value of one who will help to lift us out of our misery when we go ashore.

The navigator does a good job, and we surface on the fourth night with the high cliffs of Greece looming on our starboard side. With only a few hours left to the rendezvous with the fishing-boat all our gear is dragged to the foot of the ladder, in readiness to be passed up through the fore-hatch. We dress in battle gear while Bullock passes out face-black, field dressings and iron rations. We look like a bunch of bloody outlaws when we are fully kitted out.

'Grant!'

'Yes, sir?' I turn to find Murray standing in the doorway.

'Come aft to the wardroom. I want a word.'

I follow obediently, and we withdraw into the hollowed sanctum with the curtains closed to all outsiders.

'I'm concerned about Lieutenant Linklaker,' he says quietly.

'Yes, sir.' I'm non-committal. 'He's a bit under the weather at the moment, but he'll come out of it when he is ashore.'

'I'd like to believe that.'

'I think he will, sir. He's not used to submarines − I think it has got him down.'

'I'm sorry, Grant, but I think you're wrong. I've seen men go like this before, and they don't pull out of it as easy as all that. You know more about him than any of us; do you think he is capable of carrying out the job?'

'He's a hard old cus, sir. I've never seen him like this before, but he's taken a few hard knocks in his life and pulled through − I reckon he'll come out of it all right.'

'Could you carry out the job without him?'

I'm horrified at the thought. 'Not bloody likely!'

'Why not? You know the dredger, and you must have taken command at times?'

I shake my head resolutely. 'We were nothing more than glorified dockyard mateys, sir. It was a foreman's job − no more.'

'What about Norway?'

I feel like blurting out, 'Bugger Norway!' for I don't seem able to live down that part of my life.* 'That was a fluke, sir. I didn't really know what I was doing half the time. In any case, I had a crew of experts, who didn't have to be told what to do.'

He becomes aggressive now coming back at me with a voice heavy with exasperation. 'I'm getting a bit tired of your persistent refusal to enter into the spirit of things, Grant. It seems you will do nothing unless driven to it by circumstances or threats.'

That about sums it up as far as I'm concerned, and I can't honestly see anything outlandish about it. Didn't I tell him in Malta that I was sod-all use? 'I know my limitations, sir. I don't want to be responsible for the lives of other men when I don't know what the hell I'm doing myself. In any case, Bullock will be in charge of the shore part of the operation. Once we get over that. Half-Sh— I mean Lieutenant Linklaker will be okay again.'

'Bullock will not be in charge.'

That brings me up short. 'Oh!'

'He doesn't want the job; says he thinks it is a bad thing to keep swopping command, and, in any case, it is a Navy job. He is quite willing to go along as an advisor, but that's all. We haven't come this far, just to give up when we are knocking on the enemy's door, Grant. Linklaker's not up to it, so you will take charge all the way — understand?'

'I'm glad to be able to volunteer, sir.'

'Volunteer be damned! Errol Flynn might volunteer — you will do as you are bloody well told!'

'Aye aye, sir.'

With that he terminates the discussion, and I go out into the passage to consider the implications. Just once I'd like to have my feelings taken into consideration, but I don't deny a small thrill of excitement welling up inside — I must be a flaming megalomaniac!

I devote the next couple of hours to pumping some self-assurance back into Half-Shackle, and I believe he is coming out of his dejection by the time we are called to the fore-ends, to

* See *Ninety Feet to the Sun*

gather with an assortment of armoury strapped to our bodies, looking like 'bit' players in a partisan film.

Felix makes the biggest impact. Divested of his normal gear, wearing battledress with additional bandoliers and holsters of his own design, he looks like a Mexican bandit. I cannot help but feel a glow of reassurance as I listen to his chatter, and sense his wild excitement.

XI

The last time I found myself on a surfaced submarine in broad daylight with an enemy-held coast looming so close, it led to a series of disasters, culminating in the death of most of the crew; so the prospect doesn't enthrall me. The unwritten law for boats in the Mediterranean is to dive before the sun pokes its edge over the horizon staying beneath the surface until nightfall, with the occasional survey through the periscope for possible targets. Today I accept there is no alternative, for the fishing caique is only allowed out in daylight.

Felix reassures us by explaining that although Limos is occupied by Germans, the boat comes from a fishing village further south, which is held by Italians who have a much more lighthearted approach to the war. The rendezvous is arranged for siesta time; just west of a small, uninhabited island where we will be hidden from the mainland. The caique will 'drift' away from its colleagues while everyone dozes away the hottest part of the day before lowering her sail in a pre-arranged signal for us to surface. When I ask him if the skipper of the caique is reliable his smile vanishes, and an intense expression transforms his features as he stares deep into my eyes.

'The skipper is my father,' he says with emotion, pounding a fist into his chest to emphasise his words. 'He would die sooner than let me down. If anyone asks why I fight the occupiers of my country I need look no further than him to find the answer. For me and my English mother he worked and saved his hard-earned money to send me to Cambridge — incredible, is it not? A Greek fisherman's son going to university! Now, I join others to help you rid Greece of these aliens who would try to change my father's way of life. It is the least I can do to repay him.'

We have no more time for discussion, for I am called with Felix to the control-room, where Murray is staring through the periscope on a bearing just off the starboard bow. He notices the Greek fidgeting beside him and hands the periscope handles to him. 'There is a blue fishing-boat with big eyes painted on her prow nearby, Felix. Is it ours?'

Felix peers through the lens, taking a moment to adjust to the strange experience of looking across the sea which is only inches below eye level. He confirms that this is his father's boat, and I am invited to have a look, so that I will know her when we surface.

'Right,' says Murray, 'I don't have to emphasise the need for alacrity, Grant. If we are caught on the surface by an aircraft it will go hard for us, and the Greeks. So get it done quickly.'

'Aye aye, sir.'

'Good luck to all of you,' he adds, with his eyes already back at the lens.

We go forward to stand waiting at the foot of the ladder leading up to the fore-hatch. The torpedomen have already removed the steel 'strong-back' that spans the hatch when it is shut: thick as a man's arm, it reinforces this weak spot in the pressure hull. Hargreaves is moaning about the amount of equipment he has to carry: muttering away to Soapy while we tense up ready to go out. The orders come in quick succession, and, in moments, we are assembled in an untidy group on the dripping casing.

In the still air the noises are emphasised, and the slop of water against the approaching hull seems to fill the sky. She slides alongside easily, nudging the boat with a soft bump. There isn't going to be time for hanging about, so I lead the scramble down into the slippery bulge of the submarine's hull, to grab the gunn'ls of the fishing-boat. Everyone is struggling to get to her, while helping hands reach for us. In a moment I am on her deck, turning to bear a hand with those who follow me.

I look about to see that most of us are across the gap now. I can also see a slumped figure clinging to the skirt of the casing, as he waits for an opportunity to leap over.

'Come on, Half-Shackle!' I yell at him, hoping a familiar voice will stir him into action.

'Okay, okay, I'm coming!' he half stands on the slippery metal as the two ships roll together. Balancing precariously, and trying to judge the right moment to jump. An opportunity comes, but he misses it, to stand undecided as the gap opens up again, leaving him wavering with arms outstretched hopelessly.

I place a leg over the side, reaching down to give him a hand. 'Right!' I shout as I feel the fishing-boat rolling back towards the submarine. 'Come on!'

He makes a vague effort, and our hands touch for a second or two, then he is gone again as the boat hits the pressure hull with a resounding thud. That warns me that we haven't got time to mess about, with the bulge of the caique's bilges riding up on to the wallowing slope of the steel hull.

'You'll have to jump for it — come on! — I'll grab you!'

Someone else is beside me now; reaching down two extra hands for him. All he has to do is leap, and we will haul him to safety. I'll grant that he tries in a vague, half-hearted sort of way; but his hands are nowhere near ours, and he starts to slide down between the two vessels as they come together. I leap down onto the rubbing-strake to grab his arms as Felix comes down from the submarine's casing to help. Together we push and haul at him while he gasps and struggles in a kind of panic, until we get him over the gun'l. A burst of spray leaps up at me as I heave him bodily aft to the shelter of the wheelhouse.

A frightful scream rends the air, and I wheel to see everyone looking over the side at the gap between the two vessels. As I rush over to find out what caused that agonising sound a big man hurtles past me from the wheelhouse. Horrified, I see the top half of Felix's body being crushed between the two hulls. Blood fills his gaping mouth, while his midriff is torn apart to spread a mess of mangled entrails along the black hull. Incredibly he is still alive and conscious right up to the moment when the gap opens again, and mercifully allows him to sink out of sight, leaving behind a dazed group of shocked men, watching a small whirlpool of red disappearing in our wake. I look towards the big man as he grips hard at the rail, with his dark eyes filled with pain, and his jaw set in a hard line.

There is a shout from Murray; reminding us that life goes on, and the two boats are falling apart now, with the H-boat picking up speed as she moves away from us in a wide circle. I see the fountains of spray when she opens her vents to nose down into a shallow dive. Soon the sea is empty once more, with only the wheeling gulls to mark the spot where she disappeared. We don't ponder over the tasty morsels that have attracted them to the scene.

Beneath my feet the engine starts up to settle into a steady pulse as the bows swing towards the east to clear the edge of the small island, and show a group of brightly coloured fishing-boats bobbing in close formation. A chuckling bow-wave builds up to fan out in everwidening folds of shining water.

It is fairly crowded in the boat, for besides the crew of four there are five of us: all trying to keep out of each other's way. The Greeks withdraw into themselves as they go about their duties as though we do not exist. It all seems very haphazard to me, for our gear is strewn about the upper deck in sight of anyone who might care to look. I fidget nervously, on the brink of getting my own men to stow everything out of sight, when the skipper emerges from the wheelhouse. He has a large moustache thatching his upper lip and hanging down on each side of his mouth in a thick, wiry bush. His teeth gleam white like pearls, when he takes the butt of a cigarette from his mouth, to throw it into our wake; staring after it in a long, thoughtful look. I wonder if the death of Felix is going to jeopardise our future as I wait impatiently for him to shrug away his grief. Without his co-operation, we might as well pack up.

At last I see him square his shoulders and heave himself away from the rail; looking us over as he picks his way through the piles of our gear. He raps an order over his shoulder before coming to stare down at me.

'You have killed my only son with your stupid schemes. Nothing would please me more than to dump you over the side, but I made a promise to him, and his English mother; so I will finish what I have begun. My crew will look after you until we hand you over to Andros and his gang. I do not want to see you any more; not you, nor anyone to do with this damned war.'

He turns abruptly, to disappear into the wheelhouse; leaving us in the hands of two men who carry on an animated argu-ment. For long periods I am completely ignored as they thrash out disagreements, with wild flurries of hand-waving. Eventu-ally I get the message, and order my men to stow away the gear beneath piles of fishing nets, then send them below to stay hidden as we approach the spot where we should pick up the rest of the fishing fleet. No sooner are the men out of sight than the shapes of several fishing caiques take form about us; some with small skiffs rowing in wide circles, towing nets behind them to enclose shoals of tiny fish.

I am given a peaked cap and a scruffy old jersey to put on over a filthy pair of dungarees, to make me look like the other members of the crew, while we slide in amongst the fleet as unobtrusively as possible. Soon we are bobbing in tune with them all as we lie hove-to on a calm sea.

We have hardly settled when the roar of high-powered engines herald the approach of a German E-boat. She hurtles up at something like thirty knots; laying over in a tight turn round the fishing-boats to set them rocking and dipping madly in her wake.

Her engines cut abruptly, and she moves slowly through the fleet, checking each vessel as she moves by. I can see the crew quite plainly, standing by their weapons, studying us with bored expressions. Having counted the flock they prepare to shepherd us back to harbour, and a sharp bark from her loud-hailer brings a slow response from the boats as they start their motors, and begin to chug back home. We join in the parade as the E-boat snarls off in another burst of pent-up energy. All the way in she keeps up a series of high speed dashes on the fringe of the fleet.

Sunset is colouring the sky now, and I watch the lofty cliffs slide by in a panorama of majestic beauty. There is a golden quality to the light that contrasts deeply with the black etchings of fissures shadowed in the brown rock of the ramparts. Tufts of scrub crowd the yellow heights of these ageless cliffs, already beginning to lose colour in the fading light. In prewar days I spent a lot of time in these waters, watching these shores slide by with the same sense of invading a world of Greek gods and mythological legend. Even in these circumstances I feel the mystery of the land taking hold of me.

Passing a headland we open up a view of a small inlet, with a smattering of square, white houses climbing out of a narrow valley. The crumbling breakwater of a tiny harbour elbows out

into the deep, blue water, encompassing a small forest of swaying masts and rigging. Along the waterfront a cluster of squat
cottages drag their skirts in the sand of a narrow beach, and
dark-skinned men watch our approach with expressionless
faces. The E-boat's engines fill the valley with sound as she
makes one last circle before tucking her stern down to roar off
towards the south; relieved of her mundane duty.

The fishing fleet anchors, and throughout the evening we are
ferried ashore one by one, to merge with the locals, while trying
to blend in with the scenery. It takes a lot of effort to saunter
along disconsolately past pairs of strolling enemy soldiers who
watch every move we make with more than casual interest. If
the natives are curious, they don't show it, and I begin to
wonder how many people know who we are. It seems impossible
that they can accept new faces in such a small community without showing some interest. I find out later that they are used to
new faces here in these days of war, and it is best not to ask questions, or show too much curiosity in things that do not concern
them. Even the simple inhabitants of a fishing village learn to
lose their natural, easy-going natures, and become part of the
harsh intrigue of an occupied land.

I stride along with the Greek skipper without saying a word,
as he leads me through the narrow, cobbled alleyways, while my
belly dissolves each time we brush past members of the master-
race. The path we follow leaves the harbour to zig-zag up the
hillside between low walls, where lazy dogs guard the gates and
children haunt the shadows.

At last we reach a wider roadway, and I am led towards a
dray to take my seat beside a surly individual who broods over
the backsides of a pair of bony horses. Before my rump touches
the wood he slaps the reins and clucks at his charges, sending
them off in a shambling gait, with iron-shod wheels grinding
into the earth as they plod along.

The sweat cools on my shoulders, and my skin prickles under
the rough clothing as we roll past minute donkeys bearing
impossible loads, driven by men with chestnut arms, while
women with round faces and worn shoes watch from open doorways. The scent of olives and the taste of dust is in the air as the
hooves clump heavily into the rutted surface. It is a warm, lazy

evening, remote from the drab business of war, and it takes a party of Italian soldiers marching along the clifftop to bring me back to reality.

As we reach the apex of the long climb the sea comes into view far below, glowing red and gold. The wide sweep of a large bay opens out, and I can recognise it immediately, with the small island dominating the seaward side. The booms of the anti-submarine nets snake across the expanse between mainland and island, tended by a squat boom-defence vessel at the southern end.

I begin to pick out the landmarks ingrained on my mind by Felix when he had pointed out every peculiarity, and each prominent feature. My gaze shifts northward to where I see a clutch of moored ships, exactly where they were shown on the model. At first it looks like a group of barges nudging alongside a merchant ship with a tall fag-end of a funnel, showing her to be of vintage years. As I peer closer, however, I can see the shape of the U-boat nestled inside the barges – grey and menacing.

There are increasing numbers of enemy soldiers now, and they stare at us with open suspicion as we pass by. I grow conscious of my pale skin, and crouch forward to stare at the undulating rumps of the horses in an attempt to shadow my features. We turn off the roadway, bumping down a small track that leads away from the shore, through an avenue of waving cypruses. At the end we swing into a square farmyard to draw up in front of a plain, wooden door, flaked with the remains of green paint, and sagging heavily on worn hinges. My companion digs me in the ribs, nodding in the direction of the ground.

I scramble out without a word. The carter wheels his horses round in a stumping, jingling circle, before trundling back the way we came, leaving me standing alone and undecided. The heavy creak of the door drags my gaze in its direction, to find a tall young man glowering at me from beneath two bushy eyebrows. He is thatched with a crop of black curls that grow down each side of his swarthy face in heavy sideburns, and he wears a bandolier across his chest, loaded with ammunition. He must have bags of confidence to stand like that, even in the growing darkness.

He beckons me through the entrance, at the same time searching the surrounding country with sharp, hawklike eyes. Inside it is almost totally dark, with one small window the only source of light. A rough table dominates the interior, and two other men sit there looking up at me with unashamed curiosity.

'Wine?' offers a treble-chinned man, thrusting a tin mug in my direction.

'Thanks,' I mutter, looking from face to face; wondering what I have got myself into. The third member of their group is a wizened, little old man, with hollow cheeks and deepset eyes. He is one of those individuals who get their five o'clock shadow about ten in the morning. I grab the mug, and drink the wine slowly.

'Soon the others come,' says the fat man. 'Now you rest until Andros says we go.'

Andros must be the tall young man who led me in. He sits down, and starts cleaning his automatic rifle with more expertise than I could ever achieve. He caresses it with a loving care that suggests he has more respect for it than the human beings it is designed to kill. I ease my body into a chair, and prepare to wait in embarrassed silence.

'Any cigarettes, Johnie?' the fat man asks.

'Sorry, I don't smoke.'

They exchange looks of disgust and the fat man shrugs, 'Oh well, it is not important.'

We sink into silence again, with only the sound of Andros working the breach mechanism of his gun to entertain us. He becomes aware that I am watching him closely, and returns my gaze with an intense stare that seems to reach down into my soul. He places his weapon carefully on the table top without taking his eyes from me. 'That German submarine — you must sink her.'

I am used to most Greeks having a smattering of English, but, like Felix, this chap has hardly any accent. I am to learn he speaks no less than four languages fluently, and can make himself well understood with a couple more. Like Felix, he is a student with fire in his belly, and ideas for a brand new world once they have sorted out the mess the politicians have made of it.

'I hope so,' I answer blandly.

'Don't hope: Do it!' I almost fall out of my chair as he slams a fist down on the table with a force that slops wine from the mugs, and almost gives the old man a heart attack.

'I'll do my best,' I promise harshly.

'You had better do more than that, my English friend. We Greeks could have done it days ago, but we have not been allowed.'

The fat man interrupts with a flood of Greek, and they argue violently for a few moments before the old man barks them into silence. 'Forgive my impatient brother,' says the fat man apologetically. 'He is angry because we have done little so far to the Germans. I tell him the time will come for us. Now; it is the time for the experts.'

'Experts! Pah!' His spit lands two inches from my boot, and we glare at each other in mutual hatred. I am beginning to get riled at his attitude. I have no time for those who think war is a game of personal heroics. I concentrate on my wine, and luckily there is no time for further discussion before the next member of my group comes staggering through the door.

It is Hargreaves, and he is burning to have a go at me for the way he is being treated by all and sundry. No one, not even Andros, can silence his monologue of self-pity as he drones on and on about having to wear filthy clothes, trudge miles over dirt tracks, trying to reason with people who are too stupid to understand his language. At last, unable to stand any more of it I yell at him to shut up, in a voice that rattles the crockery, and stuns him into silence. I look about to see everyone nodding approval.

Soapy, Bullock and Half-Shackle arrive one by one throughout the evening, until we are a complete unit. Our hosts provide a meal of fried fish before we settle for a long night, tossing and turning on hard beds, while partisans come and go on mysterious errands. Towards morning they all come back to report to the old man, who accepts what they say with nods of satisfaction, then calls us to the table for a final briefing.

Andros takes the head seat. 'The dredger's crew is taken care of. At daybreak we go to work.' His voice is cold, and his eyes bore into me; defying me to put up an argument.

'We?' I ask guardedly.

'We!' affirms the old man in a way that puts me in my place. 'Without Felix you will need another leader. It is not possible to go alone. You will have a good guide – Andros. He will lead; you will follow.'

'This is no part of the plan!' I protest.

The old man shrugs, 'It is how it will have to be. He is hot-blooded, but a good man for what you want.'

I look from one to the other, angered at this sudden change of our carefully arranged scheme, and the niggling feeling that they are ganging up on me. There is a smirk on the young Greek's face as he watches my frustration with open amusement. 'Just so long as he realises who is in command,' I stress through clenched teeth; wiping the smile from his face.

'It is understood,' says the old man. 'You are in charge.'

The way he speaks makes it sound like someone coaxing a little child to take nasty medicine with promise of false rewards. A new anxiety fills my gut, and I wonder if I am on the slippery slopes of losing control of the operation. The only chance of success is for the plan to be carried out with precision: there can be only one man in command. Any independent move on the part of a foolhardy hothead will wreck the whole thing.

Huddled shapes are beginning to rise from their beds to shuffle about the place, gathering up their gear, and adjusting clothing. There is an excess of magazine rattling as the Greeks assemble near the door. They are enjoying this too much for my peace of mind. Andros wrenches open the door, and we blink in the sudden flood of sunlight that glares in at us.

'We go!' he snaps. 'One Greek – one English. Follow closely, and do everything the man in front does.'

He glares at me, challenging me to raise objections to him taking charge, but I don't rise to his bait; I am well aware that for this part of the operation we are in the hands of experts, obliged to follow his directions to the letter. I only hope he feels the same when it is my turn to command.

There is no further talk as we are led out from the village into the rough terrain; dodging through outcrops of rock, and clumps of dry shrubbery. We follow dry creek-beds, hugging close to rock faces, going ever downward until we reach a group of pine trees that straggle over a steep slope to an overhanging cliff where we can look down into a cove. The Germans have built a small concrete jetty, with a couple of huts and a pill-box guarding the seaward end. A winding road leaves the landward end of the jetty, to snake along the coast until it arrives at a sentry box and barrier that closes the entrance to the harbour. Alongside the wharf the dredger nestles, rusty and tarnished by years of abuse. I take heart when I see that she is exactly like the one we have practised with; even the lines of rust seem to be in the same places, although someone has rigged an awning just abaft the bridge.

'Come!' orders Andros impatiently; signalling us to follow him into a small copse of spindly trees, where we gather in a circle. A few words in Greek sends the guerrillas slinking off while we are left on our own to formulate the next move. Andros and one of his men are to go down to approach the sentry box by road as if they are arriving for work. The rest of us will sneak down to the overhanging cliff, and climb down behind the huts on the jetty. It all seems very straightforward and simple when spelt out by the Greeks.

I lead my section to where the trees end at the beginning of the bare headland that grows out in a long arm of rock overlooking the jetty. We crouch under cover of the last pair of pines, watching our two companions slip out onto the coast road, to saunter casually towards the harbour. I wait until one of the grey-clad figures leaves his post to go to meet them before urging my lot out of their corners, praying that Andros and his mate can keep the sentries occupied until we are amongst those huts.

We hurry over the broken ground in a sort of crouching run until we reach a fissure that runs out to the harbour. There is no time to see if the two men are doing their job at the barrier — if one of those German soldiers looks our way now it is all up with the plan anyhow. We slither down in a small avalanche of bodies and rubble, to finish up behind one of the huts. So far, so good. I pause for a moment before sliding along the side of the hut, to peer round the corner.

Andros and one of the sentries are engaged in an argument of some kind, while the other two men look on. The Greek is waving some papers under the belligerent nose of the sentry, and I can hear his voice from here as it rises in a protesting monologue. Now is the moment for us to creep from our hiding place while their attention is absorbed. I prepare to caution my group to make their movements stealthy when I realise there is another way of doing things.

While the argument goes on at the barrier we move out of hiding as though we have every right to be there, to tackle the heavy padlock on the nearest hut. Inside the oxy-acetylene equipment is exactly where Felix said it would be, and Hargreaves finds everything he needs, with a trolley to wheel the gear across to the dredger. Bullock, Half-Shackle and I stroll over to the gangway; there should be at least three members of the crew on board, for she is a self-contained, mobile unit; sent wherever she is required. So, her crew lives on board, with the exception of her skipper and the mate who, according to the Greeks, sleep ashore.

I leave Half-Shackle in the wheelhouse where he will do least harm, for he is utterly useless now; allowing himself to be shuffled about in a semi-dazed state. Bullock and I go below to find four recumbent shapes snoring their heads off in their scruffy bunks. We drag them out, waving guns in front of their wide, startled eyes as they pull on their clothes. The plan is to hand them over to the Greeks, who will keep them hidden throughout the time it takes to accomplish our mission. It is more risky than keeping them on board with us, but I have insisted on being rid of the responsibility for them. Things could get hairy later on, and I don't want their lives on my conscience. I know their skipper, and the mate are taken care of, for it is their papers that Andros is waving under the sentry's nose.

We chivy them up on deck, where two of Andros's guerrillas take them from us, and shuttle them away in random groups. I look over in the direction of the sentries; surely they must be curious at the amount of traffic in this area; but apparently not, for they are talking together about subjects more interesting than a scruffy old dredger preparing to slip her moorings, and Andros is already on his way across the gangway. A cold feeling grips me — things are going too well; I'm not this lucky.

I order Bullock aft, and persuade Andros to go forward on his own. Looking about me at the familiar surroundings I begin to feel more confident, until I notice two grey shapes moored in line astern alongside the new pier. They are the stub-nosed trawlers, with their sterns loaded with depth-charges, and short range weapons bristling everywhere else. I can imagine the hell they can produce when turned loose. I try to ignore them while I grab the wheel in readiness to cast off.

Bullock is waiting for my signal, so responds immediately to my wave by flicking the rope hawser off the bollard with a deft movement. The more inexpert Andros is less successful, and the marine has to leap ashore to lift the eye clear as a swirl of water spreads aft in response to the propeller when I yell for 'half astern' down the voice-pipe: there are no refinements like telegraphs on this barge. He climbs back aboard as we begin to slide out from the berth.

The screw drags the stern to port, so I let her go on her own, swinging in a wide circle until the bows are pointing seaward. I shout down for 'half ahead', and she spins on her axis as the rudder bites. The surface of the bay is like a sheet of glass, and only our bow-wave disturbs the glossy sheen. I spare a glance astern to see the two sentries watching our progress with casual interest, while another scruffy individual emerges from the hut, sniffs at the morning, scratches his ample belly, before spitting into the water, then goes back inside again. The whole scene is one of peace and tranquillity as we churn slowly across the expanse of sparkling sea, towards the centre of the bay.

I turn to Half-Shackle who slumps against the bulkhead, staring gloomily out of a side window. His face has crumpled like old putty, with jowls sagging each side of his loose mouth. Somehow I have got to jerk him out of this.

'Here! take the wheel!' I tell him, grabbing a fistful of jersey to heave him into position. 'This is your bloody job. Go straight for the boom − I've got other things to take care of.'

He turns dull eyes towards me, while his mouth opens and closes soundlessly. I take the edge out of my voice:

'Go on, mate. Steer for the boom − I want to look at the target.'

I place his hands on the spokes, while his lifeless eyes search mine in a kind of questioning plea. I nod towards the bow, urging him to take an interest. He fondles the polished wood for a moment, staring ahead as she starts to slew off course. I hold myself back from correcting the swing, praying he will react. It works better than I could have hoped. He feels the wheel buck slightly, and it wakes an inherent response to a familiar situation. The wheel spins to compensate, and his eyes liven up. In a moment he is steering; coming alive to the dredger's needs, so I can back off, leaving him to it.

There is time for me to study the clutch of barges, and the parts of the U-boat visible between them. Men wearing white overalls are moving about the casing; they puzzle me for a minute or so, before I realise they are in the process of fuelling her. According to Brigginshaw, this is a very exacting procedure, for the mixture is dangerous, and must be handled with almost clinical precaution. 'High Test Peroxide' they call it, and they have had all sorts of problems to overcome; even to the extent of lining fuel-tanks with synthetic rubber because of its aversion to the slightest sign of corrosion. I smile to myself; she should go up with a nice healthy bang when we plant a torpedo in her midriff. It shows there is not a lot of time to play with though, for they would be fuelling her only if she is almost due to sail.

I return to the wheelhouse, to stand behind Half-Shackle as he begins to shape up to something like his old self. Bullock enters with a report that all is ready, and I can see Hargreaves and Soapy burning through the steel girders. It means that there is nobody watching the engines, but they must be satisfied with its performance, and we will not be making any demands on it for a quarter of an hour or so. Andros is still in the bow, enjoying the scenery as it glides by. I curse his independent attitude, but there's nothing I can do about it.

We are steering easy now, at about four knots, churning our way towards the boom. This is the first crisis that must be faced, and I call down a warning to Hargreaves, who sends Soapy back to the engine. We have been told that the dredger usually signals the boom-defence vessel with a long blast on her siren as she approaches. So, with great deliberation, I yank on the lanyard, and the deep blare of her foghorn reverberates across the bay. Christ! she sounds like the *Queen Mary*.

We are gulping up the few remaining yards, and there is no movement on the other ship yet. I don't know if I can cope with any untoward snags now, so I pray that they will open the net before I have to heave to. A glance in the direction of the landward side shows the ominous shapes of the trawlers nudging impatiently at their moorings; full of menace as we grope our sluggish way through the enemy camp. Relief floods into my veins like whisky as I see a couple of disconsolate men moving to their stations. They are well-practised in their duty, and a gap is opening even as we come up to the nets, so we go through with feet to spare on either side.

There are no waves, nor any sign of acknowledgement as we pass through. Just utter boredom, and mutual contempt from both sides. Greek and German have little in common; even the bondage of the sea holds no weight here. This is no more than the hard relationship between oppressor and oppressed.

Leaving them astern, I watch the island for a tall pinnacle of rock to come in line with a tower perched halfway up the cliff. Keeping those two in line will take me right to the position where *Hobo* should be waiting later on. All I need to do is hold my course until the other two markers on the mainland line up in order to find the exact spot. I wonder if she is there now, sitting quietly on the bottom while our screw pulsates over the top of her. Now I must work the dredger into position to go through the motions of clearing the entrance to the river. Half-Shackle and I take turns on the crane, hauling up buckets of dripping sludge, and dumping it right through the open hold, trying not to soak Hargreaves and Soapy as they cut away the steel.

They work well those two, and the second girder splashes into the drink before mid-day. We make things look good by moving in and out of the creek as if we are carrying loads of silt away, to be deposited on the seabed. I hope there are no knowing types watching us; for they must surely become suspicious when the dredger's draught stays the same. Sixty tons of soggy silt should make her sit well down in the water.

During the afternoon we manage to cut away all obstructions

from the hold; far more than we had anticipated, and by three o'clock the hold is free of all encumbrances with all the gear stowed away. The time for our rendezvous with *Hobo* is sixteen hundred, so we raid the food locker while we wait.

XII

With fifteen minutes to spare we move out of the creek for the last time, and go through the motions of dumping the final load clear of the estuary. Now is the time when all our practice will come to fruition if I can only locate the marker. Half-Shackle is on the wheel, concentrating all his efforts on the steering; as though hanging on to the helm is his way of crawling out of the miserable sense of failure that submerges his spirit.

A new sound sends a thrill of fear through me, and I swing to stare up into the sky where the black shape of a diving aircraft is almost on top of us. It is an Arado 196 float-'plane, used for reconnaissance by the Italians. It looks like a clumsy old pelican as it roars overhead, waggling its wings. The pilot seems to be enjoying our reaction as he catches us unawares after coming in from the sun in a silent, gliding dive. He opens the throttle now with a deep-throated roar, and the aircraft sweeps away in a climbing arc, leaving me a shattered ruin, with my nerves in shreds.

'Stupid bastard!' growls Hargreaves, as he pokes his head up out of the engine-room hatch to see what the noise is all about. 'Just like the bloody air force – always pissing about, scaring the life out of their betters.

I'm too choked to reply, automatically taking the wheel from Half-Shackle as my stomach settles back to something like normality. A glance shows the aircraft winging in a circle over the land. Looking forward across the bow I can see we are coming on to our position, and as though to confirm my thoughts, Andros yells out that he can see the marker. He's right too, for I can recognise the piece of rubbish floating innocently on the blue sea just ahead of us. *Hobo* must be hearing our screws now, and Murray preparing to join up with us. I take the dredger in a wide circle to line up with the boat, unable to trust

Half-Shackle with this part of the operation. Everything must go right, because we are under the eyes of watchers from shore who will become curious if we carry out all kinds of strange manoeuvres.

'Look at that bloody plane! growls Bullock, and I peer up through the glass at the aircraft coming in with his floats skimming the surface on a sweep that will take him right over our bow.

'Do you think they've seen anything?'

I exchange glances with him as the same thought occurs to me. The water is clear and translucent here. *Hobo* must show plain as day to anyone who looks down from overhead.

'Christ!' I blurt out, 'we are leading them straight to the submarine!' For a moment I consider altering course, to lead them away from the boat, but decide it will be more practical to place the dredger right over the top of her now that we are this close. The lump of flotsam is coming closer all the time; there is nothing for it now but to carry on with the approach as though the aircraft did not exist.

Bullock goes to stand with Andros by the rim of the hold. The shadow of the plane sweeps across the dredger as it roars overhead; so low that it almost clips the short mast with one of its floats. Straight out over the marker it goes, and I comfort myself with the thought that the crew will not see the submarine directly under the fuselage. I breathe easier when I see it settle on a course for the anchorage.

Now I must concentrate on the final approach. The marker is under the bow, and the sea is like a mill-pond. If the bloody *Tirpitz* was to come round the corner now I would have to ignore her for these last few vital yards. The old dredger steers like a flat-iron at anything less than three knots, so I keep the speed up all the way in.

We must be over her stern already. Andros is staring down into the open hold with Soapy, who has come on deck to give a hand; and Bullock uses a long boat-hook to 'fish' the marker — complete with telephone — out of the water. I should be with them; standing by that phone, ready to contact Murray as quickly as possible. One look at poor old Half-Shackle convinces me that I cannot leave him on his own however, and I decide to hang it out to the last second.

'Stop engine,' I yell down to Hargreaves, as Bullock hooks the marker, and hauls it inboard. Andros is almost dancing with excitement as he sees the submarine coming into view under the hull.

'Half astern!' I must be careful. We don't want the screw dragging the arse-end over to port, so I stop the engine the moment the way is off her. The wheelhouse and upper works is between the well-deck and the shore to hide the goings on from prying eyes. There is no time to waste, and I leap down to the steel deck to grab the hand-set from Bullock, looking into the hold where *Hobo*'s bridge is perfectly framed. . . . There will never be another moment like this.

'This is Grant — surface now!' I shout into the mouthpiece.

They don't hang about. Voices are rapping out orders, and even up here we can hear high-pressure air roaring into the tanks as she lifts to come up sweet as a nut, water spilling from her bridge as she rises like a huge leviathan. The upper hatch clanks open and Murray climbs out, followed by several seamen, who begin passing up the heavy wires. The whole deck is a hive of activity, with the winches turning as the slack is taken up, marrying the two ships together.

Everything falls into place better than we could have hoped. Unladen, the dredger is high enough out of the water to hide *Hobo*'s bridge from anyone watching from shore, and Murray is blinking about him as though unable to believe it has all come off so well. He turns to come up to the wheelhouse, wearing a smug grin on his face.

'I knew it would work, Grant,' he gloats. 'Well done! It seems to have gone without a hitch.'

I'll take that prim smile from his lips. 'We have had a seaplane hovering about, sir. Flew right over the top of you.'

I might have told him the sun was shining for all the effect it has. His smile just broadens. 'Didn't see us then — good! They will probably ignore us now they have had a look.'

'We were lucky, sir,' I tell him coldly. 'I could see you; just by looking over the side.'

'Could you now?' He is about as interested in what I have to say as a turkey is in the twenty-fifth of December. 'Oh well! put your wheel amidships, and secure all the wires, then let us get the hell out of here!'

He's a casual bastard all right. To listen to him, no one would think that we are fiddling about under those cliffs, with a thousand pairs of eyes peering at us. The enemy most likely has a series of range-finders and long-range telescopes scanning this area day and night; all geared up to alert their anti-submarine defences, but it doesn't seem to worry him at all.

I order the seamen to keep their heads below the gun'ls, laying great emphasis on each word in the vain hope that he might be dragged out of his complacency. He ignores me as he sorts out the telephone he has brought with him, so that he can relay messages from the bridge, directly to *Hobo*'s control-room. The dredger has become no more than a piggy-back rider now, though we have to keep her engine turning all the time to fool the German hydrophone operators; but it is the submarine's electric motors doing most of the work.

Murray ignores Half-Shackle after an initial effort to bring him into the conversation. Andros doesn't impress him much either, and he has a go at me for bringing him on board the dredger, despite my insistence that with Half-Shackle turning out to be utterly useless the Greek is a valuable addition to the crew.

I stand at the wheel while Murray orders 'slow ahead together', and the wires creak when the strain comes on them. Bullock and Andros dodge about with the seamen, watching the wires tauten up as we begin to move through the water. The lessons we learned in Egypt come in handy now as we settle on course for the entrance to the bay, and by using both helms together we are able to steer nicely. Everything is shaping up well when the snarl of aircraft engines under full throttle comes blaring out from the anchorage.

'That bloody seaplane! — it must be taking off!' I swear anxiously. 'If it flies over us it can't fail to see the submarine's bridge.'

'We'll have to hope and pray that it doesn't then, won't we?'

I stare at him in disbelief; coolheadedness is one thing, but I can't come to terms with this sheer nonchalance.

'Grab the wheel!' I yell rudely, brushing him aside as I heave my body through the door.

The sound has grown to a crescendo now and I can imagine the aircraft skimming along the water, gaining flying speed with a wake spreading out on either side. In seconds she will be airborne and I know she is going to come our way. I hoist myself up into the cab of the Priesman 40 crane and press the starter before my backside touches the seat. The diesel rattles into life and settles to a steady throb. Controlling a hot panic that threatens to turn my muscles to jelly I handle the levers that swing the jib amidships, to centre above the submarine. Someone on her bridge looks up as the shadow of the bucket passes over his head, then quickly dives into the hatch when he realises what I am doing.

I lower the jib right across *Hobo*'s periscopes so that the bucket crashes down on the deck just in front of the bridge. God knows what damage I've done to them, but my only thought is for the secrecy of the operation: Anyway, if things go to plan, we don't need the periscopes for the attack. That's my main concern; what happens thereafter is in the laps of the gods.

Optimistically I reckon the jib will disguise the shape of the submarine's bridge so that only a close examination will reveal her. Even as I make my way back to the wheelhouse the seaplane swoops up out of the bay to swing north — totally ignoring us.

Murray nods at me as I come through the door. 'Good thinking, Grant. I can see you're entering into the spirit of things.'

'Hope I haven't damaged the periscopes, sir.'

He peers over the front of the bridge. 'I don't think so. The jib came down just right, and the framework missed the stands completely. I knew you would find your enthusiasm once things got started.'

My only response is to glare at him with a sour expression. If he thinks for one moment that I have any enthusiasm for this lark, let him get the idea right out of his tiny mind. I'm in this under protest, and I resent the way my life has been disrupted by his wild scheme: His lust for adventure holds no sway with me. With set jaw I watch the German boom-defence vessel heaving aside the nets to allow us through. If anything, the submarine's twin screws are an improvement on the dredger's single propeller, but one look at the straining wires shows how close we are to total disaster. If just one of those bar-taut hawsers part it could wreck the whole thing.

Murray's orders are passed from a sitting position as we go by the German ship. Only myself and Half-Shackle stand upright, and to any outsider it looks as though there are only two men on watch when we glide slowly past the boom.

'Well I'm damned! We've done it!' exclaims Murray. 'We are through the bloody nets!'

I glance at him and wince at his joyful features. Surely he realises this is only the beginning? It's like a fly celebrating because he has got himself caught in a spider's web. As if to confirm my thoughts the boom-defence vessel toots on her siren, and I have the presence of mind to respond with ours. She is closing the net behind us; trapping us inside the enemy camp.

'Port ten!'

Murray's cool voice starts a slow swing to port. He must remember every detail of the chart now, and keep us away from the shallows with easy helm orders and a touch of help from *Hobo*'s propellers. Soon the island will slide clear to unveil the targets, but before then we will be passing quite close to those trawlers and the pill-box on the end of the jetty. Looking at the U-boat and her consorts I can see movement everywhere, as though they are making final preparations for sailing. I reckon they are getting ready for trials in the morning, and when I suggest this to Murray he is inclined to agree.

We are the only moving vessel in the bay; probably attracting more than just a casual interest from certain quarters, for they must be on full alert now that the 'Peroxide boat' is so close to her proving trials, and we are diverting from the normal pattern when we edge away from the course we should take for berthing. I'm tensed up now; trying to look in all directions at once as we move towards the centre of the arena. Murray stands upright, setting up the special torpedo sight he has made for this operation.

'Stand by all tubes!'

Down below the TI will be making last-minute preparation. He has never had more time to process his torpedoes, and never before have we been allowed the luxury of lining up on a stationary target at close range, in full view of its crew. If Murray wishes he can take us within a thousand yards before firing.

The bows are coming round slowly to port, lining up to point right at the centre of a mass of ships, and the settings on the torpedoes will ensure that they pass under the flat-bottomed barges and hit the soft belly of the U-boat. Surely nothing can stop us now!

My attention is drawn to the launches patrolling the area, and I watch one sweep out on her own to turn towards us in a flurry of broken water. It could be she is just making an extra wide sweep, but anxiety tightens my muscles as I watch her approach, for there are half a dozen armed seamen sitting bolt upright on her thwarts with their faces turned in our direction as they study the dredger with intense concentration – this is more than a normal patrol sortie, and my suspicions are confirmed when the coxswain leans against his tiller to bring her round in a long curve that will bring her alongside.

'Get out of sight on the port side!' orders Murray tersely.

Andros, Bullock and I slip down into the stern and try to merge with the upper-works. The sound of the launch is growing steadily as she makes her turn, then cuts to a slow mutter. We exchange glances; there is no doubting her intentions now.

'Stand by for boarders!' Murray calls quietly, and my hands clutch the hard metal of my sten as my stomach cramps with a surge of hot panic for a second or two before it dissolves, to leave me clear-headed and surprisingly cool when the launch's engine goes astern. Beside me Bullock works his bolt stealthily, reminding me to check my own weapon. His body is tight against mine, and I feel the tension of him as he crouches like a coiled spring. I have a crawling feeling in my spine as I glance over the gun'l at the trawlers. They are still at their moorings – oblivious of the drama taking place half a mile away.

Murray's warning whisper causes me to react as though he has poked a gun in my ear. My nerves are jumping and my insides are churning like a washing-machine. One look at Andros shows that he is suffering no such trepidations as he contemplates the forthcoming affray with a glint in his eye that bodes ill for some luckless German. Bullock shows his teeth in a half-grin: they make me feel that I am the only weakling in the group.

'Wait until they are over the side!' breathes Murray. 'Come out of hiding when I yell.'

The launch must be on her last few yards now, and the dredger is nicely lined up on her target. Soapy has arrived to stand openly on deck, hiding an automatic in the folds of a shirt he holds in his hand — he will need to move fast when the action starts.

'Stand by!' comes Murray's hoarse whisper. 'It's up to you, Grant. I'll be busy firing the torpedoes.'

These are the final few seconds, for I catch a glimpse of the German coxswain as he heaves his tiller over to swing her stern in against the dredger.

No need for Murray's yell. We move out when the launch bumps alongside and scrapes along the metal.

'Come on!' I scream as the ear-splitting rattle of Bullock's gun crashes in my brain to send me leaping out of hiding with my sten jumping in my hands, bullets spraying into a mass of lumbering shapes, struggling in a confused heap in the waist. All about me weapons are stuttering. The Germans don't stand a chance as they are caught in a hail of flying lead.

Forgetting all I have been taught about firing in short bursts I empty my magazine in one prolonged burst until I am left with a useless gun, frantically searching my pouches for a reload.

Somehow I get hold of one, clipping it into place before switching my attention from the dredger's waist to the launch, to join the others firing into the bleached woodwork. A man stares at me with a look of despair as my bullets rip into his chest, convulsing his body with their impact. There is a madness in me now as I search for a new target and find the tubby shape of the coxswain frozen in the midst of it all with his hand still holding tight to the tiller.

For a moment we stare into each other's eyes — two strangers from different parts of the world with nothing in common but the smoking sten I'm pointing at him. I see a hopeless prayer in his face as I squeeze the trigger, holding the gun steady as the bullets tear into his belly, freezing that expression forever as he buckles into a crumpled heap in the sternsheets, to lie with dead eyes staring up at the red sky of a dying day.

'Cast off!' yells Murray, shaking us back to reality as he clambers down from the wheelhouse, urging us towards the gaping hold. 'Come on; get those wires off her!'

Automatically I begin to release the wires that hold *Hobo* to the dredger; checking to make certain no loose ends are left trailing to snag the props as they come slack. We work with a desperate urgency for the enemy must come alive, and time is running out if we are to get the submarine clear of the dredger. Scurrying figures are everywhere as we scramble for the small hatch that leads down into the sanctuary of the control-room.

'Come on! Come on!' Murray keeps repeating; driving us into the hold with his urgent cries. 'Come on! Let's get away from here before they realise what's going on.'

I'm in the act of casting off the last wire when a violent explosion tears the world apart. It seems to suck the air out of the bay, leaving a vacuum and a few seconds of stunned silence as all eyes focus on a great gout of debris hoisting up into the red sky before the blast echoes back from the hills to shake the dredger. A sheet of intense crimson flame leaps out of the centre of the ships to engulf the whole area as a series of lesser explosions come in quick succession. A hot blast of air breathes over me as the dredger lifts to a surging wave moving under us, and I can hear the two hulls grinding together as spreading swells reach out to us from the core of those expanding forces.

A cacophony of hooting comes from the direction of the small jetty as I hastily finish what I'm doing and go to follow the others down into the submarine. Nothing ties the two ships together now, although *Hobo*'s conning-tower is still thrust up into the open hold. The only two people I can see are Murray and Hargreaves, whose shoulders are just about to disappear below the rim as he goes down the conning-tower ladder. Murray gives one last glance in my direction to ensure that I am on my way before following the ERA.

I almost reach the hatch when a shape comes bundling out in a panting eruption of sweating panic to stand blinking in the bright light of the raging fires for a second or two before running aft to the wheelhouse.

'Half-Shackle!' I shout at him, 'what the hell are you doing? Get back in the boat — we're getting under way!'

Wild eyes stare back at me for a moment without comprehension. He stumbles back into the wheelhouse door, shutting it firmly behind him. I hesitate, looking from him to the open hatch with self-preservation fighting a battle with a crazy notion to help the poor old devil. Eventually I have to go after him, dragging open the sliding door. He stands in a corner, cringing away from me, and holding both arms across his body as though to protect himself from me.

'Come on, mate,' I urge coaxingly. 'There's no point in staying here now.'

He shakes his head pitifully. 'No, Ben — no — never again. You're not going to get me down there again. I'll die up here in the sunlight if I have to — but not down there, in that thing.'

Now I don't know what to do. I should leave the silly old sod here to stew in his own juice; but a surge of pity for the cringing, terrified bastard moves me to make one more effort, and I enter the wheelhouse after him. At this point there is a shout from the submarine's bridge and a glance shows Murray beckoning me back to the boat.

'Get back here, Grant!' he yells. 'I can't hold her like this. Come on, you bloody fool, or I'll have to leave you both behind.'

That is when my brain deserts me; for I find myself replying, 'Go on then; I can't leave him here on his own!'

For a long moment he looks at me, then an anxious shout comes from below and he disappears. I can't believe they will really leave me behind; but the bridge is getting lower in the hold, and gouts of vapour explode from her open vents. In a few seconds she sinks beneath the surface.

I'm stunned by my own actions, standing there looking down into the gaping void. The full weight of what I have done descends on me with sickening pressure. I grip the warm wood of the bridge-rail, looking towards the shuddering figure of Half-Shackle. A movement in the window behind him startles me when Andros and Bullock slide open the other door to enter the wheelhouse. It looks like a grand total of four idiots have elected to remain to face the full might of the Kriegsmarine.

XIII

We look at each other for inspiration; an abandoned little group with no immediate plans for any sort of future, except semi-retirement in a prisoner-of-war camp for the next few years. Minor explosions are taking place, and a pall of billowing black smoke hangs over a floating pile of wreckage where flames leap up to show that a fight for survival is still going on. A lot of men have died over there, and the survivors must be anxious to get as far away from the scene as possible.

An urgent whooping from one of the trawlers drags my attention in that direction to find that they are beginning to sort themselves out now. Men are working on the fo'c's'les as puffs of dirty smoke from their funnels indicate that the engine-rooms are producing power for the coming affray. They must be in a confused state however, for the rattle of small-arms fire from the dredger that first put them on the alert has been superseded by thunderous detonations and spectacular eruptions of multi-coloured flame. How long it will take them to couple the two together and cast suspicious eyes in our direction is anyone's guess. In cases like this the culprit is usually a submarine; although they may assume that the extremely volatile fuel has exploded of its own accord. Not for long though, for the launch is drifting clear with its cargo of recumbent Germans spilling blood all over the place. Right now panic is taking charge, and there is an urgent need to reach those wrecks to rescue some of the screaming survivors.

'Let's get this old bucket under way!' Half-Shackle's gruff tone takes me off-guard for a moment. He stands glaring at me as of old; in total command of himself, without the slightest sign of fear on his craggy features. Gone are the tremulous lips and frightened eyes.

Before anyone can adjust to this sudden transformation an

indignant Soapy climbs with a great clattering out of the com-
panion-way leading down into the engine-room. 'I'm still waiting!' he explodes, spittal flying in all directions.

'Christ, Soapy!' I exclaim, 'what the hell are you still doing
here?'

'You might well bloody ask! I've bin waitin' fer someone ter
tell me what ter do. Sat on me backside while bloody great
bangs goes on abaht me.'

'You silly sod!' I shout at him. 'Everyone's gone back to the
boat except us, and she's shoved off!'

He looks skyward in exasperation. 'Blimey! Nobody tells me
nothin'. What am I supposed ter do now?'

His face is a picture as he looks from one to another for moral
support, to find nothing but unsympathetic grins.

'You'll do as you're flaming well told − that's what you'll do,
me old mate,' snarls Half-Shackle. 'It's your own fault for not
taking more interest in what's going on about you. We need a
bloke down in the engine-room; so get below and let's have some
power.'

'It's nice ter be allowed ter volunteer!' moans Soapy, as he
sinks out of sight again, but within seconds the engine comes
alive to settle to a healthy throb. Half-Shackle calls down the
voice-pipe for 'full ahead', and a surge of foam spreads from her
round stern as the screw bites, to push the old girl through the
water in a tight circle, away from the floating carnage. It is to be
hoped that the enemy will think this is the natural thing for us to
do − get away from the scene of disaster as soon as possible.

The first of the trawlers is already moving out from her berth,
pouring on power as she steams straight toward the stricken
vessels. At least she ignores us, and we roll to her swell as she
pushes by at full speed. Her mate is swinging out slowly in a big
arc at a speed that suggests she is probing the depths with her
detection gear.

Every minute gained is a bonus for us, although to my eyes we
seem merely to be prolonging the inevitable as we turn through
one eighty degrees and settle on a course directly away from the
disruption. No one can accuse us of breaking any harbour speed
limits as we churn along at snail-pace. The most we can hope for
from this old tub is about six knots, and by the sounds coming

from below the throttle is wide open, as Soapy busts a gut to push her to the limit.

Andros is working at his sten-gun as always, while Bullock stares back at the first trawler as she begins to fish bodies out of the water, with a smile on his face, and a flicking tongue wetting his lips as though sampling the taste of vengeance. I am more interested in the other trawler; watching the methodical way she goes about the job — surely she must pick up *Hobo* if she carries on like that?

'Sod it!' growls Bullock. 'Look over there!'

His arm waves in the direction of the boom where the sleek shape of an E-boat is roaring in under full power.

I hear the wheel being hauled over, and turn to find Half-Shackle staring across the bow, lining up on something. Following his gaze I stare straight at the boom-defence vessel as she begins to close the nets. She plays a minor role in all this, and must be feeling somewhat guilty at having allowed an alien presence to penetrate the anchorage. No doubt there will be recriminations when there is time to work out what has happened, but right now she assumes the part of silent observer, though not for long if Half-Shackle has anything to do with it, for I can see what he is up to now, as the dredger's bow settles on course and we plunge on towards the low waist of the German ship with the obvious intention of ramming her.

A startled wail comes from her siren as she realises what our intentions are. Men run to and fro in disarray about her small deck, and someone has the temerity to open fire from her bridge with a small automatic weapon. They are desperately trying to cast off now, to get out of our way. It is hopeless, for there is nothing to stop our blunt, solid bows as they charge in towards her vulnerable belly.

A string of signal flags climbs to the spindly gaff on the boom-defence vessel's only mast as she bleats out pathetic hoots on her siren, calling attention to her plight. But we are aimed straight for her heart, and it doesn't require Half-Shackle's warning to make us brace up for the impact. White faces are peering at us as the last few yards disappear beneath the bow. Shouts of alarm are coming from the crew as they dash about the deck in total confusion.

There is no dignity in anything this old bucket does, and the way she climbs up over the waist of the small ship is no exception. We mount that waist like a randy old mongrel trying to get to grips with a reluctant bitch. The bow climbs as the keel drives over her with a screeching of metal on tortured metal, and a great clattering of loose tackle. Even at six knots the sheer weight of the dredger carries her on over the stricken vessel, bearing down on her, to tear a large hole in her side. Water pours into her while the scrambling hands of her crew grab at our rails to get free of their wrecked ship.

Bullock and Andros race out on to the wing of our bridge to begin firing into the defenceless crewmen before Half-Shackle and I are able to stop them. Screams of anguish and fear come from the panicking seamen as they dive for cover, cringing behind anything that offers the slightest protection, yelling at us to stop firing, and pleading with us to accept their surrender. Bullock and Andros are deaf to all their pleas however; their weapons chatter madly as streams of bullets fly in the direction of anything that moves. It takes almost physical restraint to put a stop to the mindless slaughter, and the look I get from Andros when I finally grab his arm to quell the shooting is one of wild-eyed malice, directed as much at me as the enemy.

The boom-defence vessel is sinking beneath us with her back broken, but we have not got off without damage to ourselves, having ripped open our own plates as far aft as the hold, so the sea is flooding in, and the old dredger will soon join her victim if we don't do something about it.

'The net! — Open the net!' yells Half-Shackle above all the rumpus, and I race forward to grapple with the unfamiliar boom rigging. All I can think to do is knock off as many clips as I can find, and release the brake on her winch. It must be the right approach, because we surge back from the other arm of the boom to leave a widening gap.

The locked ships rotate together as the dredger's engine takes us clear of the net. The grinding, rending entanglement wrenches apart at last with a prolonged screech that sets my teeth on edge. Soapy bursts out of his cavern, determined not to be left behind on this occasion, while his engine churns away at full speed ahead. The bows slip off the crushed waist of the waterlogged ship, and we swing clear towards the open sea with no one at the wheel — as though the old girl is determined to save herself from the ignominy of sinking with her victim.

We haven't much time, for the dredger is filling rapidly and getting lower and lower in the water. The bow is already awash as she rolls with that sluggish, unstable manner of a waterlogged ship. Half-Shackle is making a dash for the wheelhouse again as the sharp crack of a gun warns us that the Germans are alive to what is going on. The first shell hits the sea close by, sending a column of water high, to deluge spray across our deck. There is a gurgling sound from astern as the boom-defence vessel disappears beneath the surface with an undignified belch, and a gout of sooty smoke from her funnel. Beyond, the menacing shape of the E-boat lays over to the bite of her rudder as she hauls round to come in our direction. On her bow the gun's crew balance against the swing as they fire steadily, to send more shells whistling through the air at mast height. I have time to look beyond her to see trawler number two building up speed, with heavy smoke pouring from her stack as she forgets all about submarines and comes across the bay with a growing bow-wave under her blunt nose. We are in for it now, and I wait for Half-Shackle to give the order to find something that will do as a white flag so that we can save ourselves from the inevitable destruction about to overtake us.

The silly old sod! He has no intention of doing anything of the sort. This is a totally different Half-Shackle to the one who cringed in the wheelhouse with frightened eyes and terror in his voice. He is searching the passing coastline of the island as we plough along with our fo'c's'le scooping surf with every dip of her bow. He handles the wheel with the old skill that is more than a match for the unwieldy ruin as he steers for a sandy cove, offering a smooth, soft surface on which we can run her ashore.

It is touch and go whether we will make it however, for the next shell explodes amongst the winches at the foot of the mast, smashing every window in the wheelhouse, and slicing a chunk of flesh from my arm. Half-Shackle's face is a mass of blood, but he grips the wheel hard, eyes focused on the cove. We are gliding in past a long outcrop of rock on our port side, while miraculously, a high cliff rears up close to starboard to hide us from our aggressors for a few vital seconds. I am too engrossed in watching the E-boat to realise how near we are to the shore. I am thrown off my feet as we drive up unto the beach.

'Get ashore quickly! Come on, you lazy bastards!' yells Half-Shackle as he comes bundling forward from the empty wheelhouse. The rest of us trail behind to drop over the bow unto the firm sand. It's every man for himself – including the German survivors, and I scramble up to take cover behind some rocks at the head of the cove. I'm up to my knees in a pool, but at least I am hidden from seaward, from where all the trouble is likely to come.

Looking about me, I see two other heads peering across the top of sheltering rocks; but before I can recognise them a shell smashes into the cliffs above, showering me with dust and gravel. A large boulder hits the deck feet from my head, and my hiding place doesn't seem so healthy any more. Nosing in towards the creek with a couple of her crew standing nervously on the bow watching the shallows, but with half an eye on us lot, the E-boat attempts to push up to the half-submerged dredger, to use her as a pier.

A long burst of fire from someone hidden on the other side of the bay causes chaos on her deck as everyone dives for cover. I join in the shooting with someone else on my side so that a vicious cross-fire brings a change of heart as the Germans realise the futility of it all and back out of the cove, with a murderous burst of fire from their close-range weapons.

A body blunders into my pool, to splash down with a hefty grunt. It is Soapy, and he is looking anything but pleased with life as he snuggles up to me for protection.

'I never volunteered for this lot, 'swain,' he moans indignantly.

'Well, laddy, just nip out and tell the Germans that,' I tell him drily. 'I'm sure they'll take that into consideration and let you shove off home.'

'Ha ha – bloody ha ha!' he sneers. 'Anyway, what are we supposed to do now?'

That is the question I have been asking myself ever since I dropped behind this boulder. Now that I have had a minute to look about I can see that Half-Shackle, Andros and Bullock are crouched behind a parapet of broken rock further away to our left, and that some of the Germans who came with us are dodging about agitatedly in a narrow gully in between some more rocks half way down to the sea. All they have to do is keep under cover until their mates arrive, then join up with them, but right now they're getting fired on from both sides. I've got no sympathy for them; they're a miserable lot really, and their lives seem as grey as their uniforms. They started all this, so they haven't got a legitimate moan for being in this mess like I have.

A shout from Bullock shakes me out of my reverie, and I turn to find him waving at us; pointing towards a deep cleft that disappears behind a huge pile of solid granite reaching halfway to the top of the cliff. Sometime, in another age, an earthquake has split this chunk of masonry from the cliff to form a sheltered pathway, boulder-strewn, and filled with sparkling pools of clear water where a million tiny aquatic entities swim about amid voracious sea-urchins with waving tentacles and sucking mouths.

Without hesitation we dodge away from our hiding place to scramble in his direction. With one accord we accept his leadership — when no one really knows what to do, leaders are easily found. We are spurred on by a further shell smashing into the cliffs above us, breaking away a huge piece of rock that falls with a cloud of debris unto the beach below.

'This way! — this way!' urges the marine, with his arms flaying about like windmills. 'There's a cave at the other end — we can fight them off from there.'

We follow like a flock of frightened sheep. It is hard to imagine that bottling ourselves up in a cave while the Kriegsmarine blast hell out of us will prove much of an advantage, but there are not many alternatives about at the moment. It isn't even as though we are able to keep our movements secret, because those German sailors we left behind on the beach will be only too eager to tell their mates where we have gone.

There are a lot of big boulders strewn about the place, and we work to build them into a defensive wall in front of the cave mouth. Anyone who tries to approach us will be forced to come through the gully, so we will be able to pick them off one at a time without too much trouble. If we had a couple of years supply of water and food, we could survive the war quite easily. As it is however, all they have to do is sit out there, watching our waistlines go down, and our tongues hang out.

Just as I am trying to locate the best place to hang out a white flag something hits the back of my head, and I look up to see a rope ladder hanging down the cliff face.

'Follow me!' orders Andros — everybody's having a go at taking charge today. 'One at a time!'

'It might be a German ladder,' I warn cautiously.

'No — it's a Greek ladder,' he insists. 'The Germans would have lowered it away from the entrance.'

That makes sense I suppose; why does everyone else have the brains? Obviously, if the enemy try to climb down a rope ladder one at a time, all we need to do is shoot them in the balls in rotation as they swing above us.

A prolonged burst of automatic fire comes from above as our new-found friends persuade the enemy to keep his head down. There is a great deal of shouting from either side in a mixture of languages that mean nothing to me. The rope ladder I can handle, so I climb up steadily, with a prickly feeling running up and down my back as I try to ignore the guns that might be aimed in my direction.

I arrive at the top unscathed, except for a number of bruises and a pair of grazed knuckles. Strong arms reach down to hoist me unceremoniously over the rim, to be deposited like a sack of rotten spuds in a corner beneath an overhanging rock. The stone is still warm with the heat of the dying sun, for this cavern looks out towards the west, and I guess the way to freedom lies in that direction, if only we can find it. I shake myself back to the present, going to help other members of the party to climb over the edge in various stages of exhaustion.

My own weariness acts like a powerful drug, sapping every vestige of strength as I strive to remain alert to what goes on about me. It is an effort to keep things in focus any more as my brain decides it has had enough for one day, and refuses to function. My body is recumbent as my muscles relax, to wallow in the sheer luxury of having nothing to do. We all desperately need rest after hours of violent exercise, with our nerves stretched to the limit. I look at Bullock. He stands near the rim of the ledge looking down with a couple of the partisans. His training stands him in good stead now, and he probably regrets the lost opportunity to whip us into shape. He has a group of deadbeats to nurse along now, when there is a need for extra zeal and agility.

There are a dozen or so partisans on the ledge, going about the task of getting our party up with quiet efficiency. Andros seems to hold some authority as he bustles about giving orders to everyone. Half-Shackle has found the climb a killer, and lies sprawled in one corner wheezing air into straining lungs. Soapy watches the Greeks with a bewildered expression on his face; he has done well for a youngster, keeping the dredger's engine going right up to the end and doing his bit with quiet acceptance.

As I begin to recover I am able to take notice of what the Greeks are doing now that they have tucked us safely away. The E-boat must have landed in the cove, for Andros and his mates are hurling handgrenades over the edge to fill the evening with reverberating explosions that echo through the caverns and crevases of the cliffs. My mind absorbs it all through a haze of tiredness while I try to press my body into the sanctuary of the rock.

There is no respite for me, however: why should there be, with everyone else going mad about the place? I hoist my body upright to peer out at the expanse of limpid sea that lured so many pleasure-seekers before the war. The E-boat has been joined by one of the trawlers, to lie off with her engine stopped, lobbing shells at the cliff with gay abandon. The heavier thumps of the eighty-eight on the E-boat's bow punctuating the rattle of small-arms fire. The rock vibrates under the barrage as showers of splintered stone fall with heavier chunks of granite into the gully below, causing more distress to the German landing party than to the Greeks.

From here I can see the sunken boom-defence vessel and the wide gap in the net itself. If *Hobo* could be brought out now she would escape without too much trouble, for it seems the enemy have not rumbled to the full facts of the situation. It doesn't surprise me: who in their right mind would connect a submarine with a rusty old dredger? All their effort is devoted to reaping vengeance on the enemy they can see.

I try to visualise Murray in the control-room trying to weigh the chances, as the one trawler still remaining inside the bay goes about its task of rescuing the survivors of the wrecked ships. Dare he risk the periscope? Is the gap big enough to allow him through the net? Will he find the other sub-chaser waiting for him outside the gate? He must be tensed up with indecision as daylight fades. That control-room seems a thousand miles away now as I sit in a strange cavern amongst foreigners who seem to thrive on fury and hate.

Andros comes over to stress the need to move out while we have a chance to get clear. It is only too obvious that the enemy is trying to keep us pinned down until the army can bring up reinforcements to attack us from the landward side. He leads us out of the cavern, along a narrow path which seems man-made and carefully excavated into the cliff face so that we are hidden from above and below as we go along in single file, keeping in tight against the inner wall. There are two paths leading away from the cleft and this is the least obvious. The main party of Greeks go off in the opposite direction with the intention of diverting the fire from us.

I have an unreasonable outrage at the way we are being nursed along by this scruffy bunch of part-timers. The initiative has been taken from me, and although I can appreciate the superior knowledge Andros has of local conditions I am loath to let go all of my authority.

'We've put your mates in one hell of a mess, haven't we?' Bullock asks Andros, echoing some of my thoughts.

The Greek grins back at him. 'These men have no homes or identities now. They live in caves and are as much strangers amongst the villagers hereabouts as the enemy. We don't even have the same reasons for fighting the Germans, and I know there are some who would just as soon be fighting you if you were in occupation. They, like me, want Greece for the Greeks. Some day we will bring it about. Until that day each of us has the sentence of death hanging over him. You have destroyed a vital part of the enemy war effort, so we will do our best to repay you for that — we want to be under no obligation to any foreigners. We know that the British can be every bit as arrogant and domineering as the Germans given half the chance.'

With that he turns away to plod on in silence, leaving us to study his back as he leads us away from the sound of battle. No wonder there is a harsh coldness in the way they pursue their aims, and a cruel intolerance for anyone who show signs of being less than fully committed to killing Germans and Italians. Theirs is not a war of uniforms, drills and ethics. It is one of total commitment; a way of life, like a hill farmer carving out an existence in a continual battle with elements that are determined to crush him.

Daylight has given way to night, but a bright, full moon hangs like a gold medallion, to bathe the landscape with a blue glow; gleaming across the black surface of a placid sea in a path of brilliance stretching away to infinity. The barren rock is replaced by scrubland as we reach the cliff-top, with gnarled and twisted trees draping skeletal branches to arch over the track, trapping a million buzzing insects that swarm about our heads on their last fling before they settle for the night. No one speaks as we trudge along, stumbling over loose stones with our limbs aching in protest. Only Andros and Bullock keep going with no sign of exhaustion.

The air is scented and sweet, with a soft wind tugging at our clothes, stirring the tough, spiny grass growing in patches of scrub amid the dry dust. It is beautiful here. Black silhouettes of rocks and trees etch intricate shapes into the purple sky, while far below the murmuring surf plays amongst the boulders. Tired as I am there is still time to savour the potency of its mysterious power as secret sounds of nocturnal life come from every side. The distant noise of conflict is muffled behind the bulk of this sleeping island, sprawling like a huge basking mammal while parasites crawl about her wrinkled skin. The partisans are leading the enemy away from us, towards the east.

Soon we are moving away from the shore on a hardpacked lane that leads into the wide entrance to a shallow valley sloping towards the centre of the island, before angling off to the left in a direction that must take it to the nothern extremity and the narrow strait between the island and the mainland. As we descend the strain of music filters through the groves stretching out on either side of the road. It is a pulsating rhythm, throbbing beneath a thin, reedy lilt of pipes. We quicken our pace with Andros and Bullock drawing ahead, to leave us straggling in disarray. I lead the second batch with Soapy scuffing beside me, and Half-Shackle wheezing as he tries to catch up with us.

I can smell wood fire, raw and pungent in the soft air. Trapped between the invisible, rolling hills rising each side of the valley. There is a glow in the sky ahead and I can see the shadowy shapes of sleeping caravans, square and stark in the circle of flickering light. Figures move about the open space while spectral wisps of smoke drift across the trees, alive with sparks and yellow light. It is a gypsy camp nestling in the half-moon of flat scrub, edged by ghostly shrubbery.

'What the—!' I exclaim.

Andros pushes me aside, hushing me quiet as we wait for the stragglers to catch up. We crouch together in a small, huddled group, hidden from the shadowy figures by the bulk of the nearest caravan.

'This is where we rest,' whispers Andros. 'I will go ahead to see if it is okay. These people live only for themselves: the Germans don't like or trust them, but the Italians tolerate them, so they are able to carry on almost as normal; but their caravans are frequently searched by the Germans. If we stay clear of their camp and pay for what they can offer us we should be alright.'

He moves off, leaving us to slump gratefully into the scrub amongst the trees. The sky is spangled with a million stars between grey islands of cloud moving slowly towards the north. Soon he returns to crouch with us.

'We stay here,' he breathes. 'It will be warm and safe behind that wall over there. Eat your iron rations. I have brought water; it is all they have to give us.'

'You mean we don't have to pay for it?' I ask sarcastically. 'I don't see the point of staying near this lot.'

He comes to stand over me, seething with outrage. 'If you were the enemy, where would you look?' When he gets no answer he goes on, 'in the dark corners of the island, my friend. That's why we stay here. As for paying for the water – be grateful for anything you get from these people, for it is said that almost three hundred thousand Greeks died from famine last winter. Think about that while you rest tonight, and be prepared to move out early, before they break camp.'

He slumps off and the night goes dead as I ease my body into a sleeping position. That'll teach me to open my big mouth in another man's country.

XIV

Despite Andros's promise the chill wakes me to a black night. The moon has set and the cloud has thickened to hide the stars. I ease cramped limbs, listening to the growing wind stirring the branches above me. I feel refreshed by my sleep, but there is nothing to tell me how long I have been asleep, although the gypsy fires have died. Bullock is on watch and the others are beginning to stir. It is hard to recognise anyone, for the darkness is solid. Andros draws us together with a harsh whisper.

'Get ready to move off again,' he orders. 'We must get to the ferry before dawn.'

'What ferry?' I ask.

'The ferry to the mainland. If we are clever, we will be able to cross with the morning crowd. There is always a lot of people crossing at that time and then will be our best chance.'

'What then?' I persist. My faculties are fully recovered now.

His voice is impatient. 'We haven't time for a conference; let's go!'

'Hang on,' I say firmly. 'I'm not moving, and neither are my mates, until I know where we are going.'

He sighs heavily. 'All right, chief. If we can get across to the mainland I'm going to take you back to the village, where with luck a fishing boat will take you to one of the islands where we will be able to arrange a pick-up.'

'I see.' I harden my tone. 'Well; I'll tell you what we are really going to do. If I know anything about Murray he is not going to desert us. *Hobo* is out of the bay; I'm certain of that, and there is only one place she will use as a rendezvous – the only spot we established in the whole scheme. I'll bet right now she is out there charging her batteries in readiness to come back tomorrow morning to the position where we picked up the markers.

Somehow we have got to be there at daylight to contact Murray with the underwater telephone.'

'Bloody hell!' blurts Bullock. 'There's a lot of ifs in that lot!'

'If you don't like it you can go with Andros — but I'll remind you that you volunteered, and to my mind the job isn't finished yet.'

'How's that?'

'There will be another submarine back here, if I guess right. They are not going to waste the installations they have built in the creek. The dredging was almost done, so they are ready to use the new berths. If we could sabotage that lot the job would be complete.'

'How d'you get out to the submarine, chief, even if she is there?' asks Soapy.

I'm glad the darkness hides my discomfort. 'I'll work that one out when we get to the coast.'

'No need,' says Andros. There an edge of respect to his voice now. 'There is a small village close to the tower and the Germans allow the youngsters to go out in their small boats to dive for sponges, or whatever else they can find. Sometimes those urchins bring back archaeological bits and pieces which are pounced on by German officers. I'm sure I can work something out when we get there.'

'Sounds fine.'

'Just one thing,' he says quietly. 'I think it would be better if I do the job. I don't reckon you will last five minutes on your own.'

I shake my head. 'No good, Andros. I have got to talk to Murray. This is naval stuff, and it would be a waste of everyone's time trying to work something out with you. No hard feelings, but you haven't a clue when it comes to what can or can't be done with a submarine.'

Bullock interupts, 'I suggest we get started then. We can work out the details on the way. Only the three of us though — no point in all of us trooping round the countryside.'

'No, sergeant, you will stay here with the others.' My voice is firm.

'Like hell I will!'

'You'll do as you're bloody well told. I'm in charge now.' My brain is clear and my confidence is back. 'It was you who said that there should be only one leader, and I'm it. These blokes will need you if things go haywire.'

For a moment he looks like giving me an argument, then his face softens. 'Don't make a cock of it, that's all − and, chief!'

'Yeah?' Even in the dark I know he is holding out a hand.

'Good luck to you, mate. If this comes off I'll take you to my little boozer in Gosport and you can drink all the beer you want on me. I'll even introduce you to my missus; you'll like her.'

I'm glad he cannot see my face when we shake hands. 'Come on!' I say to Andros, striding away without waiting for him to reply. He seems to have eyes like a cat, moving quickly along the track while I stumble in the dark, aware of a host of strange sounds coming from the undergrowth, where all manner of weirdies lurk; imagined or otherwise. At last we climb a lane between two high walls and I guess we are getting close to the sea once more. At the top the lane bears round to the right, but we leave it to go down a wheel-rut that leads along the side of a sloping field, where a crouching building broods in the darkness on the edge of the cliffs. At the end of the rut we pick up a small path zig-zagging down towards a beach, enclosed in the arms of two headlands. The fact that I can see all this makes me aware that dawn is growing out of the hills to inject life into the blackness.

Andros points to the left, indicating the tower that we used as a marker when we picked up the buoy. Suddenly the path jumps a hedge to fall into a lane dropping away to the right. I can see rooftops reflecting the first glow of the rising sun. Small boats bob playfully at their moorings in the bay, while early risers are already shuffling about the tiny hamlet.

Close to the first house Andros shoves me into the shadows where the crumbling walls of several pigsties provide a hiding place. He indicates that I should remain here with the pigs while he goes off to arrange for a boat. Any argument I might offer is shortlived, for a troop of eight German soldiers march up through the village, but by the time they get abreast of my hiding place I am grovelling in muck, with an outraged sow taking exception to my intrusion. Nudging me with her snout to drive me into a corner, where she decides I am soft enough to make into a bed; laying her great bulk on my sweating body.

I am at the end of my tether when Andros returns to tell me he has hired a boat. All I have to do is keep my mouth shut and pretend I am a scholarly type, doing a spot of archaeology. This is not uncommon, even in wartime, and the Germans accept it. They tolerate quite a lot in the cause of cultural achievement; high-ranking officers accepting the occasional 'find' from the locals in return for allowing them to search for sponges and other, more valuable things that lie on the sea-bed. Of course special permits have to be obtained from the authorities, but there a lack of liaison between German and Italian commands which allows for a certain laxity at local level.

Our two adolescent boatmen wrinkle their noses when I turn up, but accept me as an eccentric boffin whose world is wrapped up in his search for old relics. All I am required to do is sit in silence, looking sage-like while they row us out into the bay. Andros persuades them to leave us to our delvings while they join their mates from several other boats to dive for anything that might be of value. We have to keep them away from the area where *Hobo* should be lying, because they will not fail to see her in the translucent water if they dive close by.

The tower stands out clearly on the cliff, with the rock pinnacle coming into line. We row out, keeping them in line until the other two markers on the mainland match up. A big doubt weighs heavily, for it seems too much to hope that Murray has thought the same way as I have and everything else has happened as I have guessed.

I offer up a silent prayer of gratitude when I see the marker wallowing in the gentle surf right on the bow. Andros sees it too, getting all excited as we draw near, quickening his strokes on the oar to bring us up to the flotsam. I reach down to find the canister with the handset safe inside.

'Steady!' he warns before I drag it into the boat. He is scanning the area, searching every crevice in the cliffs and the vacant sheen of the placid sea. 'Okay!'

I unscrew the wing-nuts and remove the lid. '*Hobo!*' I say into the mouthpiece.

There is confusion at the other end for a moment as I take the listener by surprise. The odds against me thinking the same as Murray must add up to a very long shot, so the sound of my voice coming down through the line must shake him. There is a clatter as he juggles with his set.

'*Hobo!*' I repeat. 'Grant here — Get Lieutenant Murray to the phone, will you?' The madness of the situation hits me for a moment. Here I am in the middle of the Ionian Sea, making a telephone call to a British submarine, five hundred yards from an enemy shore. A shiver stirs my spine — sunny it might be, but a chill grips my innards for a moment.

'Grant!' Murray's voice sounds welcoming. Andros is staring down into the depths, using a glass-bottomed bucket, burbling about the way he can see the submarine lying clear as day below us. I squash his enthusiasm when I tell him how easy it will be for an enemy aircraft to spot her too. The sooner we are away from here the safer for everybody.

Murray must feel the same, for our conversation is short, and to the point. He goes along with everything I say, with only a couple of minor points to argue about. The pick-up rendezvous is worked out and timed for midnight tomorrow. You can't put very much emotion across over an underwater telephone, but I know he is going along with me; warming to my determination to see the scheme through, with no loose ends. That's enough for me. There will be time for talk later if all goes well. Right now it's time we were gone from here, before nosy watchers begin to get curious. The flotsam is detached from the wire, leaving only the small canister which will sink a couple of feet or so beneath the surface as soon as *Hobo* gets under way, and her speed will keep it there until they are out of sight of shore. It may break surface on occasion, but there is no method of reeling it in without surfacing, so the risk must be accepted.

Andros and I row back to pick up our Greek lads, trying not to look too anxious or impatient. Mid-morning is a busy time in the village, with people going about their business as usual, taking only a token interest in the two strangers that come ashore with the chattering boys to take the hill leading up on the opposite side to the pigsty. Before we reach the top Andros diverts, to cross an area of scrub and trees until the sound of surf fades, to be superseded by the hum of insects as we scramble through thick brush, brittle in the baking sun. Soon we pick up the lane leading down to the grove where Bullock lies in wait.

He breaks cover as soon as we are recognised; coming towards us with his sten held across his belly, as though he can't even trust his own eyesight. The sun is high now; if we are to have a chance of doing anything to those installations we must move fast. The first obstacle is the ferry crossing. Andros is not too optimistic about our chances, but suggests that the best thing to do is get down there and sort things out when we see the lie of the land.

The ferry is no more than a flat barge hauled across by chains, big enough to cope with three ton lorries, but no more. Each day a procession of islanders makes the crossing for all sorts of reasons, ranging from shoppers to goatherds. German guards stand at the point of embarkation, studying every face and searching anyone who as much as looks sideways. We withdraw into a gap between two huts to watch the proceedings despairingly. There seems little chance of getting across here. I am about to suggest we go and find a less populated spot where we can steal over under cover of darkness, when a large, overloaded dray approaches the landing, drawn by two oxen who stump into the dust, leaning into their yoke as they struggle with the load. People move aside as the cart gets near, with the drayman urging his charges on with his whip.

Everyone, including the sentries, watches enthralled as the dray descends the slope leading to the short ramp. There is a growing anticipation of impending disaster as the heavy wheels crunch deep into the gravel. Several Greeks take up position to lend their weight to the strength of the bullocks as their hooves hit the solid wood of the ferry-ramp.

Shouts, whips, heaving shoulders are all brought to bear as the wheels roll on to the sharp incline, hesitate, then rock back to come to rest in the ditch at the bottom. Everyone joins in what must be a fairly regular occurrence. Greek and German yells merge in a cacophony of threats and abuse as the oxen strain and slide in their endeavours to heave the dray over the hump. Suddenly, through total lack of cohesion, one wheel jumps the gap and the dray slews sideways, dragging the oxen with it, so that they are plunged into the shallows, wallowing with great bellowings of outrage as the load shifts to deposit half the contents on the ramp.

Utter confusion reigns now. The ferryman curses the dray-man, and the Germans curse the ferryman. Children wail, dogs bark, and everyone mills around. Amid the chaos no one notices half a dozen extra hands joining in the rumpus. We set our shoulders to the lower side of the cart with the oxen stumping back up the ramp, blowing great blasts of air from their wet nostrils as their huge horns roll from side to side. This concerted effort is more than a match for the dray. It is wrenched back on to the timbers and manhandled on to the ferry, where every-one's struggles are put into reverse to prevent it running straight over the other end. The Greek version of a cheer goes up while we all slump in utter exhaustion beside the dray. The ferry creaks away from the shore with the German guards staring after us in disgust. They are glad to be rid of us, and I echo their sentiments entirely.

In twos and threes everyone goes his own way once the other shore is reached. Andros leads us off to the right, along a road that skirts the bay before opening out on to a low, marshy expanse of land that separates the bay from the estuary. Several huts stand in various stages of decay, and he takes us to one which is tucked away behind its neighbours. Inside we stand in the gloom amongst an aromatic array of fishing gear. Tar, paint, tools, rubbish of every kind festoon the walls, and clutter the deck amid a mass of huge cobwebs. Andros slips a heavy piece of timber into slots each side of the door before facing us.

'We will be safe here if we make no noise.'

'Good!' I say, relaxing in one corner. 'We haven't much time to hang about. I want to have a good look at that place before it gets dark. Can we get close enough to have a look?'

'We'll have to go up through the trees at the back of the hut. There's a place halfway up the cliff where we can look down on the other bank.'

'Let's go then.'

'Just a minute!' Half-Shackle's voice stops us before Andros can open the door. 'There's a couple of things I want to get straight with you. First; I'm no chicken, and it almost killed me climbing up from where we left the dredger, but I don't intend to be left here while you go off chasing about the place, not knowing if you are coming back or not. So, you've got two choices. Either you take me with you, and put up with my slow progress, or I give you a headstart before going along to the village to give myself up to the authorities.'

'There's no need for that,' I say coldly, 'if you give yourself up, the enemy will know you're not alone and the whole place will be swarming with German squaddies. Right now, they probably think only a few Greek partisans are involved – you could ruin the whole thing. Better Andros takes you to the pickup point where you can wait for us, or if we don't get there, Murray will pick you up with *Hobo*.'

'Ah, yes. Well; that's the other thing. You're not gonna get me back inside that bloody submarine. If you can't trust me to wait until you're clear, then I'll have to come with you.'

I square up to him. 'You brought this up, Half-Shackle. I had no intention of leaving anyone behind this time, but I've got the lives of the other blokes to think of, so you will have to keep up as best you can – I suppose that burst of energy you gave in Egypt was just for show, was it? We'll work out the bit about the submarine later.' I turn to the others. 'All right, let's go! We've pissed around long enough.'

In silence we move out, skirting the marsh before climbing up into a sloping bank of conifers that lean back against the gradient, hiding us from above and below as we go on a slanting course towards a hummock overlooking the creek. Bullock tells me it is four o'clock, so we have plenty of daylight left as the estuary comes into full view. Looking inland I can see that the so-called river is no more than a small stream at this time of year, with criss-crossed patterns of dried clay on either side. On the other hand, the estuary is a big expanse of deep water, ideal for a U-boat base. A long stretch of grey scars the opposite shore where they are building a wharf, with huge fuel storage tanks dominating everything. Square, functional buildings huddle together against the high bank, and several vehicles occupy a parking area at the landward end of the complex. A tall, metal fence bars entry from a road that winds down from the riverside, and on the seaward side, huge concrete bunkers and gun emplacements crouch each side of the entrance to the creek.

The place will be impregnable when it is completed. My heart slumps – there is nothing our puny efforts can achieve against this lot.

'Well, what do you think?' I ask everybody.

'It ain't gonna be easy,' observes Bullock gloomily, eyeing the sentries that patrol the fence, while dozens of workers toil away under the supervision of well-armed guards.

'Oh, I don't know,' muses Soapy. 'We're only outnumbered about five thousand to one – we British are used to long odds.'

I'm hardly listening as I watch a lorry grinding down the road, rocking and rolling with a heavy load of rubble. The sentries wave it through with no more than a casual glance at the driver. It crawls along the wharf, right past the three tanks until it reaches the unfinished part of the quay. The workers stand well back as the driver reverses his lorry to tip his load into the water.

'Where do those lorries come from?'

'There are small quarries further inland. They are bringing loads of stone down from there to fill in a foundation for the quay, as you can see.' Andros looks at me. 'If you're thinking of stealing one of those and driving it into the complex, forget it. The German sentries know every driver.'

'What about if one or two dropped in on them from a great height?'

Everyone follows my gaze, focussing on the overhanging cliffs above the installations.

'Wouldn't they fall clear of the quay, and into the water?' asks Bullock.

'Not if they are just toppled over. Can we get to the edge of the cliff, Andros?'

A gleam is growing in the Greek's eyes. 'There is a road running close to it. There are several anti-aircraft gun positions, but all we have to do is drive across a couple of groves. We would have to do it in daylight though. Nothing moves at night around here. We could ambush a truck or two – I can drive, and I know exactly the right spot. We could pack explosives into them before dropping them over the edge.'

'Where would you get that from?' asks Bullock.

'The partisans have plenty — they just don't get the opportunity to use it.'

'What about those poor bastards?' asks Half-Shackle morosely; nodding towards the complex, where groups of foreign slave-workers are busy.

'Oh hell! I'd forgotten about them,' I exclaim. 'I had thought of doing it at night originally.'

'No chance!' states Andros. 'The moment you start an engine after dark half the German army will come down on you.'

'This is bloody war!' stresses Bullock, grimfaced. 'If the target is important enough you have to shut your mind to everything else. Every day thousands of civilians are getting killed in air-raids.'

'There is a way,' says Half-Shackle in a dead tone.

We all look at him. His face is heavy; lined with fatigue as his eyes stare vacantly across the estuary. He is a sad old man at forty; out on a limb; having tried and failed. His inadequate body has been driven beyond its limit, and he is filled with shame. Brigginshaw has dragged him into a situation without giving thought to the long years the skipper spent peacefully plodding about the back-waters, in tune with the soft eddies of tranquil streams where river birds scud through reedy shallows, and the highlight of each week was checking his pools coupon. He could have performed a useful task with his boom-defence vessel, making his contribution to the war effort to assuage his pride. The medal he purports to need so desperately is nothing but a symbol; a way of cocking a snoot under the nose of a bellicose old man who plagued him with stories of valour, and derided his complacent ways. Circumstances and the commander have played him false. He is a broken man with no fight left in him.

'If someone was to open fire on the complex from this side it should cause them to take shelter, and distract the Germans from anything going on above them.' He looks into my eyes with an expression that allows no argument. 'I'm not going back into that submarine, Ben. I'll give myself up when it is all done, and take my chance.'

'Some chance!' I tell him. 'It's bloody suicide.'

'I could stay with him,' offers Bullock. 'We could make it back to the boat afterwards, with a bit of luck.'

'No!' Half-Shackle almost shouts. 'We would lead the enemy straight to the rendezvous. I'm not going to argue, Ben. It's my way of doing things.'

'I know.' There is no point in objecting further. 'There is just one more thing, though.'

'What's that?'

'If it all comes off I'll see to it that you get your bloody medal.'

His face brightens. 'Promise me one thing.'

'What?'

'Show it to my old man – he may not be there by the time I get back home.'

'Done,' I tell him.

It is surprising how much more feasible impossible schemes become when someone volunteers to die to make them happen. What had been a 'pie-in-the-sky', hare-brained plan suddenly looks as though it might have a chance of success. Andros takes us beyond the trees where low hedges line open fields, strewn with loose stones, glowing red with the dying light of day. We arrive at a tiny group of houses huddled into the gentle sloping flank of a shallow valley. Our hiding place this time is a small lean-to in the corner of a grove, where he leaves us to go off in search of his mates. That ever faithful old moon rises to light the scene with its baleful glow, and I think of Half-Shackle alone in the gloom, waiting for the dawn of a new day – possibly his last.

I must have slept, for when I am wakened by a cautious nudge from Soapy sometime during the night it takes a moment to acclimatise. Bullock is at the window, peering out with his knife held ready in his right hand. I tense up, straining my ears for any sound that might explain what has alerted them. There are only the whisperings of the night, carried on the soft warmth of the breeze sweeping in from the sea.

'It's Andros,' breathes Bullock. He seems disappointed at not being given the opportunity to put into practice some of his training. He is in a different league to me when it comes to the killer instinct. The marines have turned him into a fighting machine.

'Is he alone?' I ask.

'No – he's got a bloke with him.' He leaves the window to ease open the door and allow two shapes to enter. They settle into a corner, leaning their backs against the timber wall, where they crouch down.

'Did you get some grub?' asks Soapy hopefully.

'Grub!' snarls Andros with heavy sarcasm. 'Perhaps you would like a menu? Do you know how many Greeks died through the winter for lack of food? That food you were given when you arrived was all we could spare, and you will never know what that cost us.'

'All right – all right – I only arsked!' protests Soapy, 'Bloody hell! yer can't open your bloody mouth 'ere.'

'Shut up, Opie!' I snap at him. 'Well, Andros?'

'I have brought the head man of the local EAM resistance with me. He speaks no English, but he and his men are more than willing to help us, and he thinks well of your plan.'

There is a small flurry of mixed greetings between us, only part of which is interpreted by Andros, who is anxious to cut short pointless formalities and get on with the nitty gritty.

'There are three British three-ton Bedfords hidden away close to the village; left here by the Allies when the Germans chased them out.' He makes no attempt to hide his contempt for the inferior qualities of our troops, but I let it pass, and Bullock manages to keep his feelings down to a sharp intake of breath.

'That's fine,' I enthuse. 'I take it we can use them?'

'On condition you go along with the rest of their plan,' he warns guardedly.

'What plan?'

'There is a weir across the river about a mile inland, with sluice gates, used to divert water into a reservoir and an irrigation system. The Germans have closed them while they are completing the wharf at the complex. If those sluices are opened a flood of water will descend into the valley to flood the workings. It will destroy the incomplete construction and prevent any further building until the water level drops again. It will not be very dramatic, for the effects will take a couple of hours to show, but by the time the enemy realises what is happening it will be too late to stop. Believe me, I have seen what happens when the gates are opened wide – the whole estuary fills. It will ruin everything for the Germans.'

'Bloody marvellous!' I exclaim: 'Couldn't be better. I'll go along with that.'

'Not so fast, Englishman!' he growls. 'It isn't as easy as all that. First, the enemy patrols the cliff-top above the complex, and there are concrete bunkers spaced out along the shore-line. We will have to drive those lorries through olive groves and a tobacco field until we reach the edge. They are used to a fair amount of traffic along the road, so we must time our movements to coincide with their convoys. It will hide the sound of our engines until we reach a point where we can release the brakes and allow them to roll over the rim – remember; we cannot drive them over at speed or they will fall away from the complex. The partisans will tell us when to move, and their commands must be obeyed to the letter. Now: who can drive?'

'I can for one,' I offer.

'So can I,' says Bullock.

'Shit!' blurts Soapy. 'That leaves Joe Soap out on a limb again, don't it?'

'No, it doesn't,' says Andros. 'You will be with the partisans – not many of them can speak any English. You will take up position with those on the seaward side of the operation. I will drive one of the lorries, and if all goes well, we will rendezvous with you afterwards, then make our way down to the creek, where you are due to be picked up tonight. You'll have to do your best with sign language.'

'Flaming heck!'

'Don't worry, Soapy,' I reassure him. 'We won't leave you behind.'

He doesn't look too happy, but I haven't anything better to offer.

Andros couldn't care less about Soapy's problems. We are just pawns in the game as far as he is concerned. He goes on to explain the time-table, with occasional exchanges of Greek with the surly man, who studies our faces with little enthusiasm. It is clear that he would much prefer to be working with his own kind. Anyhow, we get it sorted out and he goes off on his own, leaving us to follow Andros out into the night, to creep through olive groves and currant bushes, clambering over low walls, until we come to a huddled group of square buildings standing isolated where four walls converge at the end of a rough track.

Shadowy figures move about in the gloom, totally ignoring us when we creep in out of the night. Three square bonnets peer out of their hiding places, blinkered headlights staring at us in mute protest, as though they know that fate has little time left for them. The Greeks are busy stowing explosives into the cab, and there are several experts with the knowhow to place fuses in position. All this is taken out of our hands, and we are just chauffeurs.

By the time the first streaks of a new dawn comes, we are ready. Andros tells me that the enterprise is timed to tie in with the floods, so the sluices will be opened at ten o'clock. We will move out two hours later, at midday, when it is hoped the enemy will be dashing about in a panic as the water encroaches their installations.

There are some friendly blokes amongst this lot of Greeks, but mostly they are dedicated to their own cause and haven't much time for us. The EAM is a communist organisation, and they have visions of a Greece freed from the yoke of capitalism. As far as they are concerned we are a means to an end, and just as alien to their ideals as the Germans; the only difference is that Hitler's mob will have to be driven out by force, whereas the British should disappear of their own accord.

I hate starting the day with an empty belly, but there is no chance of any grub from this lot, so I try to ignore the protesting rumbles of my stomach when the sun comes up to scorch the dust and turn the tin-roofed buildings into ovens. The Greeks have donated almost the whole of their stock of explosives to the enterprise, and I am very conscious of the fact that I am sitting on a quantity of dynamite when Andros tells me all is ready and I climb into the driving seat. There are men posted all along the route to guide us through the olive trees, and ensure we move only when the enemy is out of earshot, or when other vehicles hide the sound of our engines.

I'm in the second truck when we pull out of the building, to bump along rubble-strewn avenues with clouds of dust rising from the wheels, as we grind along in second gear. One by one we pick up the partisans stationed at strategic positions. They wave us through with impatient gestures before running off to new duties. We have to cross a dirt road just before we get to the short stretch of open scrub leading to an area of junipers and spindly conifers. We are guided into a small ravine to wait for the right moment to cross. The Greeks show signs of nervousness as they watch the road; weighing up the possibility of getting us to the shelter of the trees before something comes along the road.

It is Soapy who saves the day as he comes racing up through the gully to tell us that a small convoy of half-tracks are growling down from the north. He takes his place beside me, determined to stay close now that he has managed to escape from the morose partisans. The noise of the approaching vehicles fills the atmosphere long before we see them, for the rough earth track allows only slow, low-geared progress, with over-heated engines struggling under the hot sun. When they pass I can see their dusty crews staring rigidly ahead through their goggles, with their mouths and nostrils covered.

No sooner have they moved out of sight than we are signalled out of hiding with urgent waving. It is a wild, scrambling race over the open ground with engines roaring in protest as we push down on the throttles in a desperate effort to reach shelter before we are seen or heard. I aim for an opening between two gnarled and twisted cypress trees. My wheels wallow in soft dust, skidding with smoking tyres as I tread hard on the pedal, with no thought in my mind other than the need to get clear of this open ground. After what seems an eternity I shake, rattle and roll into the welcome shade, jolting to a shuddering halt, to slump over the wheel as the other engines die amid an eruption of thick dust.

Andros is elated. He pats the side of my truck with loving hands, acting as though it is all over bar the shouting. To me it is far from over; in fact, it is about to begin now that we have arrived close to the cliff-top where the enemy must be fully alert, watching for anything that might threaten the complex far below.

'Now what?' asks Soapy, in tune with my thoughts.

'Hang on — I'll find out.' I leave him sitting there while I climb down to join Andros and a small bunch of exuberant guerrillas. It is several minutes before I am able to break into their excited chatter. When I do Andros tells me we are exactly where they had planned; only a few yards from a slope that curves down over the cliff edge in an easy gradient. He takes me through the trees to where a goat-track runs along an haphazard route to the rim. All we have to do is manoeuvre the lorries into a clearing to the left of the copse, line them up, and release the brakes.

An excited brigand interrupts the general euphoria when he arrives breathless, with news of a patrol coming along the cliffs. A short exchange satisfies Andros, who explains that there are four German soldiers in the party, and they will have to be taken care of when they arrive at the trees. He is pleased that they have turned up now, for we know they will not come along in the middle of everything.

'You want to kill a German?' he asks suddenly, and I go cold. For a moment I consider telling him that I have already been party to killing several Germans, and am quite happy to give his men the pleasure but I know I can't let it go at that. A stupid pride makes me volunteer the services of Bullock and myself; so I find myself creeping to a position near the edge of the trees with my knife held in a sweaty hand, while Bullock whispers instructions on exactly where I should place the blade.

We outnumber them seven to four, but we must despatch them without any noise, and that is what worries me more than anything. I whisper as much to Bullock, who shrugs away my worries with a reassuring gesture. It is arranged that we take the first German between us while the Greeks pounce on the others when Andros gives the signal.

Bullock pats my shoulder. 'I'll grab him from behind to make sure he doesn't shout; you shove your knife right inside his ribcage like I told you. It'll all be over in a split second if you do it right – if you don't, I'll have to strangle the bastard.'

I gulp down a mouthful of saliva. The knife feels loose in my hand, as though I cannot grip it tight enough to overcome the lubrications of my own sweat. I control my breathing as I lie with the others, listening for the first sounds of approaching boots. We hear voices first; light in the warm air, and relaxed as they discuss general topics, as soldiers do when engaged on boring duty.

The boredom ends abruptly when Andros gives a coarse command. I move out with the others, heading for the leading German who is in the act of turning to look over his shoulder when I reach him. He wears a belt with two shoulder-straps and ammunition pouches. My point of aim is just above where the left shoulder-strap joins the belt, and I drive the blade in with an upward slant, carrying him back with the weight of my body, so that we fall together, to roll down a slope into a gorsebush. I wrench the knife free and drive it in again and again, until Bullock's hands pull me clear.

'Come on, mate. He's good and dead; you don't have to turn him into a colander.'

I stagger upright, panting and shaking with emotion. 'Where the hell were you?' I gasp.

'Bloody hell, Grant! Chance would be a fine thing! You were on him before I even got clear of the trees.'

My right hand is sticky with blood, gripping the knife while I stare down at my victim. His empty eyes stare into the sky with his head rolled back on his shoulders. The Greeks are dragging bodies into the shadows as the birds take up their refrain once more; aloof from the affairs of men as they dart in and out of the foliage. I wipe the blade in a tuft of dry grass before slipping it back into the sheath.

'Andros!' My voice is gruff; thick with mucus when I call the Greek to me. Something in my tone brings him quickly; looking into my eyes with a puzzled expression. In fact everyone's attention is focused on me as I straighten up with my mind clear at last.

'I'm going for Half-Shackle,' I declare, giving no opening for argument.

'What!' demands Bullock in an outraged voice.

I don't bother to look at him. 'You heard. What has to be done here can be done without my help.'

'I'm comin' wiv yer!' states Soapy.

I look at the youngster's face staring at me with an intense eagerness. He looks so much like Miller at that moment. Kids! That's all they are, with chins that have barely felt the edge of a razor. Somewhere, a couple of thousand miles away a mother is dusting an empty room, musing over the trappings of a boy hardly out of short trousers who comes home dressed in his sailor-suit with his cuffs rolled back to impress the local girls. If she could see him now, surrounded by death, with the harness of war strapped to his youthful torso, she would choke on the memories of the short years she had to shape him for manhood, just so that the Navy could turn him into a killer.

'You're going with Sergeant Bullock to the rendezvous – he knows the place. If I don't get there by midnight, you're to board *Hobo* and get away.' I put up a hand to quieten Bullock's protest. 'I haven't time to argue. It will only take one of us to find the silly old sod. Your job is to get Soapy back to the boat.'

'You'll need a guide,' says Andros. 'You'll never find your way to him.'

'I'll go the way we came.'

'No, you won't. The water level is already rising to cover the place where we crossed the river. I can halve the journey for you; and we'll need to be quick if we are to find him before the Germans do. I reckon we have an hour before he will open fire. I can get you to him in less than that if we go now.'

'It's not your job.'

'Come on,' he says drily, and stalks off down the slope towards the head of the estuary. Without another word I follow, leaving the others to stare after us. The heavy scent of flowers mingles with the busy hum of bees as we follow the goat-track into a tunnel of overhanging shrubs. The going is easy, for it is all downhill, and Andros doesn't bother too much with taking precautions now that he knows where the patrol is. Soon I catch glimpses of the estuary through the bushes, and it has changed a lot now that water has spread across to cover the muddy flats.

'They must be chasing about down there now,' says Andros. 'The water-level must be up above the scaffolding.'

'Will it flood the workings?'

'No, only the temporary staging they've rigged to build up the wharf. Just below the waters will disperse over the estuary, and you won't know the difference to look at it. The damage will be done, however. They haven't finished shoring up the outer wall, so all the filling will be washed out. They will have to clean it out and start again. If the trucks do their job it'll be months before they can get the complex working.'

We go silent as we come close to the road that leads along the base of the cliff to the quay. We do not have to cross the road, for Andros takes us over the top of a small tunnel to the river-bank where we creep inshore for several yards before coming to a rusty old pipe that spans the main stream. The current is swift as we take to the water and use the pipe to drag ourselves over to the other bank. Once there we slip into the undergrowth and make our way to the path we used last night to backtrack towards Half-Shackle's hide-out.

So far we have taken little more than half an hour to get here, and now that the dock comes into view we can see the water-level is well above the workings, although there doesn't seem to be much in the way of excitement over there. Why should there be – they know damned well where the trouble is, and I've no doubt there's hell to pay up at the sluices.

We hear the old skipper before we see him, for he is flat on his back, snoring his head off. When we wake him he is outraged, spitting invective at me for going back on our deal and not leaving him to his own devices. In vain I tell him that his intervention will not be needed now that work has stopped on the complex and the workers have been withdrawn until the tide is stemmed.

'Anyway,' I accuse, 'you would probably have slept through it all by the look of things.'

'Balls! I was just taking a short nap – there's ages to go yet.'

'About ten minutes I reckon,' I say sardonically. 'Anyway, we can settle back and watch the pyrotechnics. Afterwards we will have to stay hidden here until it gets dark before working our way along the coast to the rendezvous.'

'The sooner you're gone the better.'

'Don't you believe it, mate – you're coming with me.'

He rounds on me with fury distorting his red face. 'I've told you, Grant; I'm not going back into that submarine.'

'Oh yes you are, Half-Shackle. If I've got to drag you by the bollocks I'll get you there. The Greeks are in enough trouble already up at the sluices without the Germans getting their hands on you. I wouldn't give you five minutes in their clutches before you come out with the whole story.'

His face collapses. 'That really what you think?'

I can contain my disgust no longer. I stare straight into his eyes, shaking with rage. 'You came here for a medal you say: I'd give you a medal, you old bastard — for conduct over and above anything I've ever heard of to wreck the efforts of your mates. Your old man had you figured out good and proper — you're fit only for working a dredger — dragging filth from the sea-bed. I'm taking you back, you old sod! You're not gonna sit out the war in some cosy prisoner-of-war camp; you're coming with me, and you're gonna put on that pretty uniform you worked so hard to get and face the music.'

His mouth is working in his bemused features as he struggles for words. Before he manages a syllable there is a gigantic explosion, and we look to see a mass of debris falling into the water near the wharf, even as another truck falls from the lofty heights of the scraggy cliffs. The fuse on this one must have been short, for it explodes halfway down, so that the remaining lorry tumbles through an erupting mass of cliff-face. It hits the deck beside the tanks as the blast from the first washes over us. It is like an earthquake when the fierce heat of the dynamite expands the latent mixture until it rips the tanks apart with thunderous detonations. From a quarter of a mile away we feel the heat as flames roar up the cliff to lick at the dry vegetation near the top. An avalanche of falling rock destroys what remains of the installations with a bombardment of heavy boulders, and we are stunned into silence while the dust settles.

'Wow!' Andros is wide-eyed. 'We've done it, Grant! Better than we could have hoped — we've done it!'

I'm speechless. Nowhere in my wildest hopes had I expected so complete a success. I can only stare at the devastation as the normal sounds of the estuary tentatively test the atmosphere and the violence subsides. There is movement over there now. Men scrambling over piles of rubble looking for life or staggering about in dazed circles, their minds numbed by the concussion. I settle back to soak it all in. Nothing matters now. Miller, Felix, the blokes in Malta; they've all been paid back to some degree, and I've washed away some of my own failings.

Now I will complete the job by taking Half-Shackle back and regain some of my esteem. Shallow motives perhaps, but important to me.

'What do we do now?' I ask Andros. 'Hide here till dark?'

'You're the boss,' he says with a smile, and there is something new in his attitude now, a respect I haven't seen before.

'The biggest obstacle is the estuary. Where's the best place to get across?'

'Right down where that arm curves round towards where the dredger was working. There is a bunker on the top, but it faces towards the sea. I reckon we could creep along the water's edge until we get to a gap, then use those rocks to ease our way out to the main channel. Can you swim?'

'I can't,' asserts Half-Shackle with great satisfaction. 'If there is any swimming to be done, you can count me out.'

I ignore him. 'That hut we hid in; is it close by?'

'Less than a mile from here,' replies Andros. 'It would be easy to get to without being seen; especially now they're chasing about the countryside looking for partisans.'

'Come on then.' I rise to my feet. 'There was some rope in there.' I look down at Half-Shackle. 'We'll use it to drag you across – sir.' I grab his armpit and hoist him upright. 'I'd better get used to calling you "sir", hadn't I? After all, you'll be strutting about in uniform soon if all goes well.'

He is like a whipped dog as he follows behind through a rich mixture of aluvian shrubbery, alive with insects of all kinds that swarm about our heads when we disturb them. It is an un-inhabited area; a sort of 'no-man's-land' between the small village near the ferry and a smattering of tiny hamlets sprinkled along the river.

We find a coil of tarred rope in the hut, and some cork floats to make a sort of life-belt for Half-Shackle. Saving him has become an obsession with me now. There is no better driving force than self-contempt when you have as much to live down as I do, and no better way of using it than pouring scorn on some unfortunate bastard who fails to come up to the mark. I'm too close to it to realise what I'm doing, and Andros joins with me to badger the shambling old man along with merciless derision for his weak efforts to keep up. Between us we make his misery complete, and when we find a hiding place close to the crossing point he slumps down like a bundle of old rags, closing in on himself while we wait for the day to end.

Suddenly the full weight of my exhaustion takes hold, and in the warmth of mid-afternoon I am unable to keep awake. When I open my eyes again it is dusk, with leaden light fading the sharp colours to the softer shades of evening. I am immediately aware that the wind has risen considerably, to drive foam-crested waves in through the gap. It blusters and moans through the crevices and wakes in me a feeling of disquiet.

My stirring wakes the others, for they too have succumbed to the hypnotic languors of a Peloponnesian day. We are stiff and cramped as we stretch our limbs to force use back into them. I have mixed feelings about the weather, for the wind will hide our sounds with its blusterings, but *Hobo* will not wish to come close in to a lee shore with a force eight gale.

Half-Shackle looks even more pathetic when I tie on a mess of old cork floats and tarry rope. Several days' growth of beard and sweat hasn't improved anyone's appearance, but he has a head start on everyone else, for he looked scruffy to begin with. I'm none too gentle when I fit him out for the crossing, and he submits in a dispirited manner that increases my intolerance. If I could stand outside and look at myself I would cringe with shame, but exhaustion plays havoc with my faculties, and I have a backlog of self-recrimination to live down — Half-Shackle is an easy target.

I stuff some of the cork into my pockets for added buoyancy and wait for Andros to decide it is dark enough to hide our movements from sentries stationed in the bunker. We move out to wade through the broken water, roped together like mountaineers with the old skipper in the middle. The water is cold, for it is mixed with mountain streams. It drags at our legs and courses round the smooth boulders to meet the wind coming in from the sea, breaking up into wild flurries of turbulence in the conflicting currents. We are waist-deep, yet the waves encompass our heads and shoulders when we struggle to the last bastion of rock before the empty void opening up before us. It is a boisterous cauldron of black wildness, waiting to toss our puny bodies about when we try to broach it.

Any form of communication is impossible, so I launch out into it with legs and arms working to drag my waterlogged body across the twenty yard gap. Even with the added buoyancy of the cork floats I find my mouth under water more than not, so I have to gulp a mixture of air and water whenever I can and press on with blind determination, with the rope dragging behind like a sea-anchor. The struggle seems endless, and the vague outline of the opposite shore keeps its distance as my limbs become heavy with exhaustion, aching with the agony of movement. There isn't another yard left in me when my foot touches bottom and I reach down to find sharp-edged rocks within my depth. I batter my way through breaking foam until my hands find the welcome shape of a solid rock standing firm in the current.

I am too whacked to struggle on yet, but I have the presence of mind to wrap the rope round the scraggy pinnacle of the rock before giving a couple of hefty pulls on it, hoping Half-Shackle will get the message and heave himself across, with Andros to follow. I allow the current to hold me against the stone while I grab mouthfuls of air and rest my agonised muscles.

Eventually I am recovered enough to take in some of the slack on the rope. It comes in easy for a few feet before it wrenches at my hands with a strength that rips it through them with a speed that burns my palms.

It is like struggling with a wild animal as I heave in inch by inch against the pull of the current, taking turns on the pinnacle to hold what I have gained before it is wrenched away again. Suddenly it goes slack, sending me tumbling backwards. Desperately I haul in the rope until the frayed end shows where it has parted. For a long time I hold it to me, unwilling to believe what it means. At last I force my body into movement, scrambling from rock to rock until I reach the shore, where I am able to drag myself out of the grip of the flow to find shelter in a gully out of the wind where soft sand offers a resting place, and I can strip away the rope before lying on my back, to regain my composure and sort out my mind.

It is a wild night all right. Demonic forces are venting their fury on the seaward side of my haven, and I'm supposed to work my way along the base of the tall, sheer cliffs for almost a mile until I reach the outskirts of one of the small villages where there is an old, stone landing — no more than a flight of steps hewn in the solid granite. I have no doubt the enemy will have some sort of token defensive position set up, because it is the only place where the towering ramparts relent, and a narrow valley cleaves its passage to the sea. Between me and it there is nothing but sheer precipice from what I've seen, with an occasional outcrop of rock carved out of the shore by an insiduous sea. In our simple way we haven't taken into consideration anything other than a calm, serene ocean in our plan to negotiate the journey, or perhaps no one really thought anyone would be stupid enough to get to the rendezvous any other way but by the inland route that Bullock and Soapy are taking.

I have made up my mind that I will not see either of my two companions now. I don't even want to think of what might have happened to them in that boisterous channel. Therefore, it is necessary to gather my strength, and I resolve to drag my unwilling bones out of this hiding place. It is going to be a lonely passage, and I don't rate my chances very highly of accomplishing it.

When I leave the shelter the wind tears into me like fury. Clutching at my clothes and battering my body as though it has a personal vendetta. There are low, ghostlike clouds scudding across patches of starlit sky, but the moon is nowhere to be seen, and I have the choice of trying to climb clear of the bursting waves to try to find a way along the cliffs, or staying close to the base, half clambering, half swimming through the surf. I decide to play it by ear and use a fifty yard section of boulder-strewn beach to reach the first outcrop of rock. Beyond that the cliffs fall vertically into the sea, with no visible means of ascent. Through the spray I can just see the vague froth of bursting waves blustering over a reef about fifty yards away. In normal conditions I can swim fifty yards with no trouble, and with my pockets stuffed with cork I decide it is worth a go.

One deep breath and I launch into the sea, making fair progress for the first few yards before I am hurled against a hidden rock, just under the surface. Desperately I try to hold on to it, but the sea rips away my slippery handhold to batter my body against the sharp-edged stone. I scream as pain knifes through my right arm, and it becomes a useless appendage as I struggle to stay afloat. The sea takes over now, allowing no respite as it hurls me from the rock towards the sheer cliff. There is no way I can fight against it, and my body turns over and over at the mercy of ten foot waves rolling in to explode against the brutal stone.

Successive swells roll my torso about as my will breaks and I can no longer struggle. The blind agony of my broken arm drags gurgling groans from me, and only the cork keeps me from sinking down into merciful oblivion. The sea will not give me rest, or allow me to drown peacefully. With sadistic malice it deposits me on a sloping shelf where I lie in an agonised posture while successive waves burst over me. The fingers of my one good arm claw at the hard stone and my face is hard against the rough surface of the shelf. Nothing exists but the anguish of the broken bone. I sob and moan into the solid rock until blackness comes.

I come to in hell. A cold merciless, malevolent hades of relentless torment. Torrents of heavy water hurl down on me while other forces throw my legs about, and I pray for death. My senses must be going, for in my delirium I fancy I hear the voice of Satan himself crying out of the surf. I chuckle insanely into the granite with hot tears coursing down my cheeks. The voice comes again; vague but persistent, from the depths of the storm. It won't stop filtering into my tired brain, and I scream for it to stop, to let me sink away from the griping agony of staying alive.

The screaming seems to help. It drives away the pain if I screech loud enough into the wind.

'Grant!' The call comes above the roar of the wind and through the crashing thunder of the waves. 'Grant!'

'Shove off!' I yell into the gale. 'Let me go for Christ's sake!'

A mixture of sounds comes now, but I can beat them with my insane laughter and my wild screaming. The tumult swirls about me as I feel myself slipping into a vortex of noise and torment.

Something solid hits my back to wrench another scream from me as a searing stab of blinding agony shoots through my arm. I am being bundled about mercilessly by something more than the sea.

'Try and hold still,' a voice is telling me while I splutter protests at the treatment I am receiving. I struggle against strong arms that try to wrench me away from my rock, and a serpent is winding its sinuous coils round my shoulders.

'Easy, chief, easy, or I can't do anything,' persists the voice as the owner tries to drown me. The fight goes out of me when the coils bite into my chest like a noose tightening as it hauls me into the surf. My yells are lost to the wind, as I surrender completely to the battering ocean, gulping a mixture of air and water, impatient for the end to come.

It isn't going to be easy though. The persistent, cruel pull of the serpent will not let me die peacefully, but heaves me against yet another solid mass of hard stone while more voices torment me with their stubborn, intense urgings.

'Alright, I've got him − leave him to me.' Even Half-Shackle has come to haunt me.

'Careful; he has a bad knock on the head, and I think his arm is broken.'

That is Andros. What kind of nightmare is this? I always thought dying was easy once you gave into it. Yet, far from sinking into a black abyss of nothingness, I am dragged across tortuous rocks with a constrictor crushing my ribs.

'You go for help while I strap his arm,' says Half-Shackle's voice, as the coils ease and I slump to rest on a flat surface. My mind is clearing as I choke gallons of hogwash out of my gullet. Clouds of spray sweep over me, but the sea no longer has me in its clutches.

'Hold on, Ben,' says Half-Shackle's voice. 'I'm gonna straighten your arm and strap it to my sten.'

I manage only half a scream before merciful oblivion blankets me. There are voices all around me when I recover enough to take in what goes on. The piercing agonies of my arm are reduced to a dull ache, and it no longer flaps about with every move I make. The comforting folds of added clothing are wrapped round me to cushion my body against the bumping I receive as I am borne along none too gently by gasping, toiling bearers. I try to tell them I am conscious, but they are too busy carrying on a disjointed conversation of their own.

"'E don't look very well, does 'e?' says Soapy in between pant-
ings. He seems to have hold of my feet.

'Nor would you if you half drowned at the bottom of those
cliffs,' growls Half-Shackle. 'If he'd waited five minutes he
could have come along the same way as we did; always was an
impetuous bastard.'

'Don't talk so much,' advises Andros, 'we've still got half a
mile to go.'

They lapse obediently into silence and the bumping goes on
for some time before Andros speaks again. 'Take it easy now,
we're almost to the steps.'

'Thank Christ for that!' complains Half-Shackle. 'He's no
featherweight.'

'Set him down then, and don't make too much noise. The
Germans don't bother too much with this part of the coast – it's
too precipitous for a landing, but they might visit the village
from time to time, and the little pier is only a quarter of a mile
away.' Andros talks in a heavy whisper now and sets the tone for
everyone else – including me, for I think it is time I got through
to them.

'Help me up,' I croak harshly. 'I think I can manage to walk.'

Their whisperings stop as Half-Shackle bends to bring his
hairy face down to mine. 'There's only a few yards to go, Ben,
and it's all downhill.'

'Right – just put me on my feet.'

Together we manage to get me perpendicular, swaying about
a lot until I find stability. They wait patiently, watching my
efforts with hands held ready in case I drop.

'Ready,' I assure them, and take a wobbly step to prove it.

'Follow me,' says Andros, and with arms steadying me I
stagger down rough steps cut into the rock face, until we reach a
small jetty set against the sheltered side of a headland. It looks
abandoned now, but it is enclosed in the half circle of quiet
water, cut off from the gales that buffets the other side of the
peninsula.

'Well done, my lads.' Bullock's encouraging voice is hushed
by an anxious Andros, 'Sorry, mate,' says the marine. 'Glad to
see you, that's all – seems a hell of a time since you came and
took Soapy away.'

'How is the time?' whispers Half-Shackle.

'Just past midnight by me,' states Bullock. 'What do we do now?'

'Wait,' I tell him, 'that's all we can do. The chart shows twenty fathoms right up to the landing here, so it is up to Murray to bring *Hobo* as close in as he can get. It's going to mean a swim – but then, you wouldn't have been chosen if you weren't buddings Tarzans.'

'What about you?' asks Soapy.

'We've still got the rope! That's good enough to drag me across.' I recall something, 'By the way, how did you get across without it, Andros?'

'Half-Shackle got me across. I was going to swim over on my own once you began to haul him over, but I got washed off the slippery rocks. He got hold of me, but the rope broke when we put both our weights unto it. He wouldn't let go though, and we struggled across together. I knew you had gone the wrong way when I saw the rope still tied to the rock at the cove.'

I go silent, thinking about some of the things I have said and done to the skipper. 'What about the submarine, Half-Shackle?'

'There's plenty of booze in her wardroom. I'll drink myself stupid if I get on board; then I won't care where the hell I am.'

'Listen!' warns Andros, and we all hold our breath as the vague sounds of the storm come to us. It is another noise that stiffens us into tense attitudes; the dull clank of metal out there in the empty expanse of sheltered water, and I stare intently at the shadowy darkness to see a shape taking form.

'Blimey!' exclaims Soapy, 'It's *Hobo!*'

His young eyes are keener than mine I expect, but I don't reckon he sees her much before I do. There are men on her forecasing with heaving lines held ready as she noses in slowly towards the pier. A line comes snaking across to be grabbed eagerly by Bullock. Soapy helps him to haul it in until they are able to get hold the manilla hawser and pass the eye over a stone bollard.

The hawser goes taut as the small capstan takes the strain to heave *Hobo* bow-on towards the jetty. Murray brings her right up to the wall and there is no need for anyone to swim. Within minutes we are aboard — all except Andros, who casts off the rope and stands alone, watching the submarine sliding out astern. He doesn't wave or give any sign at all; he just stands looking at us fading into the night as Murray orders everyone below, anxious to get away before an enemy patrol comes.

Willing hands help me down the fore-hatch and into my bunk. I lie back, relishing the warmth of my blankets as I stare up at the tangle of pipes with their coloured markings. They are solid metal tubes carrying air and liquid to different parts of her body like my own veins and arteries; nothing more.

'Here you are, 'swain.' Soapy is holding a heaped plate of eggs and bacon.

If you have enjoyed this book and would like to receive details of other Walker Adventure titles, please write to:

Adventure Editor
Walker and Company
720 Fifth Avenue
New York, NY 10019

ELSEWHERE

ELSEWHERE

a journey into
our age of islands

alastair bonnett

The University of Chicago Press

The University of Chicago Press, Chicago 60637
Published 2020
Printed in the United States

29 28 27 26 25 24 23 22 21 20   1 2 3 4 5

ISBN-13: 978-0-226-67035-5 (cloth)
ISBN-13: 978-0-226-67049-2 (e-book)
DOI: https://doi.org/10.7208/chicago/9780226670492.001.0001

First published as *The Age of Islands: In Search of New and Disappearing
Islands* in the United Kingdom by Atlantic Books, 2020.

Library of Congress Cataloging-in-Publication Data

Names: Bonnett, Alastair, 1964– author.
Title: Elsewhere : a journey into our age of islands / Alastair Bonnett.
Description: Chicago : The University of Chicago Press, 2020. | Includes bibli-
    ographical references and index.
Identifiers: LCCN 2020013170 | ISBN 9780226670355 (cloth) | ISBN
    9780226670492 (ebook)
Subjects: LCSH: Islands. | Artificial islands.
Classification: LCC GB471 .B66 2020 | DDC 909/.0942—dc23
LC record available at https://lccn.loc.gov/2020013170

♾ This paper meets the requirements of ANSI/NISO Z39.48-1992
(Permanence of Paper).

CONTENTS

Part Three: Future

Color illustrations follow page 154.

Introduction

T HIS IS THE age of islands. New islands are being built in numbers and on a scale never seen before. Islands are also disappearing: inundated by rising seas and dissolving into archipelagos. What is happening to islands is one of the great dramas of our time and it is happening everywhere: islands are sprouting or being submerged from the South Pacific to the North Atlantic. It is a strange rhythm, mesmerizing and frightening, natural and unnatural. It is imprinting itself on our hopes and anxieties: the rise and fall of islands is an intimate and felt thing as well as a planetary spectacle. I want to navigate this new territory and try to grasp what it tells us about our relationship – our vexed love affair – with islands.

This is the story of that adventure. It won't be plain sailing. I know that for certain now because I'm writing this in Nuku'alofa, the slow-moving, weather-battered capital of the Kingdom of Tonga, and I'm feeling just as tired as any of the sad-eyed dogs that hunker on the hot and empty road outside. This morning the wind blew unexpectedly hard, and 15 kilometres from shore the hull of the unexpectedly small motor launch on which – many weeks before and many thousands of kilometres away – I'd booked a passage to a newly emerged and as-yet-unnamed volcanic island began to fall in sickeningly slow blows, hammering every valley between every green wave. 'We must turn back,' hollered the captain, the faded tattoos of whales and dolphins writhing with the spray along his bare arms and chest.

So, yet again, I'm holed up, WhatsApping friends and family: 'Didn't make it to my island.' I've come 17,700 kilometres for nothing. A cyclone is hitting this patch of the Pacific tomorrow and I guess I will never reach that impossible fleck on the horizon.

'My island'. What a strange conceit. Islands get under your skin like that: splinters of longing, or escaped territories, they lodge themselves deep. As the gathering storm spits down its first heavy drops, I treat myself to another splash of whisky and trawl my memory, not for the first time, for what set this long and often lonely journey in motion. I remember my seventeen-year-old daughter standing in the kitchen, toast-in-hand, wise, steady and unimpressed. 'You're fundamentally dumb,' she warned me with icy authority, adding: 'All you're doing is globalizing your male menopause.' But then she smiled gloriously: 'I want to come!' Others were less generous, narrowing their eyes in the presence of some unfortunate but undefined species of post-colonial self-indulgence.

Yet chasing these scattered and unmapped points of change feels urgent to me. I keep waking suddenly in the small hours, obsessed with some wayward, unanchored detail, only calmed when I have scribbled out a map or illegible note. I guess I need to cool down and tell this story slowly, to work out why the rise and fall of islands matters.

There is no place better to start than the South China Sea. To the north and west the coastlines of China and Vietnam bulge into its warm waters; to the south and east lie Malaysia and the Philippines. This is one of the world's great trade routes – said to be worth $5.3 trillion a year – and it is one of the cockpits of contemporary geopolitics. The Spratly Islands, the once-pristine and untouched reefs and tiny islands that sprinkle this sea, have been horribly mutilated: squared off and concreted over; a dozen or so have been crammed with military firepower and turned into audacious forward placements in a new cold war. China is bolting together the majority of these Frankenstein islands and it is winning control of the entire sea.

Satellite and aerial images show how the reefs are latched on to by long black snake-like pipes that curve through the water. They wend back to boats that are grinding up the sea floor – sand, coral, crustaceans, everything – into building material. This marine paste is squirted onto the island. Later come the concrete mixers, the airstrips, naval harbours and the missile silos. One of the latest victims is Johnson South

Reef. It has been snared by an inseminating predator. In its early stages it is bulked up. Later it will be squared off – a hostile alien in a beautiful blue sea.

The tragedy of the Spratlys has been spread across headlines in East Asia for some years. In the coming decades much bigger and more peaceful Chinese islands will grab the world's attention. Spectacular new leisure and entertainment islands are emerging just minutes from the shore of a number of coastal cities. Like the artfully shaped new islands sculptured in the Gulf States, these are sites of turbo-charged consumerism. However, since they are made by gouging out the seabed and planting rows of offshore and improbably shaped, air-conditioned hotels, these apparently carefree shopping and holiday destinations can be just as environmentally damaging as their military cousins.

Our power to reshape the planet is stark on new islands. Each of them shouts: 'Look what we can do!' But the age of islands has another face. New islands are rising up as old ones are going under. Today the spectre of disappearance stalks low-lying nations. Thousands of the world's islands are only centimetres higher than the surrounding sea and most are shrinking year by year, month by month. The roll-call of the vanished is already a long one. The rate at which dredgers and engineers can fabricate new islands is increasing but so is the speed at which natural islands are being swallowed up.

En route to the capital of the Solomon Islands for yet another conference on climate change, the then UN Secretary General Ban Ki-moon peered out of his aeroplane window and saw what may, at first glance, have appeared to be a couple of undersea reefs and, in the background, some small islands. In fact, it was the remnants of one large island that had been almost completely swallowed up, with only the highest ridges left. About a dozen islands in this part of the Solomons have gone the same way. Islands today feel fugitive and uncertain: an atmosphere of doubt surrounds them. Their stories hold a mirror up to our alarming era.

Islands are changing fast but they have a primal allure. I love islands. They offer the possibility of newness, of hope. Staring at the white, lifeless heap that is Johnson South Reef or the vestiges of the Solomons, that might sound very odd. But the idea of utopia clings to even the bleakest island. The first image of 'utopia' was an island. It is telling how insistent Thomas More was in the book usually simply titled *Utopia* – his travel fantasy that gave us the word – that Utopia had to be an island. More tells us that the founder of this uniquely perfect realm, King Utopus, 'made it into an island'. Originally it was part of the mainland but Utopus 'ordered a deep channel to be dug' in order to 'bring the sea quite round'. Only in this way could a flawless and completely new place be born. Utopia is a space apart, a jewel in the sea, a distant sight towards which one longs to steer.

More describes the island as 'not unlike a crescent: between its horns, the sea comes in eleven miles broad, and spreads itself into a great bay, which is environed with land to the compass of about 500 miles'. It's easy to imagine sailing into that generous harbour. One of the alluring things about islands is that we can picture them whole in our mind's eye. Hence we can imagine them perfect – complete and completed.

Anyone who travels to new islands has to deal with hope. Not timid, doe-eyed hope but outrageous, gleeful, turbulent, confident hope. It's there in the fast-mutating island polders of the Netherlands and the off-kilter leisure islands of the Gulf States and China. Despite the fact that most new islands are environmental disasters, it's still, perversely, impossible to detach them from hope. So it seems inevitable that I devote the last section of this book to *future* islands – places that are likely to be unveiled over the next few decades or so.

Another memory is rising to the surface. My first 'new' island. I went there a couple of years ago. I recall it like the face of an old friend. I need that memory now for the rain and wind are pounding the roof. Best not to listen as the palm trees clatter and twist, their limbs snapping and skittering skywards. Many people on Tonga are spending tonight in flimsy canvas tents donated by aid agencies in the aftermath of the last cyclone, often camped in their own wet gardens. Casting back for comforting memories, I retreat to a happier place.

A light heave on the oars. The water is calm, silky. This is how all island journeys should be. With that last pull, the pretty green rowing boat I've rented for the day grates a few inches onto an underwater rim of hefty round stones. I splash out and begin busily surveying, pushing a yellow steel tape measure through a tangled knot of shrunken alders and over the grizzled corpse of a putrefying sheep. (How did it get here?) My unnamed island is 19.5 metres long and 10 metres wide. High above it heavy black power cables sag across the width of the loch: dark arcs drawn on a summer sky. It is a windless day.

The island is one of many on Loch Awe, a freshwater lake 40 kilometres long in the west of Scotland. I had no inkling that it marked the start of something. My yellow tape measure, wielded with faux-professional aplomb, is nothing more than a protective talisman, fending off the pointlessness of a wayward mini-break. Squatting down on this islet's western shore beside a mini-vortex of plastic rubbish – coagulated food packaging and fishing lines – I baffle myself with questions: 'Why have I come here? Why do islands lure me?' Staring down at all that plastic, other questions soon come: 'What is happening to islands? Why, today, are we building so many of them and misshaping many more?'

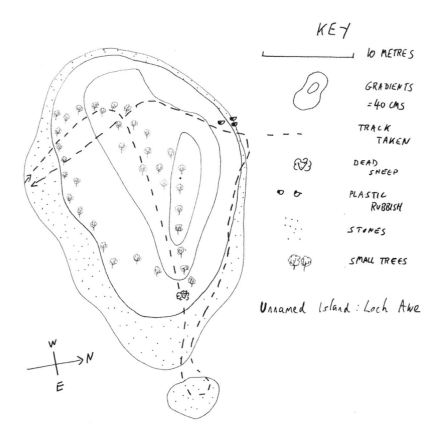

KEY

|—————————| 10 METRES

GRADIENTS
= 40 CMS

TRACK
TAKEN

DEAD
SHEEP

PLASTIC
RUBBISH

STONES

SMALL TREES

Unnamed Island : Loch Awe

This cloud of question marks might seem out of place in such an anonymous and peaceful place. But my island holds a secret: it was built by people. So were nearly all the other islands I can see from its shore. The two dozen or so that are still visible in Loch Awe were all constructed somewhere from 2,600 to 600 years ago. Surrounded by high hills, back then people used the rivers and lochs as their transport routes. They were water-based in almost everything they did and island-building allowed them to live on their economic and political 'main street'. Logs were driven into the shallows and large stones placed on top. Communal round houses were then built on the islands alongside small pens for pigs and goats. These ancient artificial islands are called crannogs. Only handfuls have been excavated. Scotland has about 350 existing examples; Ireland has many times that number and there are similar ancient lake islands in dozens of other countries. They are intriguing places: perplexing yet immediately understandable. Humans have an insatiable curiosity about islands and a deep-rooted desire to shape and create them.

After that trip out on Loch Awe I drove back home to Newcastle, the city in England's far north where I have lived for thirty years, and tried to put my feelings into some kind of order.

I began doodling all sorts of island shapes, just like I did as a boy: fat and fiddly ones; ones with lovely sinuous inlets; ones with villages and ones with mountains; ones with caves and treasure. I also started drawing up a list of the world's newest and most rapidly changing islands – both the natural and unnatural. These came from conversations at work, back in Newcastle University's Geography Department (where I first got word that the main part of Svalbard, in the high Arctic, was revealing itself as two islands as the ice sheets melt away), and news items (latest pictures on the bulked-out and militarized Spratlys in the South China Sea and a menacing-looking new volcano rising from the sea north of Tonga). I also relied on readers of my previous books on 'off the map' places. Had

I heard of the new artificial islands in Korea? Did I know about the 'Trash Isles', or islands that are poisoned, exploding, becoming uninhabitable, crowded with giant crabs?

So many islands. I'm not sure it helped to find a copy of the *Island Studies Reader* and learn that there are 680 billion islands on our planet. It turns out that figure includes 8,800,000 islets and 672,000,000 rocks. I wonder who counted them. It sounds like guesswork. I was becoming overwhelmed: unsettled by islands' fractal endlessness and the fast pace of change.

Trying to clear my head, I stopped spending my evenings on Google Earth (which is often years out of date when it comes to new and disappearing islands) or checking my email (*ping*: 'I saw this on the BBC News App and thought you should see it: "The island that switches countries every six months"'). I wanted ideas that would anchor me. I kept coming back to an idea that proved seaworthy and still guides me, namely the Janus-faced nature of modern islands: they are both frightening and beguiling; they offer security but also vulnerability. Here are some of my more cogent scribblings from when I was just back from Loch Awe.

Islands = crisis: the drama of so many issues – climate change, species loss and extinction, overpopulation, nationalism and pollution – is played out with a special intensity on islands. The disappearance of an island occasions genuine grief, a real sense of loss, in a way that ordinary flooding does not. When an island goes it is like a complete thing, a whole nation, has been eradicated. Islands are often small places but they pack a big punch. Conquering or creating new ones is a big deal. Countries are greedy for them – in part because they can claim 200 nautical miles of territory from the shore of every single one. They offer a radical leaping outwards of national power. If you are looking for places that are intensely occupied by military firepower or have been bombed to nothing, then islands are the places to go.

Islands = freedom and fear. They seem tailor-made for experiments and a fresh start. Perhaps that's part of the tingle when the boat nudges the shore, the possibility that this is a new world where things, finally, can be made right. The twenty-first century is throwing money and ideas at islands. The rich like them because they offer security and status. But in an era of rapidly accelerating sea-level rise and worsening storms, islands are fragile. They are the first places to be abandoned. The dream becomes a nightmare and the island a prison. Islands are often used as dumping grounds for the unwanted. They lure us but they can easily and quickly become places of dread.

The windows have started to shudder and the wall plugs just sparked. 'No way you're flying out this week,' my Tongan captain forewarned me. As the cyclone gathers, I'm shrinking and hunching, trying to get small. My notes about islands suddenly feel like very thin gruel. They may contain some truth but they don't feel vulnerable enough. Our relationship to islands goes well beyond political and ecological headlines or clever paradoxes. I try another memory; I reach back, much further.

I'm standing with my brother and sister in an old wood – it is called Wintry Wood – at the northern end of Epping, the town on the eastern outskirts of London, where I was born and grew up. I've got my bright red wellington boots on; sometime later one of them will be sucked down and lost in a nearby patch of bog. Before us – Paul and Helen and me, the youngest – there is a dark, quiet pond hazy with flies and in that pond is an island. The pond and the island must be very old but they do not look natural: dug out for reasons long forgotten and of no interest to us. The island has our full attention: it is our destination. It is maybe 100 square metres in size and dense with beech and silver birch trees. Thin, finger-like branches reach down and paddle the water, beckoning children. Generations have taken up the invitation. We edge sideways down one particular muddy bank where an uneven causeway of sticks has been strewn – branches and twigs thrown into the water by those who came before us. It's likely at least one of us will get a welly full of stinking, leaf-matted water and have to beat a wet retreat. But not this time, not in this memory. I can't help smiling: we've all made it, holding hands across the tricky bits.

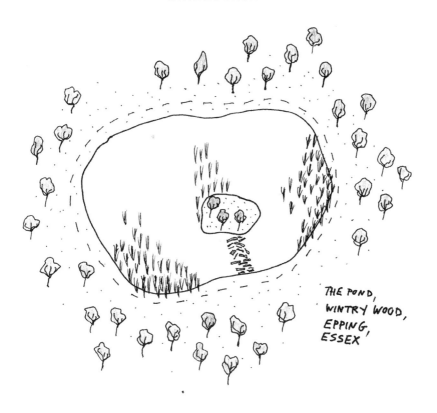

THE POND,
WINTRY WOOD,
EPPING,
ESSEX

But once on the island, what to do? There's a glitch in my happy memory. The triumphant three stand aimless, patrol proudly, going nowhere. The island offers elation and restlessness; soon we're splashing back to the mainland with a sure sense of accomplishment and a tale to tell.

The voyage to an island stays with you, moored inside for reasons that are hard to explain. I think I knew I wanted to become a geographer when I came across a book called *Topophilia* by Professor Yi-Fu Tuan that recognized the depth of this mystery. Tuan wondered why 'Certain natural environments have figured prominently in humanity's dreams of the ideal world.' And he names them: 'the forest, the seashore, the valley and the island'. His list pointed to the natural advantages of these landscapes and so referenced the work of another thinker interested in why we are attracted to some landscapes and not others. This was Jay Appleton, a poet-geographer who died in 2015 and who worried away at the question of why people find high mountains and islands alluring. We stumble around trying to pin down our feelings about landscapes, said Appleton, using words like 'happiness' and 'grief', even though we know they don't really fit. We are, he said, 'using a second-hand terminology to describe a relationship which we do not properly understand'. For Appleton it's a relationship that goes beyond language for it is based on atavistic instincts of fear and safety. He devised what he called 'prospect-refuge theory' to impose some order on this uncertain terrain. Humans, he argued, have an 'inborn desire for places where they can assess threats from a place of safety'.

It makes some sense and our fascination with islands, especially small ones that we can observe all at once, is, in part, explained by Appleton's 'prospect-refuge theory'. A less scientific take on this allure is found in D. H. Lawrence's story 'The Man Who Loved Islands'. Based on the real-life island-hopping of the novelist Compton Mackenzie – who, in the 1920s, leased or bought a series of ever-smaller British islands (first Herm then Jetou, which are Channel Islands, then the Shiant Isles in the Outer Hebrides), each of which was his sole domain – Lawrence wrote that 'an island is a nest which holds one egg, and one only. This egg is the islander himself.'

During a long, sleepless night and all morning Cyclone Keni bruised Tonga. Like everyone else, I peep out of my door in the afternoon when it feels safe. The windows of almost every building had been boarded up so there is not much glass on the streets. Taking to my hire car, I soon come across schools and government buildings marooned by new lakes, with kids whooping and splashing in the warm water. Although large white defensive rocks are piled on some northern shorelines, this water has poured straight down from the sky and now it lies all around in shining sheets. It is so humid that I have to keep on wiping tiny rivulets running down my glasses. After thirty minutes driving I end up at the island's most western point. An information board proclaims it was here that Dutchman Abel Tasman 'discovered' Tonga in 1643. This afternoon, the spot is colonized by a giggling and friendly group of gay and transgender youths. They are dancing round a tiny speaker, enjoying the return of some sunshine. Their first question is the same question all Tongans ask of strangers, asked in the same quiet way with an uncertain, shy smile: 'What do you think of Tonga?' I can tell they are steeled for a put-down, expecting to be hurt. Each time I'm asked this kind of question I freeze. I can't tell the truth because they wouldn't believe me. The truth is that l think it is beautiful, unique, and it feels like a huge privilege to be here. We all laugh, I mutter something about the weather, and I guess they go away believing that my opinions about Tonga can be reduced to the words 'it is very wet'.

Weeks later, years later, I wish I could go back and explain, get it right. The least I can do is to dedicate this book to them and to all those who love islands.

PART ONE

RISING

Why We Build Islands

I N A DARK bar on the shores of Loch Awe a tall, beery fellow leaned into me and slowly explained that the crannogs – the ancient homesteads sprinkled in the lochs of Ireland and Scotland – were the very first artificial islands. I nodded meekly. It seemed likely and he was staring at me with red-eyed certainty. If I'm ever up that way again I may have the courage to lean back and put him right. The truth is that artificial islands are found across the world and that trying to claim any one as 'the first' is like trying to locate the first firepit or the first hut. Although often overlooked today, they are just too common to be easily or usefully tracked down to a single original source.

What are they for? Sifting through the layers of island-building history, the main reasons why people built them can be organized as follows: for defence and attack; to create new land for homes and crops; as places of exclusion; as sacred sites; and finally a rag-bag category of islands for lighthouses, sea defence and tourism. If we drill down into each of these purposes, we start to see continuities to our modern age of islands but also differences, not just in terms of number and size but in how they are used. For the majority of the world's new islands have no pre-modern predecessors. These are the rigs and turbines, dedicated to oil, gas and wind power extraction, that dot so many horizons.

Defence and attack

Many of the reefs of the South China Sea have been bulked out and squared off to house missile silos, naval docks and runways. Although there is a long history of new islands born of strife, the oldest have nothing to do with sabre-rattling. In the Solomon Islands, the Lau fishing people built about eighty islands in a sheltered lagoon by paddling out – year after year, for centuries – and dropping lumps of coral into the water. The Lau built these islands to escape attack from mainland farmers. Many are still inhabited. Their defensive function has ceased to matter but they still offer protection from wild animals and malarial mosquitoes. Elements of this story can also be heard on Lake Titicaca in South America where another fishing community, the Uros, built a similar number of islands many miles from the shore in order to be safe from aggressive neighbours. Unlike the Lau's solid structures, the islands of the Uros are made of reeds and float. This design reflects the building material to hand but also allowed the islands to be moved if under threat. Reed islands last about thirty years and need to be continuously remade. The Uros maintained these woven structures across hundreds of years. Today they are much closer to the shore and attract tourists from all over the world.

Ancient defensive artificial islands were small, occupied by families not soldiers, and never had much, if any, weaponry. In Europe the construction of more robust and professional artificial island fortresses began in earnest from the seventeenth century, and over the next three hundred years imposing stone forts were built on numerous reefs and sandbanks, usually to guard important ports. Some of the grandest were built by Louis XIV, such as the horseshoe-shaped Fort Louvois. Foundations for Fort Louvois were sunk into a muddy rise in the sea near Rochefort on 19 June 1691. At high tide it still looks startling: a castle rising from the water. In fact, Louvois saw only brief bouts of active military service. The last came on 10 September 1944, when it was shelled and briefly occupied by the fleeing German army.

Like a lot of militarized islets, the history of Fort Louvois is largely one of inactivity. Their main role has been as deterrents: they look big and bold in order to make invaders think twice. Peter the Great, having founded St Petersburg, sought to defend his creation with a series of spectacular sea forts. The first was Fort Kronshlot, built in shallow water during the winter of 1703. The most famous of the Petersburg forts is Fort Alexander, an immense oval begun in 1838. Fort

Alexander was big enough to accommodate 1000 soldiers and 103 cannon ports. Like so many other dramatic off-shore forts, Fort Alexander quickly became outmoded and, in military terms, useless. Having been demoted to a storage depot, it was given a new lease of life in 1897 when it became home to the research laboratory of the Russian Commission on the Prevention of Plague Disease. For twenty years this isolated, stone citadel caged a variety of animals used in plague experimentation, including sixteen horses whose blood was used to produce plague serum.

Their military life may be brief but the story of any well-built sea fort is rarely a short one. Cut off from the bouts of demolition that afflict the mainland, they often last a long time and see a range of uses. Many European nations are still trying to work out what to do with the military islands that freckle their coasts. Many stem from the busiest period of European island-building, which came in response to the threat of Napoleon and his heirs. Napoleon built his own islands, the most striking of which is Fort Boyard, an austere oval – resembling a giant napkin ring cast into the sea – that was built between 1809 and 1857. For many years it lay empty, but in the 1990s Fort Boyard began a new life as the setting for a French 'escape the castle' television game show that has had a number of international spin-offs.

Across the English Channel, Victorian sea forts are simi-larly intriguing but have been equally hard to find a modern use for. Occasionally they come up for sale, such as 'Number

1, the Thames', an address also known as Grain Tower Battery. This bizarre hodgepodge of Second World War gun emplacements stuck onto a mid-Victorian military island sits in one of the widest reaches of the Thames estuary. In 2014 it came up for sale for £500,000. This sounds like a meagre asking price given that islands are usually one of the most expensive types of property. However, while old sea forts may look good, they come with colossal maintenance bills. A similar problem kept down the price for the five forts built to defend Portsmouth in the 1860s. With 4.5-metre granite walls and armour plating, even when newly built they combined magnificence with obsolescence: at the very moment of their completion, the threat of the French invasion they were built to repel disappeared. In 2009 three of the forts were acquired for conversion, one into a museum (Horse Sand Fort) and two into luxury hotels (No Man's Fort and Spitbank Fort). After huge investment, ten years later all three were being advertised for sale again.

Some fort-islands are so large and remote that their commercial opportunities are limited. Fort Jefferson is 19 hectares in size and 109 kilometres west of Key West in Florida. The largest brick building in the Americas, it was constructed in 1847. After being used to blockade the Confederate States during the Civil War, it had a limited life as a military prison and was abandoned in 1906. It is now an out-of-the-way tourist attraction set within the Dry Tortugas National Park, one of the most inaccessible of America's National Parks.

Many sea-forts do not even function as quirky tourist destinations and lie totally abandoned, breaking slowly apart under a weight of weeds. The hexagonal Fort Carroll is one such place. It lies in the Patapsco River in Maryland. Built to defend Baltimore in the 1840s it was bought by a family in 1958 and left to become what it is today, a stone wilderness and home to thousands of nesting sea birds.

Nineteenth-century fort-islands were built of stone or brick. During the First and Second World Wars military engineers began to use metal and the result was an array of raised – and, not long after, rusting – structures. The most famous is Sealand in the English Channel. On 2 September 1967, retired army major 'Paddy' Roy Bates climbed onto it and declared it was an independent country – a claim that is maintained by his descendants to this day. Sealand was one of a range of sea forts built off the English coast in 1942–43 that resemble oil and gas rigs. Some, like Sealand, have two rotund supporting legs while others rise on thin stilts and have a number of interconnected platforms. Assailed by stormy, salty seas, examples of the latter have not fared well. A few dilapidated examples linger on and had interesting afterlives, such as Shivering Sands Army Fort, which in 1964 was turned into a pirate radio station by the eccentric politician Screaming Lord Sutch.

After the Second World War, island-building shifted to the Pacific. The USA began reshaping atolls for military purposes. Johnston Island was bulked from 18 to 241 hectares in order to accommodate a landing strip. Today it is a long, unnatural-looking rectangle. At its peak about 1000 personnel were stationed there. The island was used for nuclear weapons testing in the 1960s and has a 10-hectare landfill full of toxic material, including drums of Agent Orange from the Vietnam War. To add to the poisonous brew, the island hosted an incineration plant for chemical weapons, including Sarin nerve gas.

New land for homes and farms

The most common form of ancient artificial island is a small homestead. The crannogs are one example. The homes of the Ma'dan, or Marsh Arabs, are another. Since the fourth century BC the Marsh Arabs have been building floating islands made of reeds in a junction of the Tigris and Euphrates rivers in Iraq. Their way of life was almost destroyed when Iraq's president, Saddam Hussein, drained the marshes. Since Hussein's fall, there have been determined attempts to restore the marshes, and small groups of Marsh Arabs have chosen to return, fitfully reconstructing their former way of life.

Numerous homestead islands may accommodate a lot of people but each is a small and simple affair. A pre-modern counter-example is the island city of Tenochtitlan, the site of modern-day Mexico City. The invading Spaniards couldn't believe their eyes when they saw it. They called Tenochtitlan 'a very great city built in the water like Venice'. Bernal Díaz del Castillo, writing in 1576, told how the Spanish marvelled at Tenochtitlan's size and beauty and at how it was a:

> wonderful panorama, as picturesque as it was novel [...] on account of the great towers and temples and buildings rising from the water, and all built of masonry. And some of our soldiers even asked whether the things that we saw were not all a dream.

Tenochtitlan was built by the Aztecs in the early fourteenth century and was home to around 500,000 people. It was semi-artificial, being extended from a natural island to spill out over several islets establishing a 13-square-kilometre platform connected by 20 kilometres of canals and raised roads. Historian Gerardo Gutiérrez tells us that 'Moving through the city of Tenochtitlan would have involved a combination of canoes and walking through a complex network of streets and alleys connected by hundreds of bridges.' Tenochtitlan linked together numerous artificial farming islands called chinampas. Chinampas are sometimes called 'floating gardens' though they don't actually float; they are made by staking a reed fence to the lake bottom then piling on material until an island emerges. In Tenochtitlan, with the help of the chinampas, farming was urbanized, with hundreds of rectangular field-islands, all artificially created, linked in rows and bedded into the fabric of the city.

The 'floating city' is one of the many labels given to Venice, whose 118 islands are knitted round a network of canals and bridges. From the fifth century AD settlers fleeing raiders from the north began living on the region's marshes. Later generations drove wooden stakes into the mud and created basic wooden platforms and buildings. From these simple beginnings the city of Venice emerged, perfecting the art of the semi-artificial island. To give an idea of the effort involved it is enough to note that, in 1631, to build Venice's church of Santa Maria Della Salute, 1,106,657 4-metre wooden stakes had to be piled into the water.

The name of Venice is conjured again and again, like a charm or talisman, in modern residential island developments. The Venetian planning model of multiple canals and houses with direct access onto the water has been rolled out worldwide. Coastal reclamation for these schemes helps explain why – despite sea-level rise – since 1985 the world has gained more land from the sea than it has lost: an area, according to the Dutch research group Deltares, about the size of Jamaica. 'The Venice of America' is Fort Lauderdale, 40 kilometres north of Miami. Once a country town, from the 1910s Fort Lauderdale began to be transformed by entrepreneurs who realized that maximizing waterfrontage for newly built homes would create upmarket sales. Canals were built, land reclaimed and soon residential communities such as Las Olas Isles and Seven Isles were attracting buyers willing to pay over the odds for an exclusive address that offered privacy, security, views over water and quick access to their own boat. Although these new communities were usually advertised as islands, they were nearly always 'finger islands' – long, thin peninsulas joined by circuitous roads to the mainland. Finger-island development was to spread up and down the coast of Florida and, later, to the more prosperous parts of the coastal world.

Another influential set of Florida islands lies between Miami and Miami Beach in Biscayne Bay: the six 'Venetian Islands' built in the 1920s and 1930s and connected by a highway. Their names pay homage to their Italian forebears, such as San Marco Island, San Marino Island, and Di Lido Island. They showed that finger islands were not the only way to make money, and that real islands (albeit connected by a highway) could also offer canny developers premium returns.

The 'islandization' of coastlines is, for the most part, a form of suburbanization. The new island suburbs are scattered wherever water, land and money collide. As they grow they join up, creating an uninterrupted string of built-up water-facing townships that stretch along the seaboard. In some places, like Australia's Gold Coast, this has resulted in the coastal landscape being transformed from a natural beachscape into a long chain of artificial residential island developments. There is a pecking order, of course: the stand-alone, 'real' islands usually have higher property values than the finger islands. The Gold Coast's Sovereign Islands are its most expensive address. Reclaimed from sandbanks and mangroves, this gated community comprises six connected islands with a single bridge to the mainland. It was formed by dredging 2.3 million cubic metres of sand from adjacent waterways, a process that both built up the land and cleared a channel deep enough for the largest of luxury boats. Many of the houses on the Sovereign Islands are like palaces. They are well away from prying eyes but they are ostentatious. With names like Palazzo di Venezia or Château de Rêves (which became famous for having its swimming pools lined with 24-carat gold tiles), they are confident yet safely distant – loud statements of wealth that do not wish to be disturbed. Today the best-known examples of this kind of development are in the Gulf States. I'll be exploring some of Dubai's most outlandish examples later, when I take a trip to the most bizarre of them all, The World.

Some planning experts claim that we are transitioning to a feverish, hyperactive state in the creation of ersatz island locations. Two geographers from the University of Bristol, Mark Jackson and Veronica della Dora, argue that the 'worldwide phenomenon of the artificial island has become a key defining imaginary and material form of 21st-century development visions'. Jackson and della Dora suggest that 'urbanizing coastlines' are seeking to 'ornamentalize' themselves. Adam Grydehøj, a lecturer in Island Studies in the University of Prince Edward Island, says that in 'today's capitalist urbanism, the coast is a place where both dreams and land come true – assuming one can afford them'.

HOW THE MALDIVES IS BUILDING A FUTURE

All of the 1190 islands that make up the Maldives are projected to be underwater by the year 2100. The Maldives are fighting back with a flotilla of new islands, including an island city, floating islands for tourists and an island that landfills the endless garbage created by its tourist-based economy. The country's tourist slogan 'Maldives – Always Natural' could scarcely be more misleading.

The centrepiece of the fightback is Hulhumalé, branded the 'City of Youth' and the 'City of Hope'. It has been built 2 metres above sea level on a coral reef. Phase one is now almost complete and, in 2013, had a population of 30,000. The target is 60,000. It's a 188-hectare urban rectangle with rows of anonymous apartment blocks. The 240 hectares of Phase two offers taller, more glitzy buildings and is designed to house a further 100,000. The idea is that Hulhumalé can become a safe home for about half the population of the Maldives. Where the rest will go is not so clear, though there is no shortage of plans, including mass relocation to India.

In the meantime the government is capitalizing on the Maldives' 'natural' beauty while it can and, in 2016, passed a law allowing foreigners to buy land in the country, as long as they had $1 billion to invest and 70 per cent of the land they bought was reclaimed from the sea. Rich foreigners can also buy property in 'The Ocean Flower', 185 floating villas built by Dutch Docklands and arranged in the shape of a Maldivian flower. Other Dutch Docklands plans given the green light include Greenstar, a star-shaped floating hotel and a floating eighteen-hole golf course that the promotional bumf claims 'will feature many water hazards and 360-degree ocean views'.

Water hazards and ocean views are not in short supply in the Maldives, though the government works hard to not shadow the island's carefree tourist image with the sombre and unpicturesque reality of living with sea-level rise. Well away from the tourists' floating playgrounds a very different sort of artificial island has been built to hide the island's trash and its most polluting industries, such as cement packing and gas bottling. The island is called Thilafushi. It was once a blue lagoon but it is now a squared-off landfill, where 300 tonnes of rubbish are shipped every day.

Islands of exclusion

Islands have been built to deposit all manner of undesirables. Venice has an archipelago of dumping grounds: San Lazzaro degli Armeni started life as a leper colony; San Giorgio in Alga was for political prisoners; and San Servolo housed the city's insane asylum. There was also a number of plague islands, such as Lazzaretto Vecchio and Poveglia where it is said so many died that half the soil is made up of human remains. Creepy legends continue to stalk Poveglia. The story goes that, when a mental hospital was opened on Poveglia in 1922, one of the doctors went mad and began torturing and killing patients before they rebelled and he was thrown off the bell tower. A more recent tale has it that in 2016 five American tourists tried to spend the night on Poveglia. It didn't go well. As soon as darkness fell a terrible presence began to harry them. Their screams were eventually heard by a rescue crew of passing firefighters.

Some islands of exclusion were also windows to the outside world. Dejima was built in Nagasaki bay in Japan in 1634 to contain foreigners but also to provide a safe place to meet Portuguese and then Dutch traders. The fan-shaped, 9000-square-metre island was ordered to be constructed by the local shogun because he feared the presence of Europeans on Japanese soil would encourage the spread of Christianity. Life on the island was strictly monitored. During its long period of Dutch occupation, the twenty or so foreign residents were watched over by a staff of more than fifty gatekeepers, nightwatchmen and other officials. The last Dutch 'overman' of the island left his post in 1860, just before the emperor began opening Japan to the outside world. Although now integrated into the rest of Nagasaki, a reconstruction project has been restoring some of Dejima's buildings, and in 2017 the newly recreated old bridge to the island opened with members of the Japanese and Dutch royal families in attendance.

Ellis Island, which sits in Upper New York Bay, is a semi-artificial island that grew from 1.3 hectares to 11 hectares, mostly with material derived from ship ballast and debris from the building of the New York City subway system. It served as a site for a gibbet, a fort, an ammunition depot and finally, in 1892, an immigration processing facility that processed more than 12 million applicants over the next sixty-two years. Since first- and second-class travellers were allowed to go straight to the mainland, most of the people it dealt with were third-class passengers. From Ellis Island, anyone whose application for entry to the USA was refused (with disease being one of the main reasons for refusing entry) would not have the option of evading the immigration authorities and could more easily be sent back home.

Sacred islands

An island is a space apart. One of the ancient reasons they were built was to create sacred sites reserved for rituals and high priests. This doesn't happen today but there remains something otherworldly and extraordinary about all islands, artificial or natural. One of the most remote and intriguing examples is Nan Madol, a complex of about a hundred artificial islands reserved for priestly and elite ritual found off the island of Pohnpei in the Federated States of Micronesia. Inevitably dubbed the 'Venice of the Pacific', Nan Madol was built from the eighth century and many of its coral stone walls and buildings have survived, lacing the shallows with an overgrown and tumbling geometry of ruins. Said to be built by twin sorcerers, Nan Madol had a complex function, providing homes for an aristocratic social caste and a cluster of fifty-eight islands dedicated to rituals surrounding the entombment of the dead.

The act – the effort – of creating a sacred island can itself be a form of veneration. This appears to have motivated the building of a number of religious islands such as Our Lady of the Rocks in Montenegro. This island, which hosts a small lighthouse as well as a church, was built by generations of sailors sinking ships loaded with stone around a rock where an image of the Madonna and Child is said to have appeared on 22 July 1452. A festival is still observed on this date: a convoy of small boats connected and decorated with branches and banners rows across and then drops stones around the base of the island.

Sacred islands are places of legend. Sometimes, like Chemmis – the fabulous floating island that held a temple to Apollo described by the ancient Greek historian Herodotus – they belong only to the world of myth. But the relationship between myth and reality has often been confused, especially when legendary sacred islands are replicated as an act of homage. This brings us to the three most important sacred islands of Chinese mythology: Penglai, Fangzhang and Yingzhou. They were searched for by Chinese emperors because, as well as being retreats of the gods, they were said to hold the elixir of immortality. Expeditions to find them returned with reports of sightings. According to the second-century BC *Records of the Grand Historian*, 'All the plants and birds and animals of the islands were white, and the palaces and gates were made of gold and silver.' Such was the utter conviction that they were real that one emperor sent a colony of young men and women to take possession of them.

Penglai, Fangzhang and Yingzhou were not only searched for, they were reproduced. Imitations of the islands were built within lakes in the palace gardens of many emperors, including in Beijing's twelfth-century imperial garden alongside the Forbidden City. These mirror islands became part of a well-known landscape-design pattern known as 'one lake, three mountains', in which the 'mountains' were the sacred islands, each topped with a dramatic temple. The Fairy Isle of Penglai is the best known of the three islands, and visitors to the Chinese city of Penglai can today enjoy a heritage park containing one lake and three 'mountains'. Although some have described the result as tacky, the historical journey from legend to ancient reconstruction to modern theme park is a powerful lesson in how sacred islands retain their hold on the imagination. Frequent mass hallucinations seen off the coast of Penglai drive the point home. One news item, relayed by China Broadcasting in 2006, ran:

Thousands of tourists and local residents witnessed a mirage of high clarity lasting for four hours off the shore of Penglai … Mists rising on the shore created an image of a city, with modern high-rise buildings, broad city streets and bustling cars as well as crowds of people all clearly visible … Experts said that many mirages have been recorded in Penglai, on the tip of Shandong Peninsula, throughout history, which made it known as a dwelling place of the gods.

Lighthouses, sea defence and tourism

Ancient examples of artificial islands used for lighthouses and sea defence do exist but they are rare. An artificial light-house-island was built in the first century AD at Portus, Rome's harbour. It is said its foundation is the concrete-filled ship that in AD 37 carried the Egyptian obelisk that now stands in St Peter's Square.

From the eighteenth century, lighthouse-building expanded in scale and ambition, creating many semi-artificial islands. By the end of the nineteenth century, completely artificial islands began to dot the shallows and reefs of major ports in seas and lakes all over the world. There are thousands of such islands and in a pinch they are still useful to mariners, though modern GPS-navigation technology has rendered most of them redundant. Lighthouse-building has become a rare event. The last one of any size built in the UK was in 1971, the Royal Sovereign lighthouse, off the south coast, which sits on a sea platform supported by a single pillar.

Protection from flooding is a very old art. One widely used technique was to build high mounds in flood-prone areas. In north-west Europe, these occasional islands were called 'terps' and their remnant small hills can still be seen across the Netherlands, Denmark and northern Germany. Using artificial islands to create barriers between the mainland and the sea is a largely modern phenomenon and, even today, it is rarely the sole function of such islands. Sea defence is *one* of the roles of the polders of the Netherlands but they also serve to provide more land for people and farms. Similarly, Toronto's Port Lands Flood Protection project, which is aiming for a 2023 completion date, will also create a new island, named Villiers Island, for homes, green space and businesses.

The importance of natural barrier islands is often only understood once they are washed away. Restoring barrier islands is a worldwide coastal priority. One of the biggest schemes has been in Louisiana, which has lost 4920 square kilometres to the sea since the 1930s. Today the rapidly eroding Bayou Lafourche barrier island complex is being bulked out and reshaped by a coalition of private and public organizations, including one with the telltale name of 'Restore or Retreat'.

Artificial islands built for mass tourism are a new thing. Older examples of pleasure islands are not uncommon but they were reserved for the very rich and are usually tiny and eccentric. The Palladian Villa Barbarigo at Valsanzibio, south of Padua, features a 'rabbit island' designed to be an attractive talking point as well as a way of keeping rabbits – considered something of a delicacy – safe from foxes. In aristocratic estates, tiny islands were also used as places for tombs and memorials, such as the monument for the eighteenth-century wit and playwright William Congreve that sits in a lake at Stowe, an English stately home and garden. The most marvellous of European aristocratic islands was built by the Duke of Anhalt-Dessau in Germany and is called Stein Island. It featured a rocky island with caves and grottoes, and an artificial volcano that, thanks to subterranean fireplaces, produced real smoke and steam. Completed between 1788 and 1794, it was designed to recreate in miniature the landscape of Naples, complete with Vesuvius. After falling into disrepair, it was restored and reopened in 2005.

In the twenty-first century pleasure islands often combine conference, hotel, marina, theme-park and residential attractions. They are now more like spectacular neighbourhoods dedicated to leisure and shopping than the small, single-attraction islands of the past. They are strange, paradoxical destinations. A taste of their sheer oddness is provided by Indonesia's 'Funtasy Island: the largest Eco Park in the world'. Just 16 kilometres south of Singapore, it caters for Singaporean tourists who can enjoy a mixture of theme parks combined with 328 hectares of 'pristine tropical islands' and an 'unspoiled natural environment'. It is, above all, fun: 'there will be many specially designed spaces that offer worlds of fun dawn to dusk'. Funtasy Island is, apparently, both highly developed and unspoilt – both untouched and luxurious. Its builders have not left nature alone but rather added nature in. They have planted mangroves, created underwater 'structures to attract small fishes and dolphins', and claim to 'plant one coral per visitor'. The importance of the 'eco' in Funtasy Island is indicative of a new trend in island-building. People want nature as a 'sight' or 'experience' and they are more likely to travel to a destination that makes them feel good about the environment. The irony – that a once-pristine reef has been destroyed and built over in order to attract visitors to enjoy 'unspoilt' nature – is unmissable.

Artificial islands are spearheading everything that is bizarre about the twenty-first century. Maybe the fact that they are such 'fun' helps explain how we square the circle. Yet islands built for fun do not have to be relentlessly consumerist or huge. In Copenhagen harbour floats a 25-square-metre wooden platform with a slender linden tree growing in the middle. Free to use and open to all for barbecuing, stargazing and bathing, it is the first of a planned archipelago of similar floating wooden islands supporting various functions: a floating sauna island, floating gardens, floating mussel farms and a floating diving platform are in the offing. After Funtasy Island it feels like a cooling balm, a dose of sanity. Perhaps pleasure islands can also be simple places and rest lightly on the water.

Rigs and turbines

There are plenty of modern artificial islands with ancient ancestors. But there are more that are entirely new. Chief among these are the platforms dedicated to extracting energy, which come in a huge variety of forms and have led to some remarkable island-building technologies.

The first offshore oil rig is a contested title, though it seems likely it was in the USA. Louisiana's Caddo Lake had them in 1911 but documents from Mercer County, Ohio record oil wells pumping far out in the waters of Grand Lake St Marys twenty years before that. Today's rigs dwarf their ancestors. Among those rigs whose legs are lowered to the seabed (called jack-up rigs), the largest so far is the Noble Lloyd Noble, with legs that are 214 metres tall. Spar platforms – where the rig floats like a buoy in the water – are anchored to the seabed and designed for deeper waters. After a two-month journey from shipyards in South Korea, carried by the world's largest heavy-transportation vessel, the main platform of Aasta Hansteen – the biggest spar platform ever built – arrived in the Norway gas fields in 2018. Norway also hosts Troll A, a 'Condeep' (concrete deep) gas platform. The tallest and heaviest man-made object ever moved on Earth's surface, Troll A stands 472 metres high, dwarfing the 381 metres of the Empire State Building. In 1996, its platform and substructure were towed over 200 kilometres out to the Troll field, north-west of Bergen.

Another giant is Prelude FLNG, which looks like a red supersized ship. At 488 metres long and 74 metres wide, the 600,000-tonne Prelude FLNG is the largest offshore structure ever built, displacing six times as much water as the largest aircraft carrier. Created to extract and liquefy gas, it combines production and processing on one huge floating site in the seas off north-western Australia.

The twentieth century witnessed ever larger and more ambitious offshore oil islands. Some went well beyond rigs, such as the four THUMS (Texaco, Humble, Union Oil, Mobil and Shell) Islands in San Pedro Bay. They were built in 1965 to house oil rigs but designed to keep visual and noise disturbance to a minimum. This 'aesthetic mitigation' meant building a phoney landscape. There is a waterfall and luxurious buildings illuminated with coloured lights at night, including a hotel known as The Condo, but they are all fakes designed to conceal the drilling rigs.

The shallow waters of the Arabian Gulf have numerous new islands where oil workers and equipment are located. In 2010 came the completion of twenty-seven drilling islands in Saudi Arabia's Manifa oil field, all connected by a 41-kilometre causeway. The Canadian and Alaskan Arctic has seen some of the most innovative oil and gas islands. The Beaufort Sea has hosted a dozen or so 'sacrificial beach islands', which are made up of beach debris, as well as gravel islands, 'rubble spray islands' and concrete and steel 'caisson islands'. The diversity of island-building technologies in these cold waters is unrivalled. Many are huge. Endicott Island, which is 4 kilometres off the Alaskan coast and covers 18 hectares, is made up of two gravel islands linked to the shore by a causeway. Another technology is 'spray-ice islands', which are among the cheapest to build. One example, built in 1989 by ExxonMobil, is Nipterk P-32. The creation of spray-ice islands in a sub-zero climate starts with hosing water high into the air. The water freezes before it hits the ground, and builds up on the sea ice. In shallow waters, after many days of continuous spraying, the sea ice is weighed down to the ocean floor. The hoses remain on until a roundish island is formed. Completed in fifty-three days, Nipterk was soon able to support a rig as well as service and housing structures.

Offshore wind turbines have no visible platform so it's hard to recognize them as islands. This form of energy production remains expensive and they have not yet achieved a global roll-out. They are only common in north-west Europe, which is also where most of them are built. As of late 2018, the Walney Extension off the north-west coast of England was the world's largest offshore wind farm, followed by the London Array in the Thames estuary. In deeper waters, 2017 saw the completion of the first floating wind farm, Hywind Scotland, 25 kilometres off the Aberdeenshire coast. Although not designed to be occupied, engineers can sometimes be stranded on turbines by high seas, so many have basic food supplies and sleeping bags. Larger offshore wind farms also have separate service and accommodation platforms as well as transformer substations, where the power generated by turbines is collected and sent on to the mainland.

Artificial islands: creation and destruction

The small scale of ancient artificial islands meant they only had a minor impact on the environment. Today's age of islands is different. Many of the new residential and leisure islands like to boast about their ecological credentials. This is mostly 'green-wash', a patina of eco-verbiage designed to convince the incurious. Nearly all modern artificial islands have a deleterious impact on the environment.

On the first island I am headed to, Flevopolder, there are signs that a more careful and considerate model is possible. However, this hopeful message must be set against a sober backdrop. There are four main aspects to the problem: first, the ongoing resources required to maintain an artificial island; second, the knock-on impacts on coasts (new islands change local patterns of deposition and erosion and can lead to rivers silting up and beaches washing away); third, the consequences of dredging on marine life; and finally, the new international trade in sand. Sand is a key resource for the modern world: it is often used to build up islands and you need it to make concrete, the production of which has increased more than thirtyfold since 1950. In just three years, between 2011 and 2013, China used more concrete than the US did in the entire twentieth century. The demand for sand is leading to the destruction of beaches, dunes and seabeds across the world. Two dozen sandy islands have already been completely dug away in Indonesia and 2000 others are at risk of disappearing. Sand smuggling is illegal but today it is a large-scale and lucrative trade.

What happens when you dredge or hoover up the seabed? A lot of islands are built on coral reefs and in places where marine ecosystems have been evolving for millennia. These ecosystems do not pop back up again. New islands often feature inlets and semi-lagoon features where the water is slow-moving, shallow, warm and salty. It may look pretty but this kind of water is oxygen-poor and supports little life. All too often artificial islands are dead zones. Trying to make them live again is hard work. This can be seen at Japan's Kansai International Airport, which opened in 1994. The building of this airport island destroyed the rich seaweeds that were once harvested in the area. The task of trying to replace them has been expensive and uncertain. Gentle slopes have had to be built underwater and seaweeds planted but it remains uncertain if they will survive.

FLEVOPOLDER, THE NETHERLANDS

The world's largest artificial island is going wild: an eco-archipelago has sprouted off a northern shore and its nature park is being reverse-engineered to become primal and untamed. Flevopolder is the place to go to see a new green chapter in the story of the age of islands.

That was not my first impression. Flevopolder is mostly a clipped grid of pancake-flat arable fields and quiet residential streets, and it is huge: at 970 square kilometres it is sixteen times the size of Manhattan – another island first colonized by the Dutch. But, sharing a cup of tea at Ans and Bas's kitchen table, I find it easy to see why they moved here from Amsterdam. The morning sunshine gilds the hand-crafted details of their beautiful, self-built home, pouring through tall windows that open out onto acres of woodland, ponds and gardens.

I can't help it: a wave of jealousy is rolling my way. It is with just a bit too much eagerness that I interrupt the polite flow of conversation to ask if they are not worried living 5 metres below sea level. They share a smile before assuring their nervous guest that the island's pumping stations make Flevopolder even safer from flooding than other places in the Netherlands. I'm more likely to end up underwater back in England.

Flevopolder is not a landscape at risk of inundation but it stages another drama. It was declared finished in 1968 but its journey is far from over. Today it is on the frontline of the battle to reimagine what 'artificial land' means and who artificial islands are for. It's a compelling story. Environmental diversity, along with wild horses and wild cattle, is being 'brought back' here.

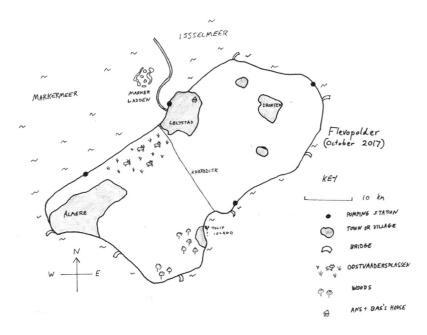

That is, 'back' to a fabricated place, to somewhere that used to be deep below choppy, cold water.

The attempt to rewild Flevopolder is an act of remorse and nostalgia but also courage. This is a landscape that has been won from the sea – shaped, farmed and populated. The Dutch could just sit back and congratulate themselves on the results of their hard work. But they don't. Instead 'artificial islands' are a source of anxious debate about the point and possibilities of human intervention. Today nature is being invited in – a long-lost friend, though perhaps hard to recognize. It's a modern parable for a modern paradox. Industrialism and environmentalism are conflicting yet intertwined ideologies; the first creates the need for the second but, like squabbling twins, each rejects the other. On Flevopolder, at last, some kind of rapprochement has started.

When you first drive over one of the unremarkable bridges from what islanders call 'old land', it's not obvious that you are entering one of the world's extraordinary places. It is just a thirty-minute ride out to Flevopolder from Amsterdam. Leaving pitiless motorways, you cross a calm river and arrive in a geometric space: broad, straight roads slice between green fields. A milky sky scrolls overhead and everything is lined up, just so, in shadowless precision. There is a dreamlike smoothness, a lack of resistance to the landscape. Even its own artifice washes away; the mind rebels against the unsettling reality that every horizon here is a human creation.

My little blue hire car is headed north-east and I soon find myself amid the spacious residential lots of suburban Lelystad, the town named after the creator of Flevopolder, Cornelis Lely. An abrupt left turn and my wheels are grumbling up an overgrown driveway. I'm hoping to find the room I've rented in what looks, from the outside, like a round water tower. I learn later that it's a folly – one of Ans and Bas's creations. Unpretentiously bohemian and wryly humorous, they are bemused by my enthusiasm for their adopted home. Explaining that selling their small flat in the capital bought them a hectare of land, Bas tells me that 'No one wanted to live here.' He pauses, evidently unsure if this attitude has changed: 'If you drive around it's not exactly exciting.' As soon as they were grown, their two children fled back to the city.

'I was crying the first three weeks,' remembers Ans, recalling the young couple's first days here back in 1994. But the regrets have washed away, replaced by a sense of promise. It is with conviction that she tells me, 'There are lots of possibilities here. If you have an idea there are possibilities to create it.'

I've already started to realize that an appreciation of Flevoland's 'possibilities' demands that I learn some more about its past. So next morning, I'm one of the first through the doors at Lelystad's *Nieuw Land* museum. On the ground out front, there's a bright blue rectangle representing the sea, out of which rises a great white head with a life-size Cornelis Lely standing on top, punching the air. As I'm admiring this homage to 'poldering', a black van trundles onto the sea. A ladder is erected and the unblinking white giant is thoroughly cleansed.

Representing Lely's achievement in sculptural form was never going to be easy. The museum is more to my taste: it is stuffed with maps of polders. I am, inevitably, reminded of my earliest days of studying geography. 'The polders' was a staple of post-war geography lessons, at least in Britain. A running joke among my cheeky classmates was the sing-song refrain 'Are we going to do polders, miss?' My love affair with coloured pencils had to remain a secret passion.

Filling in the Netherlands' 'new land' in careful shades – naming the urban areas and the agricultural produce – felt like a kind of magic: conjuring something vast in so tiny a space that it could be closed away in an exercise book. My father, who keeps everything, recently presented me with his own geography exercise book from 1945. In it is a map labelled 'HOLLAND' and its 'POLDER CROPS: WHEAT, BARLEY, RYE, FLAX, SUGAR BEET, POTATOES', and the 'ZUIDERZEE (BEING RECLAIMED)'. Little geographers have been drawing polders for generations and learning their definition (reclaimed and drained low-lying land). The technology to make them is not complicated. What matters is the long-term commitment. The pumps and sluices need to be kept in order; otherwise the water table will rise and you'll be left with a very large bathtub.

Following a major flood in 1916, which killed fifty-one people, Cornelis Lely's solution was accepted: dam and reclaim the Zuiderzee (the huge sea inlet that once scooped out the heart of the Netherlands). It was accepted, in part, because polder-building was nothing new. The oldest ones in the Netherlands date back to the fourteenth century and there are an estimated 3000 across the country. The old Dutch proverb 'the world was created by God, but the Netherlands was created by the Dutch' is no idle boast. Draining the Zuiderzee took a known technology to a new level. These polders would not only create new farm-land and living space but also act as protection barriers, preventing flooding across a huge swathe of the country. After a dam was built across the top of the Zuiderzee, the first polder, Wieringermeerpolder, was completed in 1930. It was deliberately inundated by the retreating Nazis in 1945 but reclaimed soon after. Then came Noordoostpolder, which was completed in 1942 and stretched out to gobble up the old fishing islands of Urk and Schokland. Their ghostly shores – curving, wayward – can still be traced in the midst of the surrounding geometry. Both these polders were joined to the mainland. Existing rivers flowed straight over them, causing problems of subsidence. Flevopolder was created as an island to avoid this problem. It has a dividing dyke in the middle, the Knardijk, designed to keep one half safe if the other is flooded. But there has been no flooding. When it comes to building new land, the Dutch know what they are doing.

The expertise of Dutch engineers and designers is behind new islands from Panama to the UEA to the Maldives. Chinese firms are now also acknowledged experts and can undercut on price, but the Dutch remain the respected masters. The specialism of poldering – creating land below sea level – has also gone global. Polder-making has been taken up by numerous countries with flood-prone coasts. You can find polders on the coasts of Britain, Germany, Poland and much further afield. In the 1960s 123 polders – most in the form of new islands – were built in flood-prone Bangladesh. Without them, the regular flooding the country still endures would be even worse. The Netherlands and Bangladesh are both low-lying, river-delta nations and in many ways topographic cousins. Unfortunately, over the past decade, Bangladesh's polders have run into trouble. Their walls are crumbling and the new islands are turning into water-filled rings. Water engineers in Bangladesh now argue that the solution is to work *with* the water: rather than simply keeping it out, we should let it come and go. This new approach involves controlled river flooding: managing the river's flow in, across then out of the polder.

Controlled flooding is catching on in Europe too. In the Netherlands, the 'Room for the River' programme is seeing dykes lowered and some polders, such as Overdiepse Polder (an artificial island that sits in a river near Rotterdam), being cleared of farmland to become a 'spillway'. 'Going with the flow' is the new catchphrase. It's a technical solution to a practical challenge but it mirrors a wider cultural shift. The Dutch want nature back.

Ans and Bas answer my polder questions dutifully but the subject that excites them is the ugliness of the unnatural, modern world. The new towns, Lelystad included, 'turned out really ugly,' says Bas. It dawns on me that their beautiful home – 'we wanted a house that looks older than it is, with nice old tiles' – is another island, a green retreat from a remorselessly industrial world.

It's a viewpoint and an aspiration shared by many. I hear it again a few days later as I'm sitting in a ramshackle basement that is stuffed with eccentrically crafted objects. It is owned by a large, shaggy guy called Ruud, another big-hearted Dutchman with a room to rent, this time in the medieval centre of Haarlem. He is damning about Flevopolder: 'It's got no soul, just money,' he growls before bemoaning the fact that the Netherlands no longer has any real countryside, that it is effectively one big city. He tells me about the time he visited his corporate boss in Lelystad, a town he loathes: 'He wanted to show off his things in this horrible place: I've got this and this and this.' It was all too much for Ruud, who soon fled the corporate world for a wilder, less predictable life.

In every country it's easy to find people chewing over the unappealing nature of modern planning and either finding sustenance in the resultant melancholic cud or actively searching for something better. Today the Dutch are also leading the way in the ecocentric redesign of new islands.

Back in Flevopolder, it is time to leave the *Nieuw Land* museum, especially now it's getting full of skittering schoolchildren, hunting in packs for buttons to push. Outside the weather has closed in: a steady rain smears the windscreen as I drive north, along the 30-kilometre dyke road that cleaves what was once the Zuiderzee. By the time I get a quarter of the way up, at what I hoped would be a panorama of eco-island splendour, it's pelting down. On the right is the IJsselmeer, on the left the Markermeer, two vast freshwater lakes. Lely planned a polder for the Markermeer but his scheme was finally shelved in 2003. A new, greener mood had taken hold; the prospect of another century of creating land exclusively for human use had become unappealing, especially as it was learned that the Markermeer was silting up, its sea creatures suffocating and bird life disappearing. After parking I brave the bleak drizzle, and the new solution for the Markermeer is just visible in the mist. It's incredibly bold. Wiping raindrops from my glasses, I can make out the sinuous black lines of new dam walls. They loop and roll over much of the horizon. This is a new eco-archipelago. Not an exercise in geometry but a twisting labyrinth, it's easy to envision as a maze of islands, creeks and hidden places.

The new 10,000-hectare eco-archipelago, which officially opened in September 2018, is called the Marker Wadden. The first island was begun in 2016, made by mud dredged up from the lake's silty reaches, thus deepening and clearing the lake at the same time as providing a natural habitat for wildlife. When settled into place, the islands will be covered in reed beds and low dunes and surrounded by rock break-waters to stop the whole thing being washed away. A little harbour will allow hiking day trips for nature lovers but that will be as far as the human presence goes. The results are not entirely predictable; that also is part of the design. This is planning with nature; therefore nature will 'get a say' in what happens and what the Marker Wadden looks like. Project manager Ruud Cuperus, talking to *Het Parool* news-paper, is pleased that 'herring, smelt, glass eel and anchovies are now swimming again' in the surrounding waters and he looks forward to the arrival of more bird life, including exotics like wintering flamingos and spoonbill. But he is candid that this is a journey into the unknown: 'You can pull all kinds of levers but the outcomes are not predictable.'

The Marker Wadden is not the only green archipelago being built. There are others in the Markermeer and off the other coasts of Flevopolder, including islands shaped in the form of a tulip. Sculpting shapes for aerial photo opportunities is a common weakness of island designers. A more convincing green archipelago was built adjacent to Amsterdam at the start of the century. IJburg is all about sustainable human habitation; the first residents of this ten-island complex moved in in 2002. Designed for minimal carbon emissions, with communal roof gardens and plenty of parks and trees, IJburg has proved popular – and not only because it has a mixture of prices, with plenty of low-cost rentals. Increasingly people want to live alongside and with nature; the straight lines and efficient spaces of Lely's day are no longer seen as exciting but as unsustainable and boring. There is a seismic shift underway in how the Dutch think about the purpose and consequences of 'new land'.

The most controversial outcome of this shift is the re-wilding of 56 square kilometres of northern Flevopolder. I've been saving the trip to Oostvaardersplassen until my last day on the island, though I know it is not an experience to be rushed. After all, this is Europe's best-known example of rewilding: not a landscape designed for human pleasures – including the pleasure of staring at animals – but a place to be left alone.

That said, there is a visitor centre with a cafe and gift shop, from which point you can wander off across umpteen tracks. I opt for one that is heading seaward, with just the sound of the wind in the tall reeds for company. It's so flat and wide that distances are hard to gauge, and it's difficult to imagine that this empty quarter was once earmarked for industry or that it is now a battleground between those happy to see its various species live and die here and animal rights campaigners who charge it with being a cruel and unnatural experiment where large herbivores starve to death. For some, claiming this place as 'primal' is a piece of artifice, a conceit for which the animals trapped here (there are currently no green corridors for them to move off the site) are the innocent victims. The horses and cows introduced here in the mid 1980s were selected for their archaic qualities. The Heck cattle are a hardy breed, first bred in the 1920s to resemble the extinct aurochs, an ancient bull-like species that once roamed Europe and Asia. The horses are Konik ponies, which look like another extinct species, the Eurasian wild horse, the last of which died in 1909. Along with red deer, these animals spend all year out in the open and, in warm years, their numbers have outstripped the natural feeding capacity of the reserve. Since they have no predators, rangers have stepped in to cull the animals. In 2018, local politicians decided that the number of large herbivores should be capped at 1500. They were responding to a rewilding backlash that was unleashed when photos of starving beasts circulated on social media. Protesters went so far as to compare Oostvaardersplassen to Auschwitz. Groups of them began tossing bales of hay over the fence that surrounds the reserve. Campaigners like behavioural biologist Patrick van Veen are adamant that Oostvaardersplassen is a 'failed experiment' tarred by 'machismo and deceit'.

Yet, heading further along this increasingly marshy path, it occurs to me that if Oostvaardersplassen is a failed experiment then Flevopolder is an even bigger one. After all, creating a geometrical island where unproductive nature is banished is a pretty extreme idea. You can't judge either experiment in isolation from the other. Oostvaardersplassen is one element of a shift away from just thinking about the landscape and the planet in terms of humans and their immediate needs. It's not an easy thing to do; our species has come to define itself as beyond or above nature. The bonds have broken and sticking them back together will often look fake and feel clumsy. But it's the right thing to do.

After hours of contemplative wandering, I'm back in my small blue car, ready to head off across the bridge, back to 'old land'. I pass a group of Konik ponies gently cropping a wild meadow. They must be used to sightseers as they barely stir. There is a line of parked cars ranked nearby, with cameras poking out of every window. There used to be not much to see in Flevopolder but now there is. Wild animals are exciting, alive and effortlessly beautiful in a way the human world isn't. We are drawn to them, as to every tiny plant or buzzing bee, irresistibly and inevitably. Our love of other forms of life is a self-preserving impulse: bringing nature 'back' into the picture is not just pleasing; it is necessary for our survival and our sanity.

THE WORLD, DUBAI

It was raining in Dubai as I stepped onto Lebanon. Later that day journalists heralded the stormy weather as proof of the efficacy of intensive cloud-seeding. Artificial rain on an artificial island, falling on one of only two completed islands of the 300 that make up 'The World'. The other is in the Greenland group, reportedly a gift by Dubai's ruler, Sheikh Mohammed bin Rashid Al Maktoum, to Formula One racing driver Michael Schumacher.

When seen from the window of a plane The World, sited a few kilometres off Dubai's downtown shoreline, is a plausible world map. The continents are all there, though things go a bit wonky at the top, bottom and around Australia. Each continent is made up of roundish sand islands. A lot of them are assigned to particular countries and they sit in roughly the right place. So, for example, Egypt is above Sudan, which is next to Eritrea and Chad. Some of the biggest countries, like Russia, are broken up into islands that represent cities or regions; so there is a Moscow island and islands for Omsk and Siberia.

The only way to get to The World is by boat and, so far, there are no bridges between the islands, though many of the channels between them are narrow and shallow. If I wasn't wet enough already, I might be tempted to wade over to Palestine.

The original vision of The World, launched by Sheikh Mohammed in 2003, was that the islands were to become playthings and unique retreats for the super-wealthy. Today,

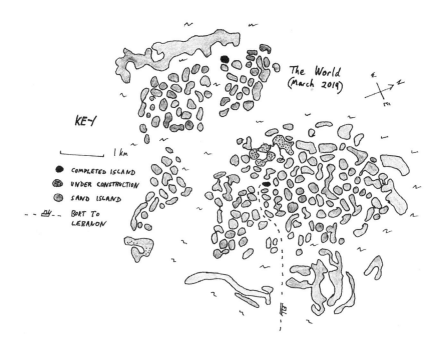

The World
(March 2019)

KEY

——————— 1 km

● COMPLETED ISLAND
◉ UNDER CONSTRUCTION
◎ SAND ISLAND
- - 🚤 - - BOAT TO
LEBANON

however, it's just me and a family of three from Glasgow on a day-return that costs £40. We are met on Lebanon's pier by its Indian manager, who is smiling steadfastly as the water pools on the little white tray he carries bearing four cups of pineapple juice. Apart from him and a few other staff, we're the only ones here.

Nakheel, the state-owned firm that built The World, initially sent out invitations every month to 'Own the World' to fifty rich, high-profile potential buyers. Karl Lagerfeld had plans for a 'fashion island'. It was said that Brad Pitt and Angelina Jolie had bought Ethiopia for their children. The photo opportunities and the showmanship were irresistible. Richard Branson posed on Britain in a Union Jack suit next to a British phone box. Turkey's MNG Holdings bought Turkey; China's Zhongzhou International bought Shanghai. Back then Nakheel's marketing people depicted The World as *facing away* from Dubai. They calculated that, like other aristocrats, the super-rich want to be at the centre of things but remain invisible.

It's easy to find critics who will tell you the whole scheme is bonkers. It is, undeniably, outrageous. But you only have to turn round and look back at the twisting, soaring towers of Dubai to understand that this sort of thing happens here on a regular basis.

Most of The World islands were turned over to buyers in 2008. Nakheel was basking in the success of another of its projects: the world's most famous artificial island, the

Palm Jumeirah. The fronds and trunk of the Palm Jumeirah stretch out over 5 kilometres and, if you include the tourists staying there, today it has a population of about 75,000. Repeating that success has not proved easy. Just after completion of The World, the worldwide financial crash rolled into town. The crash messed up building timelines for The World and a bunch of other islands Nakheel was constructing or planning. Another huge palm, Palm Deira, was downsized and lopped off into the family-friendly resorts of the Deira Islands, which are well underway. The giant sister of Jumeirah, Palm Jebel Ali, has been piled into shape but further work was put on hold and its heralded halo of islands – shaped into an Arabic poem written by Sheikh Mohammed – quietly forgotten. In hindsight, the Sheikh's would-be island-words have an ironic subtext:

> *Take wisdom only from the wise,*
> *Not everyone who rides a horse is a jockey.*
> *It takes a man of vision to write on water,*
> *Great men rise to great challenges.*

Another casualty was The Universe, a delirious, cosmic fantasy that would have wrapped The World in bands of islands forming the shape of the Milky Way and the solar system.

The World may have found a saviour in Josef Kleindienst. Once a policeman and member of Austria's right-wing

Freedom Party, he is now one of Dubai's big property developers. Arriving at the western shore of Lebanon, and looking out over the empty shoreline of what I'm told by another Indian staff member is Syria, the skyline is animated with multiple cranes slotting together the Kleindienst Group's 'Heart of Europe'. (The young member of staff also expressed irritation that the island of India was smaller than Pakistan: 'That is very wrong.') Six territories are being built – Sweden, Germany, Main Europe, Switzerland, the heart-shaped 'honeymoon island' of St Petersburg, and The Floating Venice – in order to form an interconnected upmarket resort. The golden domes of Sweden's beach mansions and Germany's modernist executive villas are nearly complete. In addition, there will be floating individual three-storey 'Seahorse Villas', some of which have already been built and which feature underwater windows.

The target audience for The World has broadened. The scale of the rising blocks shows that reclusive exhibitionists with deep pockets are no longer the key market; these are not solitary domiciles for tycoons but hotels, apartments and shops. The Heart of Europe is being built to accommodate up to 16,000 people and its promotional spiel promises 'European retail coupled with food and beverage concepts' as well as sheer spectacle, such as 'ground-breaking climate control technology which will convert narrow cobbled streets and picturesque plazas into a beautiful winter wonderland!' Again the outlandish nature of this vision needs to be placed in context: Dubai's Mall of the Emirates already has a huge real-snow ski slope and its many supersized 'shopping experiences' vie to outdo each other in showmanship.

Both Dubai and Kleindienst thrive in the meeting point between social conservatism and huge ambition. It is a fertile terrain for hyper-consumerism and artificial islands. Environmental, political and welfare concerns, which would derail such schemes in Europe, barely get a look in here. Despite a much-proclaimed shift to renewables – especially solar power – creating air-conditioned, shopaholic lifestyles in the desert eats up a lot of resources. The United Arab Emirates, of which Dubai is part, is run by a patriarchal fiefdom and its shining towers and motorways are built by an underclass of South Asian men who work in incredible heat. A local building engineer explained to me that it is illegal for workers to be out in temperatures beyond 50 degrees Celsius, 'but it is funny how the thermometer gets stuck,' he grinned at me, 'gets broke at 49.8 or 49.9, you know. It's not good but that happens.'

The environmental costs of Dubai's new islands mostly concern the huge amounts of materials and energy required to build and sustain them as hot spots of high-income, air-conditioned mobility and shopping. It's not all bad news, though: in terms of marine life, the islands may have a positive impact. Along with the protective reefs that surround them, they provide a habitat for corals, fish and other sealife that would otherwise not find a home in the Arabian

Gulf's shallow, sandy waters. Artificial reefs – made of everything from boulders to sunk trains – have been shown to encourage biodiversity in many parts of the world so it is not surprising the same thing happens here. Nakheel's most audacious reef loops round the northern reaches of The World. Over a thousand coral-covered boulders that were under threat at a port site further up the coast were towed 14 kilometres underwater. Nearly all the coral survived, and this section of The World reef now attracts divers.

I pick my way around the unoccupied beach furniture on Lebanon. Occasionally an employee will brush a few damp leaves from the sand or look out of a window from the empty restaurant. When the rain comes down harder, I head inside and become the restaurant's only customer. Delivering my sandwich and chips, the Kenyan waiter tells me about his plans. He works twelve hours a day, sending money back home to buy a supermarket. The idea is that his wife will run the supermarket and he will buy a poultry farm. That's his dream and it should be possible, he says, in three years. The manager and beach-sweepers have similar ambitions. To me Lebanon seems like a place dropped out of a scene from a Samuel Beckett play – all silences, ennui and emptiness. But I suspect this says more about me than the island: I can afford to indulge my boredom. By contrast, many of the people who build, staff and get customers to and from these resorts don't have time for feelings of 'ennui'; nor do they see themselves as victims but rather as grafters, even as would-be entrepreneurs.

With 300 play-sized kingdoms being traded to the world's richest individuals, it's no surprise that all sorts of stories – many of them true – swirl around The World. Another project that did not come to pass was Opulence Holdings' scheme for Somalia; the idea was to shape it into a seahorse and build luxury houses where residents could hit golf balls into the sea from their balconies. The owner of Ireland, John O'Dolan, had plans for a replica of the Giant's Causeway but took his own life when his debts became insurmountable. The purchaser of Britain ended up in prison for bouncing cheques. Many owners, like Baron Jean van Gysel, the Belgian hotel owner who bought Greece, are biding their time. When he bought Greece, van Gysel said that his first act would be to run a metal band around the island to protect it from erosion. As far as I know, the metal band hasn't materialized, but it throws up the question of how other owners are going to protect their islands. Or, indeed, to supply them with water, power and waste disposal. The initial plan was for fresh water and electricity to be laid on, piped from the mainland out to The World. However, for the time being, owners have been left to their own devices – which, in the short term, means diesel generators and shipping stuff back and forth.

Despite the challenges, the allure of The World is still drawing in investors. Two big green-lit proposals are for a resort called OQYANA on the fourteen islands that make up Australia and New Zealand, and for a low-rise resort village on twenty islands in the North America group. One of the more recent investors was Hollywood actress Lindsay Lohan, who is designing her own island and giving it the name 'Lohan Island'. She told *Emirates Woman* that the island will feature a 'luxury hotel, Michelin-worthy restaurant, idyllic waterfront pool and plenty of leisure activities'. Lohan also revealed that she has bought Lebanon and plans to revamp it as a 'luxury getaway'. From where I'm standing, it looks like a 'luxury getaway' already, albeit a rather damp one. But 'luxury' is a restless animal, forever feasting but never satisfied.

It seems inevitable that Dubai's luxury skyline will colonize The World and continuously shape and reshape its islands. On the other side of Lebanon to the Heart of Europe you can see the virgin lands of Palestine, Jordan and Saudi Arabia and, beyond that, the massing forces of the future, including the hazy pinnacle of the world's tallest building, the Burj Khalifa.

After a few hours on Lebanon everyone, staff included, took the boat back to Dubai. I want to see what it is like actually living on one of Dubai's islands so I've rented a room on the Palm in the home of a young expat couple called Reena and Ryan. Pointing out the shops across the busy road that runs up the spine of the Palm, Reena jokes that I might need to get a taxi. Later, edging my way along a broken and vestigial pavement, I realize she was not joking. Reena and Ryan have a three-year-old daughter, a happy chatterbox who absorbs most of their energies. She spends much of the day in the front room with views over the bright, glinting waters and the low-rise mansions that occupy the Palm's fronds. The little girl rolls restlessly between a large television that plays endless cartoons and another screen that scrolls out educational games. Both parents worry about her: she's boxed up when she should be playing and running outside. It's way too hot out there and, apart from some manicured green strips, there is nowhere to go. 'I do feel that she is missing out on something that I took for granted,' says Ryan. 'We do what we can; it is a big thing that concerns me.'

But they are not planning on moving. They tell me the compensations outweigh the costs. It's not just the money they can earn here and the zero-rate income tax, it's also the fact that Dubai is safe and efficient; there is very little crime and almost no rubbish on the streets. Ryan and Reena don't even bother to lock their front door. They've travelled widely and been to plenty of countries, including the UK and USA, and have no appetite for what they saw: insecurity, inefficiency and dirt. It's an ironic truth that, although Dubai panders to the rich, people with great wealth are insulated wherever they live: they don't need Dubai. It's ordinary people, like Ryan and Reena, who endure the hard edges of anxious, neglected places and it is they, above all, who value this modern wonderland in the desert.

Dubai is used to put-downs. Even the *Rough Guide to Dubai* is condescending about the Palm. 'Disappointingly botched,' it says, with 'densely packed Legoland villas strung out along the waterside "fronds"'. A visiting journalist for the *Guardian* describes 'rows of McMansions looking across at each other between thin strips of stagnant water'. I suspect there is an element of resentment in such dismissals. Love it or loathe it, the architecture here – mansions included – is often bespoke and frequently daring. Countries, like the UAE and China, that were once poor are poor no longer. They have seized control of the image of the modern city. Critics in the West, who thought they had the copyright on modernity, are becoming dimly aware that they are now outside the loop.

Also envious of Dubai's success, other Gulf States have been creating their own artificial leisure and residential islands. Qatar's Pearl is nearly finished; its developers promise homes for 6000 and 'a warm, welcoming community whose residents are seeking an urbane and vibrant lifestyle'. In Bahrain there are the residential communities of Durrat Al Bahrain, shaped like petals floating in the sea, as well as Northern City and the Amwaj Islands. Kuwait's Green Island led the way when it was opened in 1988, though today it is somewhat overlooked – especially now a complex of finger islands called Sabah Al Ahmad Sea City is nearing completion and is already being called the Venice of the Desert.

How long will these islands last? In Nakheel's HQ I was told that the Palm islands are built to withstand a predicted sea-level rise of 0.5 metres and that they are 4 metres clear of the water. The first figure seems conservative: most scientists predict a larger rise. And from what I could see, the islands of The World are nothing like 4 metres clear of the sea. Moreover, with 85 per cent of the population of the UAE living in vulnerable coastal areas, the threat of sea-level rise on the islands cannot be separated from the possible inundation of the urban shoreline they are plugged into. Another worry is the temperature. Climate change is predicted to make the Gulf States even hotter. It is already too hot to safely be outside for much of the year, so the question of how habitable Dubai will be in fifty or a hundred years' time is a real one.

Delegations from around the world come to Nakheel's offices to learn and copy. 'We have a lot of governments coming to learn from us,' they told me: 'from China, South Korea and now from Africa as well. We get a lot of people wanting to emulate what we have done.' The so-called 'Oriental Dubai' is called Phoenix Island in China. The axis of island-building is shifting eastwards; as we shall see in the next chapter, though, many of them are not about leisure and pleasure but more hard-nosed modern needs.

CHEK LAP KOK, AIRPORT ISLAND, HONG KONG

Having obliterated a place, modern planners like to decorate their new creation with street names and signposts that sweetly memorialize what was there before. 'Oak Tree Grove' has neither oak tree nor grove; 'Green Acres' is a jigsaw of tarmac and brick. I'm reminded of this perverse practice as I squint up at a bright white sign announcing 'Scenic Drive'. All around are shrieking roads, high wire fences and the geometric assemblages of airport hangars and terminals. I'm at the start of a day trip to an artificial island dedicated to Hong Kong International Airport. It is called Chek Lap Kok and, at 1248 hectares, it is almost twice as big as Gibraltar.

The mouth of the Pearl River is spangled with mountainous islands. On some of the gentler slopes skyscrapers jostle for every spare inch but on others subtropical forest lies undisturbed. Hong Kong has both; it is a gloriously vertiginous and idiosyncratic city-state that has an uneasy relationship with the Chinese mainland. In 1989, a few days after the massacre of pro-democracy protesters in Beijing's Tiananmen Square, a new airport was proposed by David Wilson, the British Governor of Hong Kong, which was still a British dependent territory. The new scheme was widely seen as a bid to bolster the confidence of Hongkongers fearful for their future under Chinese rule. Compounding this impression, Wilson announced a draft Bill of Rights a few weeks later. For their part, the Chinese were irked by Britain's high-handedness in piling up a tab they had no intention of paying. President Jiang Zemin responded angrily: 'You invite the guests, but I pay the bill!'

Given its size, Chek Lap Kok was built remarkably quickly: commencing in 1992, it rolled off the production line in July 1998. It was crafted by flattening, expanding and connecting four existing, natural islands (including the old Chek Lap Kok). A sizeable chunk of the world's commercial dredging fleet was involved. They dug sand from the seabed and sprayed it in great arcs until a smooth and even platform emerged. At the same time, 34 kilometres of roads, tunnels and bridges were built, along with an express rail link. In all contractors relocated 238 million cubic metres of material, which is comparable to moving a small mountain.

The new island saw the destruction of 50 hectares of mangrove and the mass transplantation of both people and endangered fauna. The old Chek Lap Kok was about 3 square kilometres in size, an ancient and hilly island that had once been a favoured hideaway for pirates. The brigands had long gone, leaving a mining and fishing community, a Qing temple and a shrine dedicated to the sea goddess. The villagers were relocated to a set of anonymous blocks called Chek Lap Kok New Village on a neighbouring island, complete with a rebuilt temple. The human population accepted their marching orders with meek endurance. The shy and secretive Romer's tree frog caused more fuss. Discovered in 1952, this fingernail-sized, dowdy amphibian is unique to Hong Kong and its uncertain fate quickly established it as an icon of Hong Kong wildlife, so 230 specimens – about half a bucketful – were transported off the island and installed in safe havens. It is rumoured that a few of the tree frogs cling on in wet patches of their original homeland. If so, they are unlikely residents of one of the world's most expensive airport developments.

For island-spotters, Chek Lap Kok is a magnificent example of an 'infrastructure island', an offshore platform dedicated to activities too polluting, noisy, unsightly and hazardous to be tolerated elsewhere. Japan led the way. It has five offshore airports, including Kansai International Airport. Completed in 1994, and situated over 5 kilometres from shore, Kansai was the world's first wholly artificial airport island. This type of island usually has a penumbra, a rim of land left empty that forms a barrier between it and the ordinary world. In Chek Lap Kok's case, this empty zone was designated as 'noise-sensitive land' – somewhere the scream of aircraft is way above acceptable levels.

It is around this benighted edge that I'm taking my afternoon stroll. A few metres from the 'Scenic Drive' sign, I'm relieved to see a walkers' fingerpost. It beckons me with unlikely promises, pointing the way to 'Scenic Hill', 'Ancient Kiln' and a 'Historical Garden'. A fierce twelve o'clock sun is stinging my skin and these nostalgic destinations suddenly appear less attractive than the cool, deep shadow pooling under the Hong Kong–Macau bridge, which shoots over one side of Chek Lap Kok on fat concrete stilts.

On the day of my visit, in April 2018, the world's longest sea bridge is not quite complete and remains silent, a slumbering colossus. It rides out seawards, 55 kilometres long, linking China's two mini-states and tying them firmly to the motherland. The bridge has two striking mid-route artificial islands. Resembling sleek ocean liners, they funnel the roadway into a 6.7-kilometre tunnel, allowing unhindered sea passage for the container ships that ply the Pearl River delta.

Chek Lap Kok and the bridge to Macau are mega-projects, heroic in scale and internationally significant. But, resting in the bridge's shade, I can't help thinking about where Hong Kong is heading and the sense of loss that comes with transformation. Perhaps these are my problems. My attraction to places no one in their right mind would want to go can sometimes feel worryingly masochistic. The 'walking track' indicated by the fingerpost is strewn with building rubble. I've yet to see another soul. Who is all the signage aimed at? Back in the unforgiving sun, I find an answer on a battered information board. In English and Chinese it natters on about the 'Airport Trail' and was presumably put up to instruct schoolchildren dragged here by merciless teachers. 'What is the purpose of the trail?' it demands. Somewhere in a hot recess of my skull I graffiti a response that I'm sure also occurred to a few of those children: 'to remove all hope'.

This reminder of educational duties triggers a more immediate anxiety. I'm in Hong Kong as a staff member on a university field trip with twenty-nine geography students – or is it twenty-eight? – investigating ideas of citizenship. Thankfully the field trip is led by Michael, the young lecturer who is enthusiastic, knowledgeable and has a generous smile that could warm the most homesick heart. He even gets up before everybody else to buy punnets of fresh fruit to supplement the students' breakfasts. It soon becomes obvious that all I have to do is stand next to Michael, not eat all the grapes and occasionally repeat what he has just said. In a tacit admission that this is neither demanding nor useful, Michael suggests I take the afternoon off to pursue my private passion for islands.

Yet the field trip has been an intense experience and I can't help thinking about the encounters it has led to. We've been speaking to pro-democracy activists and going into highly charged spaces. A year later, protests would explode into the streets and be heard around the world but, when we were there, it felt as if overt opposition had been successfully muffled and was disappearing. On our first day, Michael instructed us all to sit down in a circle on the tiled plaza beneath HSBC headquarters. This was one of the key sit-in and tent-city sites for what we, mistakenly, imagined was the high-water mark of Hong Kong protest, Occupy Central, a movement that fed into 2014's Umbrella Revolution, which saw 100,000 protesters take to the streets. Michael knew that the sight of so many people sitting down on this significant spot would lead to an appearance by the security forces. He also knew they weren't likely to be too scary. They duly arrived. After twenty seconds China's iron fist was made manifest in the form of a portly, diminutive and very polite female security guard who ambled slowly over to inform us that sitting down was not allowed. This clash with totalitarianism created quite a buzz among the students and I basked in the reflected glory of Michael's chutzpah. Later encounters were more telling: activists speaking confidentially and quietly, not wanting to be overheard: 'Is the CCTV on here?' One older man informed me matter-of-factly that 'Hong Kong is disappearing very surely.' Younger activists – one of whom had spent fifty-nine nights at the HSBC Occupy protest – spoke with raw passion about how Hong Kong was being politically and culturally eradicated and its vestiges of democracy disappearing ('It is very hopeless for us'). We heard other, less expected concerns: about the intrusion of an alien, uncouth Chinese culture ('They are so rude; they push past') and the threat to Cantonese, the regional spoken version of Chinese, which is making way for Mandarin ('It is wrong that the ten-year-old boy, my neighbour, is speaking a different language').

My footsteps begin to connect the dots. Chek Lap Kok and its giant bridge to Macau are at the epicentre of China's plans for the future: here too somewhere distinct and small is being rolled over by powerful forces. Here too I am encountering forlorn attempts to hang on to vestiges of the past while, all around, the ground shifts.

My trail does, as promised, lead to a small archaeological site and a patch of grass labelled 'Historical Garden'. I catch up with a group of five female airport employees, each wielding a bright parasol, one of whom tells me they have driven out from behind the airport's high fences to touch and smell the flowers. At the 'ancient kiln' there are rows of explanation boards that go into detail about how the 'airport retained the hill at the southern tip of Chek Lap Kok Island' where 'furnaces ascribed to Yuen dynasty (AD 1271–1368)' have been unearthed along with 'Neolithic remains' and 'ceramics of Tang and Song dynasties'. The jewel of the historical garden turns out to be a 2-metre-tall, many-toothed 'cutter head' from a 'cutter-suction dredger'. Painted a fetching blue and framed by acacia trees flushed with scarlet flowers, it squats fatly like a malign Buddha. The smiling women pose for pictures in front of this revered object.

For a moment things fall into place and I imagine a kind of balance has been struck between the old and new, yin and yang. The fantasy is soon torn apart. This island is sprouting new limbs and the wide bay it lies within is churning with restless industry. Soon after leaving the comforting aura of the parasol-holding women and trudging reluctantly towards massed cohorts of diggers and construction barriers, I'm immersed in dust and grinding gears. Coughing and leaking sweat, I round a headland and everything stills. In front of me is a panorama of truck-sized pipes; they are scattered across the shore and the shallows like penne fallen from the plate of a boorish pasta-loving giant. Land and water are radically confused: platforms and concrete plinths jut out of the sea for miles around. A little further away, shimmering in the heat, another new island is being birthed. It is a polyp of Chek Lap Kok and connected to it by a thin neck of road. I clamber my way forwards, walk inside the length of one of the pipes, and get as close as I can to the diamond-shaped 150-hectare newbie. This island is dedicated to the single task of processing traffic on the Hong Kong–Macau link and its official and only name is 'Hong Kong Boundary Crossing Facilities'.

The tediously literal place name isn't the only reason Hongkongers aren't paying much attention to what, in most other countries, would be a source of excitement and controversy. So much else is going on, and people here are well used to land being won from the sea. The shoreline across the city has been pushed forward for 150 years and there are other huge schemes afoot that are soaking up media attention. Off Chek Lap Kok's northern shore dozens of barges and dredgers are at work, building 650 more hectares for a third runway. The Hong Kong government's '2030 Plus' plan envisages a new 'infrastructure island' for an incinerator as well as a 1000-hectare urban island with a population of up to 1.1 million. Dubbed East Lantau Metropolis, it will create a new business district as well as platoons of new apartments. In a city where the average apartment costs over eighteen times the average income – and where, consequently, home ownership is an impossible dream – 'new land for new houses' is a popular vision.

But why more islands? They will be hugely costly, eating up at least half the city's fiscal reserves. The new islands are vulnerable in other ways too. Hong Kong is expected to experience a significant rise in sea level as well as an increase in the frequency and intensity of typhoons. Forecast maps show that much of Hong Kong's reclaimed land could be underwater by the end of the century.

Hong Kong's island frenzy is a puzzle. I suspect it isn't just about sensible choices and expert decisions. Even though the islands squeezed out from its 'cutter-suction dredgers' have the romance and visual appeal of a piledriver, they are still amazing. They reflect a preference for the drama of the open sea over the open arms of China.

I've been walking for hours now and I packed almost nothing to bring with me: a single banana and two water bottles. I sit down on a large boulder in the shade of another road bridge and watch some young men precariously perched on one of its piers, a concrete shelf they have paddled across to in a tiny metal boat. One of the youths, wearing only bright yellow shorts, leaps up and starts circling his thin arms, shouting to me or at me. I just stare back, aware something is amiss. What is wrong? The man calmly settles down, suddenly indifferent. Perhaps he was signalling to someone far away. It's easy to misread this place.

Getting the measure of Chek Lap Kok can't be done in its generic airport terminals but it's hard here too. The island seemed more graspable yesterday, when I took the cable car that leaps over its shoulder on the way up to see the world's largest outdoor bronze seated Buddha. The ride affords huge views. You can follow the snaking curve of the Hong Kong–Macau highway out to sea and try to count the myriad vessels piling up land for Chek Lap Kok's third runway. The island is crawling with aeroplanes, like white flies on a corpse. From high above, it looks like a landscape that has been killed and skinned. So why does it hold my attention and draw my eye down to every desiccated shape and shore? Maybe because of its sheer oddness, the way it manages to be both machine-like and magical, somewhere conjured up from nothing.

In the cable car's rattling, glass-bottomed gondola another answer occurred to me. Travelling over a fabricated island built for travellers, it felt like Chek Lap Kok was the epicentre of a global culture in which impermanence and mobility is everywhere and prized beyond anything else. The flip side of this restlessness is a yearning for the lost authenticity of place, and nostalgia for a less relentless and uprooted way of life. The Hong Kong activists I've been listening to are caught up in this same dilemma. They don't just want a vote; they want to hold on to something of value, an identity and a history that is being dug away and flattened out.

Heading away from Chek Lap Kok, back to my hotel, I make my solitary way onto another island then another. I walk across skywalks, up escalators, into subways, never quite sure if I'm ever in contact with solid ground. The ceaseless churn of this shifting city fills each moment with thoughts of departure and destination – to better places and worse.

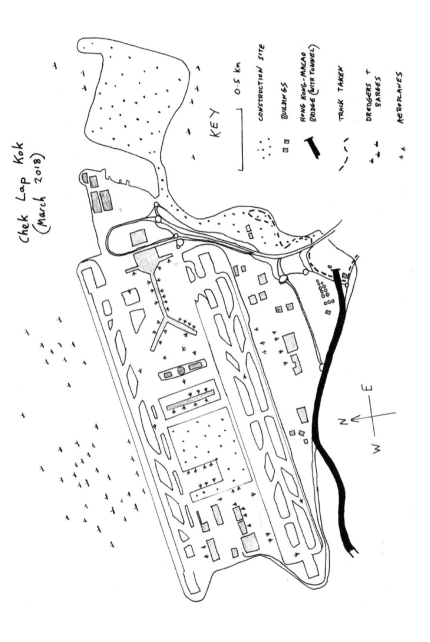

Chek Lap Kok
(March 2018)

KEY

0·5 km

CONSTRUCTION SITE

BUILDINGS

HONG KONG-MACAO
BRIDGE (WITH TUNNEL)

TRACK TAKEN

DREDGERS +
BARGES

AEROPLANES

FIERY CROSS REEF, SOUTH CHINA SEA

Of the seven remote reefs transformed into landing strips, harbours and missile silos by the Chinese military in the South China Sea, Fiery Cross is the most important though not the largest. That distinction goes to Subi Reef, which has been bulked up to nearly 4 square kilometres and is crowded with over 400 buildings. In its natural state Fiery Cross was a ragged coral death-trap for unwary ships. Today it is 2.8 square kilometres in size and China's key forward base in the region. The new island is claimed to have twelve hardened shelters for missile launchers, an early-warning radar and sensor array, hangars to accommodate twenty-eight combat and bomber aircraft, and housing for more than a thousand troops. Fiery Cross also has a runway that is over 3 kilometres long – long enough to land a Xian H-6 jet bomber, which has a range of nearly 6000 kilometres.

Military reclamation of the island began in 2014. 'Before and after' photographs show the conversion of the natural reef – full of colour and enclosing a large pale blue lagoon – into a grey rectangle with a long black airstrip and gaping square jaw. The jaw is the military harbour and is usually dotted with the black teeth of destroyers and other naval vessels. The Chinese claim nearly all of the South China Sea, leaving the other nations that surround it with residual coastal strips. Unsurprisingly, China's claim is hotly contested and the Permanent Court of Arbitration – an international body that tries to settle intergovernmental disputes – has ruled that there is 'no legal basis for China to claim historic rights'. There are many overlapping claims on the numerous islands that make up the Spratlys (of which Fiery Cross Reef is a part). Ownership of Fiery Cross Reef is claimed by the Philippines, where it is called Kagitingan Reef, as well as by Taiwan and Vietnam.

The Chinese call it Yongshu Reef. 'Fiery Cross' remains its international name – one with a suitable ring, given how perilous the current stand-off is in the South China Sea.

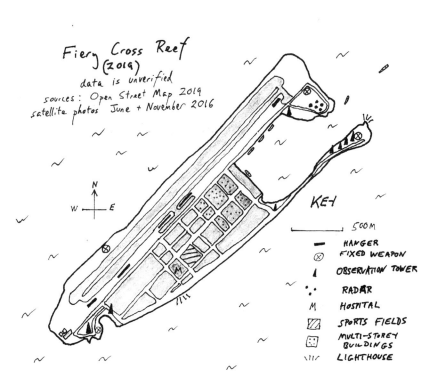

The name derives from 31 July 1855, when *Fiery Cross*, an English 'extreme' tea clipper famed for its speed, ran aground here. This part of the South China Sea is called Dangerous Ground, a reference to the number of ship-snagging reefs. With China showing no sign of accommodating its neighbours and regularly seeing off planes and fishing boats that stray near its de facto possessions, this is another newly appropriate place name.

The Chinese military strategy appears to be to establish a forward line that gives them reach over the whole of South East Asia. Taking control of the South China Sea also has economic benefits. Over $5.3 trillion worth of shipping travels through these waters every year. They contain extensive and untapped oil and gas reserves and about 12 per cent of the world's fish catch. The Spratly Islands are the aces in a high-stakes game of geopolitical poker.

The building of new military islands requires huge resources and perseverance. The first task is to find a reef that can provide stable and enduring foundations. China is not the only country that has done this in the South China Sea. Taiwan, Vietnam and Malaysia have transformed the reefs they control in the same way. Visiting them is not easy. Tourist boats from Vietnam and China do go on trips but these are patriotic missions and only open to vetted nationals of those countries. The only military Spratly Island that foreigners can visit is the one controlled by Malaysia. It is called Layang Layang and it looks like all the others: a rectangular landing strip. However, Layang Layang also has a 'diving hotel' that provides package holidays for those who want to explore what remains of the corals that surround the island.

The closest I've come to Fiery Cross Reef is looking out over the South China Sea from the palm-fringed city of Sanya, China's most southerly city. I have a local tourist map with an inset of the whole of the South China Sea. It shows a thick dotted line marking China's territorial argument and which delivers almost the entire sea to China, with little red squiggles in the centre representing the Spratlys and Paracel islands, all claimed by China.

It may seem odd that the South China Sea should be included in a local tourist map. The rest of the map is concerned with pointing out the local historic temples and surfing spots. However, tourism is not an innocent bystander in the South China Sea dispute. Pretending the islands are a tourist destination is a way of normalizing control. Flag-waving tourists are shipped out and, in 2016, China landed two commercial passenger aircraft on Fiery Cross Reef, one from China Southern Airlines and the other from Hainan Airlines.

Despite the bristling weaponry that crowds its concrete surface, a civilian presence is key to convincing the world that Fiery Cross is part of China. In 2011 China Mobile announced that residents of the Spratly Islands (of which there were, in 2011, almost none) would henceforth be enjoying full phone coverage. Fiery Cross is reported to possess a coral-restoration facility in addition to a lighthouse and a hospital. After sinking numerous bore-holes, fresh water was discovered in the vicinity, and in 2019 China's Ministry of Transport opened a maritime rescue centre on the island. The official website 'China Military Online' reports that 'fishermen who go fishing in the South China Sea can also stop on the island to find shelter or replenishment'.

The Chinese occupation of Fiery Cross did initially have non-military aims. In 1988 UNESCO asked the Chinese to build a weather observation station in the region and Fiery Cross was the chosen location. Even this was controversial. Vietnam objected and sent ships with construction materials in a bid to begin their own building work. They were seen off by the Chinese navy, one of the first skirmishes in a fractious cold war that frequently heats up.

Fiery Cross Reef reminds us that artificial islands are not just about leisure, pleasure or offshoring infrastructure; they can be key military assets. Such islands have a long history. Yet their recent history and our ability to now build them bigger, more quickly and further away from the mainland should make us wonder if international law, which gives nations with islands a hugely extended territorial range, needs to be updated. I'd argue that artificial military islands – which are weapons just as surely as the aircraft carriers they resemble – should be excluded from these generous territorial provisions. Otherwise, I fear that many other lonely reefs and shallows will be commandeered and mutilated and the seas dotted with ever more daring and ferocious forward placements.

PHOENIX ISLAND, CHINA

At seven o'clock every night a switch is flicked and Phoenix Island's pod-like towers begin pulsing with multicoloured patterns, swimming fish, exploding fireworks and scrolling celebratory messages in Chinese. Down on the sand of Sanya Bay, still warm after another sweltering day, well-mannered parties are in progress with extended families taking selfies and having picnics.

Phoenix Island has been dubbed the Oriental Dubai, though it's minuscule by comparison and will soon be overshadowed by China's newer artificial leisure and residential islands. It's just off the coast of Sanya on the island of Hainan, 'China's Hawaii', where roadsides are lined with coconut and banana trees. There are ten more artificial islands being built around Hainan's shores, including the stupendous Ocean Flower. They are all leisure and residential islands, absorbing the surplus cash made by wealthy mainland Chinese who fancy a place in the sun. South of Sanya is the South China Sea, a feverish zone of military island-building.

I'm booked into a seafront hostel on Sanya Bay with a fine view over the lozenge shape of Phoenix Island. During the day you can see that, although one half of it is complete and a hive of activity with frequent helicopter traffic, building work on the other half has ground to a halt. Sanya has a laid-back vibe. The honking of buses and scooters is incessant but punctuated by the whoops and giggles of holidaymakers, padding about in flip-flops and clasping umbrellas to keep off the sun. On my first day here, weaving through the beach crowds of a few Russians but mostly mainland Chinese, I make my way over to the bridge that crosses to Phoenix Island. It's a big moment for me. I've been planning this trip for months and spending sickening amounts of money and it all culminates here and now.

There it is: an elegant white road bridge arching across. This should be easy. But closer to it, I see there are swing barriers and half a dozen uniformed guards. I begin to walk by the barriers but I'm waved back. I have been diligent with my introductory Chinese classes but no one understands anything I say. A border official presents me with a laminated A4 sheet that reads 'The island is not open. It is open for guests.'

The next day I book a room online and am waved through. But this minor mishap tells us something. More often than not, artificial islands are not open to the public. As they proliferate so does the idea that public space – places without barriers and guards – is second best. Hainan's new islands point towards a future in which valued places exist as luxury enclaves, well away from the ordinary life of the city.

A golf buggy trundles me and a few other unsmiling residents across the bridge in dead silence past immaculate hedges blazing with azaleas and more guards, now in crisp white uniforms. The final guard, outside Tower D, snaps the driver a stern salute. The hotel is near the bottom of the tower, which shoots up from slender concrete supports. As we cram into the lifts, it is like entering a rocket ship heavy with fleeing people. The island's curving, sinuous buildings are supposed to put you in mind of the sea. The architect who designed them, Ma Yansong, told the *Hainan Daily* he wanted something that looked like it 'grew out of the sea. They should be curvy, just like coral or sea star.' But the scale is way too big for that and the whole thing points skywards. It's a place that wants to escape.

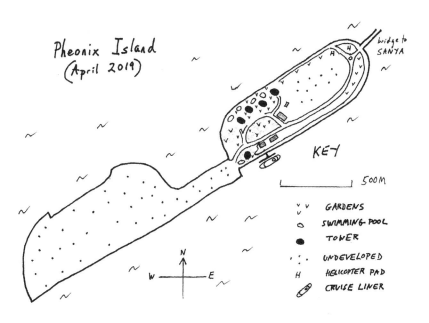

Since I've paid only £40 for my room, I am steeled for a dismal night. Instead, I'm shown into a huge apartment with its own private garden, planted with pretty flowers and inside and outside bathtubs. I flump onto the bed, slinging a friendly arm round a pile of white towels that have been skilfully folded into the shape of an elephant. My eye is caught by a cleaner, burnishing a handrail just outside this princely domain: he's moving along methodically, and when he spots a bit that isn't up to snuff, he applies himself with real energy. I head out, and pass the guard who snapped a salute earlier. He offers a broad smile, gives me a bow of welcome. As so often in China I'm having to rethink. What I took for sternness, even officiousness, was something else: a sense of pride in doing a job well. Like the guy cleaning the handrail. People here aren't just turning up for work; they are part of something: something small and particular but also spectacular and wildly ambitious. One of the most important statistics that explains China is that between 1981 and 2013 China lifted 850 million people out of poverty, with the percentage of people living in extreme poverty (living on under $1.9 a day) falling from 88 per cent to 1.85 per cent. The Chinese are proud of what they have achieved and who can blame them?

The near-disappearance of the worst kinds of poverty was accompanied by a huge increase in the number of people with enough money to afford holidays and second homes. The new wealthy are literally reshaping China, and it is their money that is fuelling Hainan's island-building boom. Pursuing a tourism- and real estate-led development strategy, the provincial government based in the capital of Haikou has been keen to welcome mainland money.

The new islands create lots of opportunities to build high-value, waterfront houses and leisure resorts. Reclaimed between 2002 and 2003, Phoenix Island opened in 2015. One of its key assets is a cruise ship terminal, offering a city-centre berth for the increasing numbers of Chinese who favour a holiday at sea. Before nightfall, I try to find out what else brings people here. There are a succession of very popular swimming pools, long tables decked out ready for an open-air barbecue, and a lot of expensive sports cars revving noisily. It doesn't take me long before I think I've seen everything. The island is set up for families and romantic getaways; the air is warm and full of contented laughter. There is plenty to enjoy here, just not for me. People look puzzled as they catch sight of me – a lone male and the only Western person, it seems, on the island. I try to look purposeful, walking quickly, pretending that I have someone to meet; I stare at the blank screen of my phone, hiding. All this empty performance is made emptier by China's 'Great Firewall', which means that all my apps and servers, from WhatsApp to Google, are blocked. Burning with self-consciousness, I settle down poolside next to splashing families, and tinker with the notes I made in Hainan's capital, Haikou, where I spent last week.

In the sprawling, dusty city of Haikou I stayed in the tallest hotel because I thought it would give me a view of two incomplete artificial islands anchored just offshore. The nearest is called Huludao, meaning 'gourd island', and has bulbous ends and a thin midriff. The low trees that have begun to colonize its scrub reveal that building work has not been continuous. China's new islands are plagued by stop-and-start construction. It's not just a Chinese problem. Expensive, complex projects like island-building are vulnerable: economic conditions change; a contractor goes bust; one level of government gets cold feet and everything is put on hold. The busy circle of boats around Huludao suggests it may be soon back in business. The master plan for the island shows swirling, sail-shaped buildings and a huge central tower that will feature 'ultra-star hotels'.

China's islands often inscribe Chinese culture into the sea. Just along the coast is Nanhai Pearl Island, shaped into a yin-yang symbol. The 'yin' half is to be a residential complex and the 'yang' a marina. On the other side of town is Ruyi Island. (A *ruyi* is a curved ceremonial baton, an ancient motif in Chinese art.) This is the most ambitious of Haikou's new islands: 4.5 kilometres from the shore, covering 716 hectares (more than twice the size of New York's Central Park) and divided up into six entertainment, wharf and residential districts. Finally, there is Millennium Hotel Island. The plans show a small island with a colossal 'seven star' hotel planted in the middle. When these are all finished Haikou will have a jaw-dropping skyline: big, brash and in the sea. Scott Myklebust, an architect working in Hainan since 2005, told CNN 'The market has been an arms race to develop the next most interesting or extreme project.'

Even the terms for the hotels to be built – 'ultra-star' and 'seven star' – are extreme. What do they mean? Opulence and 'high end' are the mantras of all these islands catering for and, supposedly, creating wealth. No one seems to doubt that there will be enough rich people to fill them. Luxury may be the common denominator but it's getting ever more bizarre. An insatiable expectation of excess has been set in motion, in which ultimately nothing can ever be good enough. Usually I stay in cheap rentals but in Haikou I'm in a Hilton and I'm finding its attempts at luxury a little overwhelming. My room has more than forty lights and light-switches and I can't work out how to turn on any one particular light. The toilet is run on so many sensors that it is on the verge of sentience; I have no control over the lid or the flush because it lifts and flushes when it thinks it is appropriate to do so. I lie in the dark, waiting for the toilet to make a decision.

Escaping my luxury room for the hotel's luxury lobby on the thirty-sixth floor, I've arranged to meet a tourism expert, Dr Fu from Hainan University. He is a young man with a ready laugh, and I like him immediately. I can tell he is not a big fan of Huludao, which is disappearing in the mist below us. 'It creates trash problems on our coast because it is so close,' he says. 'The water quality is very bad and the island makes it worse and stagnant.' He adds: 'The Hainanese are crazy for artificial islands. They want to be like Dubai. Some people say Dubai is very successful.'

Dr Fu explains the bonanza of new islands in starkly economic terms: 'The major industry in Hainan is real estate.' You might think building islands was an expensive way of selling property but, in fact, because the price of urban land is so high, it works out to be a cheap option. It can be ten times more expensive to buy land onshore than to build in the sea. Moreover, in China all city land is owned by the state. This also explains why entrepreneurs are tempted to go offshore. The sea is open to unfettered capitalism in a way other places are not.

Later Dr Fu treats me to a hot-pot lunch. While we are slipping slices of bamboo and jellied duck blood into a simmering cauldron, he talks about the place of islands in Chinese culture, especially in Chinese mythology. Islands were the home of the gods and associated with long life, and were felt to be auspicious. Moving up to date, he gets his smartphone out and shows me clips filmed by a friend who lives opposite the Ocean Flower, which is nearing completion on the west coast of Hainan. It looks like a fully formed high-rise city. From above, the Ocean Flower reveals itself as another Chinese cultural inscription in the sea. It is shaped like a lotus with scrolling leaves, the lotus being a symbol of honesty and purity in Chinese Buddhism.

The opening frame of the Ocean Flower developer's promotional film is a computer graphic but it gives a sense of the scale of the project. The words translate as 'Sea Flower Island. Filmed March 2019'. Canyons of apartment blocks dominate the Ocean Flower's 'leaves' while the lotus itself is a collection of fantasy architectures: there are European-style castles and churches sitting beside grandiose hotels and amusement parks. This is one of the world's most ambitious building projects, about 1.5 times the size of Palm Jumeirah. When complete it will have twenty-eight museums, fifty-eight hotels, seven 'folklore performance squares' and the world's largest conference centre. However, Dr Fu tells me that building work has come to a halt. The central government is unhappy. I'm curious to find out why.

Next day, I make my way over to the university campus to talk to some more experts. You don't have to wander far into Haikou's steaming lines of bumper-to-bumper traffic to see why people might prefer to live on one of the new islands. Aside from the scooters, which come at you from all angles, the driving style is patient but the roads are so packed that accidents abound. Haikou is, indeed, going the way of Dubai: a city of fantastical air-conditioned architecture where no one walks. Ironically, the two professors, Dr Xiong and Dr Li – stylish young women with polished

English – explain that in China Hainan is a byword for tranquillity and calm: 'My shoes are dirty after one day in Beijing but here it's a week.' We are talking in a busy, off-campus juice bar and they are eyeing me with amused concern because Dr Li has given me a lift to our rendezvous on the back of her scooter and it was more fun for her than it was for me. 'You seem afraid of my "*scooter*",' she chuckles, rolling the word like a delicious marble as I mop the sweat from my upper lip.

Trying to seize back my lost dignity, I ask about push-back on all the island-building. They tell me that 'there is no environmental movement here'. This despite the fact they personally would never live on any of the new islands because they are 'dangerous with land subsidence'. The push-back is coming from the top. I hear the same story again: 'The government has stopped those islands.'

Eleven new islands are being built round Hainan. I've mentioned six so far, the remaining five are all leisure islands of similar type, the most unusual being 'Sun Moon Bay'. Sun Moon Bay is already built and consists of one island shaped as the moon and one as the sun. An official news agency promises it will be 'high-end atmosphere grade, similar to the well-known Dubai World Island'. 'High-end' and 'Dubai' – these are the magic words for Hainan's developers. So what's gone wrong? The central government in Beijing has, it seems, been raining on the developers' parade and in 2018 it started cracking down on private reclamation projects all over China, citing a lack of environmental assessments and 'proper permits'. The new islands were said to be creating coastal erosion, silting up rivers and damaging ecosystems. According to the Xinhua News Agency and ChinaDaily.com, developers have been ordered to 'restore the environmental damage they have caused' and 'fulfil environmental restoration work as soon as possible'. Nearly all the island projects around Hainan have been officially suspended and 'ordered to carry out environmental impact assessments'. It's not just the developers who are in the dock. In fact, the main target may be local politicians: 'government officials who were found to have violated the law in those cases will be punished'.

I suspect this story isn't just about Beijing's new-found enthusiasm for environmental protection. It's also about cutting developers and provincial politicians down to size. Reining in confident and wilful regions is something the central government does a lot. Yet there is a momentum to Hainan's new islands that won't be halted. It's too late for that. The official slapping-down from Beijing is a temporary set-back, nothing more. The party on Phoenix Island is already in full swing and Hainan's other islands are not far from completion. China is building big – on a scale never seen before.

Back home in Newcastle, I tell people where I've been: Hainan, Sanya, Haikou. 'Where?' No one has heard of them. They will soon.

OCEAN REEF, PANAMA

Ocean Reef is a pair of Dutch-designed artificial islands that jut out from Punta Pacifica, a high-rent and high-rise neighbourhood in Panama City. It is an ultra-secure retreat for Panama's wealthiest families. Joined to the mainland by a permanently guarded causeway, Ocean Reef is not just gated, it is locked down: it has its own marine security force and is surrounded by underwater sensors that pick up anything or anybody over 40 kilos. 'Yes, it is like James Bond,' chuckles James, the affable Scottish-Nicaraguan real estate agent who is showing me round. (It turns out that James's father came to Central America from Glasgow to mine for gold.) The army of service workers that keep the place ticking over have a dedicated tunnel discreetly positioned at the entrance of 'Isla I'. Once below ground, they swap over to electric vehicles, keeping the islands quiet and free of car fumes. Anyone who has been to Panama City will know just how precious that is.

This is my first time here. The sleepless flight from Amsterdam banks down over the Panama Canal and then swings in front of finger-thin skyscrapers that form a crenulated silver wall stacked up against the blue bay. Ocean Reef is already visible, a pincer shape snapping out from the vertiginous glass and concrete shore. Slogans from its website are playing in my head: 'Live an island lifestyle within the city'; 'As we evolve, our homes should too'; 'The first man made urban islands in Latin America'. Even from this height you can tell it's something special. You'd have to be well off to live in one of those extravagant shoreline towers. But there's rich and there's *rich*. Ocean Reef – low-rise, separate, secure – caters for the latter.

I'm arriving in late October 2018 and, though the islands are built, many of the surface features have yet to be put in place. Soon the open water between the two islands will cradle a 200-slip marina designed to accommodate vessels up to 90 metres (300 feet) in length. At that size so-called 'yachts' are more like small ships. But it's not the size of the boats, nor the multi-million-dollar price tag of the apartments, that informs you this is a place apart. Far more telling is the fact that Panama's constitution, which forbids marine estate being sold for private use, was controversially waived on a one-off basis to allow Ocean Reef to be built. Panama's elite have had this place constructed for themselves and they have made sure that no rival islands are ever going to spring up next door to spoil the view.

Panama is the bridge of the Americas and provides a stark divide: on the Pacific side artificial islands are being magicked up for millionaires while, 70 kilometres to the east, subsistence farmers are watching their ancestral islands disappear beneath the waves.

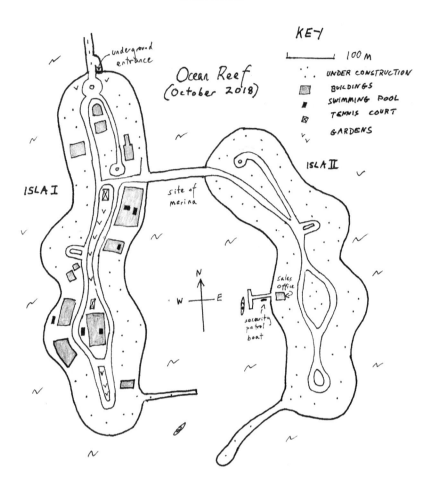

A little smaller than Scotland and just as hilly, Panama is a raw and intoxicating country. Per capita, it's the richest nation in Latin America – far wealthier than any of its neighbours. Yet outside a few pockets, it looks poor. Its capital is claimed to be one of the most ritzy and cosmopolitan cities on the continent, but it's not far from thick jungle and most of the city remains off-limits to tourists. Once you get off the Pan-American highway, driving anywhere in Panama is a trial of potholes and scrub roads. I have, however, been disabused of one popular myth: the Pan-American highway comes to an abrupt halt before Panama's legendary Darién Gap *not* because of impenetrable terrain or wild tribes but due to a long-standing feud with Colombia, the country Panama separated from in 1903.

Thankfully, for once I'm not on my own. My partner Rachel has travelled with me and is able to hold forth while I take a back seat – such as now, when sitting in a bar in Panama City's colonial old town, as we are joined by a talkative local. Dorset-born and covered with tattoos of English punk bands, he works for the minister of tourism and is delighted to find some fellow Brits to while away a couple of hours. He and Rachel are having a great time and, jet-lagged and dozy, all I have to do is offer an occasional encouraging smile. I do perk up on hearing a familiar mantra: 'Don't leave the cobbles.' The cobbles are the road surface you find in the heart of the old town, and it seems tourists are asking for trouble if they stray beyond them. It's a tall order as 99 per cent of the city is beyond the cobbles, but it's also a serious bit of advice. A few hours earlier, we were wandering 4 or 5 metres off the main drag when a young woman in a white pick-up pulled over and leaned out to give us the same warning: 'It's not always safe in those alleys,' she smiled.

Fears about safety guide our footsteps and shape the city. If we had wandered a bit further we'd be in El Chorrillo, a ramshackle, densely packed neighbourhood that was once home to General Manuel Noriega, the drug baron and de facto ruler of Panama in the 1980s. The USA invaded Panama in December 1989 in order to oust him. In the first thirteen hours of the invasion US planes dropped 422 bombs, a lot of them on El Chorrillo. Casualties are still not known but the figure is usually put at about 7000.

The invasion is still a sore point in Panama but, as in many small countries, hostility to the regional superpower is a luxury few can afford and, in the end, security is what counts. We all try to live in islands of safety. Some of us can turn that metaphor into a reality. Drive across the Ocean Reef causeway and the tension, the nagging anxiety, of living in a dangerous city melts away.

The construction of Ocean Reef was thorough. The seabed was scraped down to the bedrock and barges full of rock from the mainland were piled up in the water, then sprayed with sand. There were going to be three islands, each named after one of Columbus's ships: *Niña*, *Pinta* and *Santa Maria*. But in the end the Dutch designers recommended that two would create a more durable shape. Today they go by the prosaic names of Isla I and Isla II. Each is an organic bulging loop, with the second and further island curling just enough around the first to create a protected anchorage.

The residential plots were quickly sold and the first foundation stone was formally laid in 2010 with much fanfare. *La Estrella de Panamá* newspaper reported that 'It was a gala where the cream of society met together with important figures of the current administration' including President Ricardo Martinelli. 'In the front row were entrepreneurs,' *La Estrella* continued, 'accompanied by the Minister of Economy, Alberto Vallarino, who among light music, caviar, wines and champagne celebrated the start of the project dubbed the "Dubai of the Americas".'

The words 'exclusivity' and 'luxury' are front and centre in Ocean Reef's promotional bumf, often followed by 'tranquil' and 'private':

> Ocean Reef residents are only those who enjoy the finer things in life, for them quality is not a desire, it is a reality. With this person in mind, Ocean Reef Islands have been created. Being a member of the Ocean Reef community is a privilege. Ocean Reef will be the only place in the city where you can engage in a true island experience – tranquil, private.

The Ocean Reef website rhapsodizes in English and Spanish that 'Exclusivity and Luxury have never been so obvious in any development' while also reminding likely buyers that this is not going to be a mere resort, populated by renters and blow-ins; the properties are freehold and the buyers are nearly all Panamanian. The implication is that they will be passed down through the generations. I was told that few, if any, properties will come back on the market again.

The promotional spiel goes on to talk about the islands as an 'unspoiled refuge' set in the 'midst of timeless natural splendor'. The idea that artificial islands give access to 'nature' is a paradox I keep bumping into. When you arrive on urban exclaves, like Ocean Reef, it's easier to understand. After negotiating the rubbish-filled streets and the built-up canyons on the mainland, on Ocean Reef you can at last see the sky and stare out to sea. You can also walk on the ground. Contact with the earth is an unregarded part of our relationship with nature, but in high-rise, traffic-clogged cities it is an increasingly rare thing. To be able to walk out to see a neighbour – not in some air-conditioned tube but simply round the corner – is the kind of simple pleasure that islands like Ocean Reef allow and put a high price on.

There is another and even more rarely voiced kind of exclusivity at work in Ocean Reef, which has to do with Panama's relationship to race. Panamanians like to claim that theirs is an inclusive, colour-blind country. It isn't. The Ocean Reef publicity shots show exclusively young and good-looking white people relishing its pleasures. They mirror a wider prejudice: every billboard, every TV advert displays nothing but white people. That's striking because Panama is a very diverse country where nearly three-quarters of people are mestizo (mixed). Twelve per cent are indigenous and there is also a large black population, many of whom descend from Caribbean workers brought over to dig the canal. As a rule of thumb, the richer the neighbourhood the whiter-looking the inhabitants. Some words of caution, however: this doesn't mean that Ocean Reef is just for whites; it isn't. Or that 'gringos' – a term applied to all foreign whites these days – are part of the club; they aren't. Panama's racial dynamics are complicated but also stark. The flight to live in secure compounds like Ocean Reef has racial baggage: it's a flight away towards the safety of something not exactly white, but certainly whiter.

Visiting Ocean Reef is not straightforward. You can't just wander up. I know that for a fact, as I tried it. I walked under the entrance arch – adorned with the slogan 'A lifestyle change begins with a vision and a single step' – onto the pristine causeway lined with palm trees. Adopting the brisk 'I know where I'm going' stride that has ended in humiliation many times before, I strode past the guarded booth and the barrier arm. Perhaps I was trying to deploy some white privilege. If so the guard wasn't impressed. He stepped out and called me back, finger-wagging and repeating 'Imposible, imposible, imposible.'

Thankfully, I have a Plan B: an appointment with James the real estate agent in his offices in Punta Pacifica. I really didn't know how I'd ever get my foot in the door of Ocean Reef and so I emailed him under the pretence that I was 'interested' in buying an apartment. It is a lie that starts to come under pressure even before I arrive. Rachel has agreed to come with me and is bringing with her an ethical agenda I was hoping to avoid: 'I'm not pretending to be buying anything; that would be ridiculous.' The atmosphere in the taxi on our way across town was tense.

We are ushered into a plush back room. Everything is clad in black leather, photos of the local 'Trump Tower' decorate the walls, and beads of sweat are pricking my forehead. I run through a few scenarios – 'We'll need to know what you can afford, señor' – and a lot of them don't end well. A well-built, smartly suited and roughly handsome man joins us, clearly in charge. James is smiling warmly and my butterflies take a rest. He knows – he always knew – that I was not a client. I guess he is intrigued and keen to show off Ocean Reef.

We chat about the 'sinking' islands on the Atlantic side of the country and he readily admits that people in Panama are not that interested in sea-level rise or in climate change more generally. 'Perhaps they should be,' he muses. In this part of the world, the environmental disaster that matters is earthquakes. James opens out the colourful master-plan document of Ocean Reef and explains how computer modellers subjected the islands to 14,000 earthquake simulations. It is built to withstand anything the Ring of Fire can throw at them, which also helps explain why, rising to over 9 metres, Ocean Reef has the highest ground on the seafront.

Faced with James's friendliness, I am disarmed; more than that I'm eager, laughing and agreeing with everything he says. Rachel casts me a quizzical look; 'I was wondering how low you could go,' she tells me later. We climb into James's superior four-wheel drive, the barrier swings high, and our stately progress is met with a series of greetings and nods from roadside workers. Once on foot, the waves and greetings continue. They are all from receptionists and service workers since only twelve families have so far moved across. Isla I is not finished and Isla II (apart from the main sales building) is bare land. We take a lift onto a series of connected roof terraces and I become aware of piped music drifting through the warm air. We wander past infinity pools. I make appreciative noises, though I'm more interested in the odder sights, such as the walls plastered with plastic green foliage and a rooftop 'pitch and putt'.

The sky is overcast and threatening rain and I realize I'd better take a few photographs before it starts pouring. (It rains a lot in Panama: two and a half times more than in Britain.) I snap one of Isla II, mostly undeveloped and connected to Isla I by the bridge that will form the apex of the marina. To its left the high towers of Punta Pacifica rise in the distance, including the distinctive arc of the JW Marriott hotel (formerly 'Trump International Hotel and Tower'), foregrounded by the palms and low-density, low-rise homes of Isla I.

Back in the car, as we roll past a well-equipped and pristine children's playground, the conversation turns to the island's family ethos. James will bring his own young family to live here when the island is complete, and he has no doubt that Ocean Reef will function as a real community. It seems likely, since a lot of the families – there will be 400 in total – who will come here already know each other. It's 'selling to friends', says James.

To keep the community cogs turning, a $1000 monthly service fee buys residents into the 'island app', which is used to book gym or restaurant time and access other facilities. We drive over the bridge that leads to Isla II and park up by the sales centre. I've become nervous again: do I have to pretend to be 'interested'? However friendly and forgiving James might be, I feel like a fraud. If I sold everything I own I couldn't afford half the price of the cheapest apartment here. Yet here I am, swanning around, pretending I'm used to this sort of thing. I amuse myself with the melancholy thought that this sums up a lot of what I do. It's certainly par for the course when visiting artificial islands. As Rachel and James chat away, I try to make myself inconspicuous, taking a studious interest in various glass-boxed models that exhibit the master plan, the marina and different apartment blocks where tiny people dash about in bright casuals.

One of those tiny people could be me – waving to friends, popular at the waterfront … My reverie is broken: James has one final sight to show us. We walk out to a pontoon where Ocean Reef's security patrol boat is moored and take in the spectacular view. Punta Pacifica rises vertically to one side and on the other are the dark humps of the Pearl Islands, an archipelago that lies 50 kilometres or so out in Panama Bay. It is incredible: utterly urban yet so far away from the stress of the honking metropolis.

Next day, back in the city, a yellow taxi pulls up and we begin negotiating, trying to get somewhere we want for a price that seems fair. It's the usual thing with cabs in Panama City and it's an unpredictable process. This morning's journey is a success. It takes us round El Chorrillo, past street corners where men are making sugar-cane drink from ancient crushing machines, and past parties of Kuna women recognizable in their bright shawls and leg bangles. Our destination is a hill that overlooks both canal and city, on the top of which flaps the world's largest Panamanian flag. At one point a man calls us back and jabs his finger up: we have just walked under a branch on which a fat boa constrictor is looped, sleeping off its last meal.

At the crest of the hill a huge panorama opens out. On one side rows and columns of colourful cargo containers stand waiting for loading by the Panama Canal; on the other is the drama of Panama City. And there's Ocean Reef, reaching out into the sea – part of the city and yet free from the city, in it but not of it.

Natural, Overlooked and Accidental: Other New Islands

Natural

HUMANS BUILD VERY small, flat islands. The planet is engaged in larger construction projects: such as colliding the 103 million square kilometres of the Pacific plate into the 47 million square kilometres of the Australian plate. The former is being shoved under the latter, where it heats and melts, lava bursting to the surface to create mountainous islands. The most spectacular natural island to emerge in recent years was one of them: Hunga-Tonga.

As we worry and wonder at what people are doing to the planet, it's easy to forget that, in geological terms, we are not that big a deal. Imagine you are trekking towards a great mountain. It's looming ahead, a dark immensity. As you begin climbing you stare down in horror to find your boots are bustling with ants. Gazing about, you realize the whole mountain is covered with their trails: everywhere they are shifting and shovelling, creating huge farms and eating away at the vegetation, amassing anthills dark with tens of millions of insects. It seems odd to anyone gazing on the great mountain from any distance, but the ants think of themselves as the centre of creation: that this mountain – everything – is all about them. But being clever creatures, they have collected data and know for sure that it is, indeed, the 'era of the ant'.

Today geologists talk about a new geological era defined by human impact on the planet – the Anthropocene – though they cannot agree when it started (some say with industrialization; others believe with the first dusting of nuclear radioactivity). It's plausible: human activity *has* transformed the planet's climate and landscapes. According to Owen Gaffney of the Stockholm Resilience Centre, 'we move more sediment and rock annually than all natural process such as erosion and rivers combined'. But defining the planet around us may not be so bright. It implies that if we screw things up we can click our fingers, do something clever, and fix it again. It is necessary to be reminded, time and again, that we are dependants on rather than masters of Earth and that, even as we harm it, the planet keeps on turning and will continue to do so well after the last of us is not even a memory. And whatever we do, the Earth will continue to make islands.

Natural new islands are produced in two main ways: through volcanic activity and through changes in sea and land levels. The latter may create the most islands but the drama, beauty and headlong pace of the former is intoxicating.

The Earth is divided up, to a depth of between 15 and 200 kilometres, by seven major plates and an awkward bunch of microplates. The continents and oceans sit on these plates. They are a shifting, buckling jigsaw and they are very hot. Recent research has shown that the Earth's core is about the same temperature as the Sun. Heat energy melts the outer core (the inner core is now thought to be solid) and drives the motion of the plates. Islands are formed both where plates crash together and where they are ripping away from each other.

The Atlantic is being zipped open by a mid-ocean rift and has about twenty active volcanoes, all of which are building undersea mountains (called seamounts). The largest island created so far by this process is Iceland. The highly active nature of volcanism in and around Iceland – most famously the creation of Surtsey in 1963 – suggests something else may be going on. It turns out that Iceland is not just on a volcanic rift but sits above a 'hot spot'. Sometimes called 'anomalous volcanism', hot spots can occur anywhere and are often found well away from plate boundaries. Why magma spews up at them is still not known. The most famous hot spot is under Hawaii (other examples are Cape Verde and Galapagos), a highly volcanic island chain that is thousands of kilometres from the nearest plate boundary. In 2018 the Kīlauea volcano on Hawaii's Big Island, which has been erupting almost continuously for over three decades, flung up a new islet. It caught people by surprise. Such islands always do. We don't know the when, where or entirely why of hot-spot volcanism. What we do know is that hot spots are not fixed in place, that they rove around, and that they are not single sites but extensive. Like most volcanic islands, Hawaii is the visible part of a long chain of undersea volcanic seamounts. The 'Hawaii chain' is 5800 kilometres long and includes hundreds of undersea mountains. Some are rising but others are eroding, submerged islands that came and went long before humans were about to tell the tale.

Swim west of Hawaii, and keep going for some 5000 kilometres, and you will arrive at one of the most active zones of island production: the crunch point between the Pacific and Australian plates. It is a complicated place: in between the big plates a number of geological oddities – microplates – shove and butt up against each other. The Tonga microplate is the world's fastest, moving at speeds of up to 24 centimetres per year. Here we find the newly risen Hunga Tonga. It's not clear how long it will last; volcanic islands come and go. Another Tongan ephemeral island is Home Reef, which came into existence and disappeared again soon after volcanic eruptions in 1852, 1857, 1984 and 2006.

There are many volcanoes bubbling under Tongan waters as well as the world's second-deepest canyon. Volcanic islands often form alongside long trenches, creating the classic island arcs seen in the Pacific and Caribbean. The deepest point of the Tonga Trench, 'Horizon Deep' is 10,800 metres below sea level (for comparison, Mount Everest is 8848 metres high). Horizon Deep is only 100 metres higher than the world's most famous plate boundary abyss: the Mariana Trench's 'Challenger Deep', formed in the north Pacific and the deepest place on the planet. The best known of the volcanic islands near the Mariana Trench is Nishinoshima, which – after eruptions in 1974, 2013 and 2017 – is now nearly 3 square kilometres in size.

The most surprising form of 'volcanic island' is the floating one. One of the types of rock produced by undersea lava streams is pumice. It's so light that it floats, creating 'pumice rafts'. The largest pumice raft ever recorded was spotted in the South Pacific by the Royal New Zealand Air Force in 2012, 1000 kilometres off the Auckland coast, spread over an area of 25,900 square kilometres – or 'nearly the size of Belgium', as the New Zealand press described it. Pumice-raft islands soon drift apart but it has been speculated that animals and plants may sometimes hitch a lift and hence colonize new shores.

Island-building is often a combined effort. In the warm waters of the tropics many 'volcanic islands' are actually old, worn-down volcanoes built up by coral, an industrious animal that also creates offshore reefs. Coral can accumulate to considerable depths, being well over a kilometre thick on some Pacific islands. Another reason why 'coral islands' appear is that the weight of nearby volcanoes pushes them up. When you stomp down on a surface, you'll see the area around the impact rise up. It is the same with the Earth. Such pushed-up reefs are called 'makatea islands', named after the Tahitian island of Makatea, an ancient reef that the weight of nearby rising volcanoes has caused to lift up out of the water.

Yet most new islands are created not by volcanic activity but by changes in the level of the land and the sea or by the way waves and wind shift shorelines. Islands created in this way are so common and usually so short-lived that they are rarely named or inhabited. Most are the result of deposition: sediment rushed along rivers often creates new islands in slow-moving stretches of water or out to sea. Others can emerge over just a few days: sand-bar islands shunted into place by waves and storms. Inland, long periods of drought may give birth to another species: drying lakes usually reveal a mottled flock of brown, dowdy islands.

Sea levels have risen and fallen for millions of years, creating and destroying millions of islands. If sea level continues to rise at the rate it is currently projected, then we will see the break-up of coastal areas, such as the eastern states of the USA, as well as the fragmentation of islands created by ancient sea-level rise, such as Britain, into archipelagos.

We are currently in an 'interglacial' or warm period of the Earth's climate, a period that started some 11,700 years ago. The ice retreat and the flooding that we are seeing today compounds an existing, natural process with an unnatural, modern one. Artificially accelerated global warming is already producing many new islands, though they rarely make the headlines. On Russia's long north coast, a group of nine islands in the Novaya Zemlya and Franz Josef Land archipelagos were added to the map in 2015 by the Military Topographic Directorate; almost every year more are added. They have emerged thanks to retreating glaciers and melting sheet ice. The biggest of the new islands is 2 kilometres long and 600 kilometres wide. It is predicted that ice retreat will soon reveal that Spitsbergen, the largest island in the Norwegian archipelago of Svalbard, is not one but two islands, with open water separating the island from what was thought to be the peninsula of Sørkappland. Already, in the west, ice melt has revealed that Spitsbergen's 'Flower beach peninsula' – or Blomstrandhalvøya – is an island; it has been renamed Blomstrandhalvøya Island.

Islands created by melting ice are appearing very fast. Those caused by the land rising are much slower affairs. Around twenty thousand years ago ice sheets covered much of northern Europe and North America. The weight of all that ice pushed the Earth's crust down by up to half a kilometre. Now that much of this ice is gone, the Earth is readjusting itself; it is bouncing back. At the present rate, in two thousand years or so the Gulf of Bothnia, which separates Finland and Sweden, will close up in the middle, turning its northern arm into a lake. The Kvarken Archipelago, which lies halfway down the Gulf, is the most spectacular example of 'rebounding' land. It is made up of 6550 low islands and counting. After new land first emerges, it takes about fifty years for it to grow large enough and to dry out enough to become usable for house-building.

Although uplift creates islands, in the long run it leads to their disappearance. As the water drains away, archipelagos are turned into hilly landscapes. Off the coast of Juneau – in Alaska, and today connected to it by a long bridge – is Douglas Island. This island is steadily joining the mainland; the channel between it and Juneau is silting up. One day Douglas Island will be an island no more. When that day will be is getting harder to judge because of the way global warming and rising sea levels have complicated things. At the moment it is predicted that the phenomenon of new land creation in the far north will continue but at a slower rate.

Overlooked

In 2015 it was revealed that Estonia had 2355 islands rather than 1521, as previously thought. In 2016 the Philippine national mapping agency revised the total of islands that make up the archipelago, adding 534 to the previous tally of 7107. These aren't literally 'new islands'. In part, what is happening is that satellites and aerial photography are showing a much fuller and more detailed picture than we have ever had so that overlooked islands are being added to the map. It's also true that national mapping agencies the world over are getting keener to identify and claim as many islands as possible.

Estonia has lots of rocky islands in the Baltic Sea, the great majority of which are uninhabited. Some of its new islands are likely to be the result of glacial rebound, but most are the product of politics not nature. A small country in the far north-west of what was formerly the USSR, Estonia was once a very minor part of a huge empire and Soviet cartographers did not make detailing its shores their life's work. With Estonia's independence in 1991, a more scrupulous approach began to be taken to the national map. Since countries can claim a 200 nautical miles 'exclusive economic zone' around their islands, the incentive to bag new ones is considerable. That the new islands are sources of national pride was driven home by Estonian Public Broadcasting, whose report on the story concluded with the sardonic observation that it will 'come as a further blow to neighbouring Latvia, which has a famously low number of islands, officially at one, and that too is man-made'.

Only 318 of Estonia's islands are larger than 10,000 square metres, which begs the question: how small can an island be before we stop counting it as an island? The Filipino cartographers adopted the sensible idea that an island has two essential features: some part of it must be above high tide, and it must be able to support either plant or animal life. They need to visit their new discoveries in order to provide 'ground validation' of these two points. But does every stone jutting up from the sea at high tide count as a separate island? The requirement that an island sustains life points towards Article 121 of the United Nations Convention on the Law of the Sea. Here it is stipulated that 'rocks which cannot sustain human habitation or economic life of their own' might be islands, but 'shall have no exclusive economic zone'. Yet few islands today 'sustain human habitation or economic life' on their own, while almost every rock can be found to support some kind of life.

If you ask how many islands are in the British Isles (the main islands of which are Britain and Ireland), the number you will get will vary enormously. One recent definition came from a retired marine surveyor called Brian Adams, who suggested that an island is at least half an acre. If this is the case, then there are 4400 (210 of which, Adams says, are inhabited). However, if you go to Wikipedia you'll find that there are 'over six thousand' and that 136 are inhabited. The wrangle over how many islands are in the Minquiers and Écréhous reefs (which lie, respectively, south and north of the English Channel island of Jersey) are a lesson in how tiresome island-counting can become. These reefs have long been claimed by France but they have a huge daily tidal range and what is permanently above water varies from season to season, year to year. It took thirteen years of talks between France and Britain to arrive at an agreed demarcation. One Jersey politician involved in the negotiations described it as literally counting the Minquiers and Écréhous 'rock by rock'. The border agreement came into force on 1 January 2004. It was only then that the boundary between France and Britain was finally fixed.

The hope that all our planet's islands can be counted finally and irrevocably falls apart in Russia and Canada. You can get a sense as to why from the name of the eastern shore of Georgian Bay, which is just one arm of Lake Huron: Thirty Thousand Islands. That is a rough estimate of the number of islands that dot this low-lying, pine-clad part of Ontario. It is the world's largest freshwater archipelago, but it is also a big clue that trying to count all the world's islands may be a fool's errand.

Accidental

Many of the islands created by human activity were neither designed nor foreseen. They occur as an accidental consequence of quarrying, mining, dredging, reservoir-building or chucking waste into the seas. Pebble Lake in Hungary, where tiny islets crowded with holiday homes are surrounded by the cold waters of a flooded quarry, and the Trash Isles, are examples of accidental islands.

The fugitive island of New Moore helps us think about what 'accidental' means. New Moore emerged a few kilometres out to sea in the Bay of Bengal after Cyclone Bhola in 1970. Created on the border between Bangladesh and India and coveted by both, it looked for a while like New Moore would be a battleground. The Indians stationed troops on the island in 1981 and ran up the Indian flag. The conflict never came, however, largely because New Moore began to disappear; by March 2010 it was fully submerged. Many interpreted this story as a faintly absurd example of people squabbling over something that nature had created then destroyed.

River sediment creates islands, and natural land subsidence is gradually lowering the land under and around the Bay of Bengal. But sea-level rise and river sediment is also being affected by human activity. Road-building upstream contributed to New Moore's creation by triggering landslides that added sediment to the river. Deforestation across the region, especially the felling of mangrove trees, is also changing the coastline, denuding them of protection and stability and making it more likely that islands are created far out to sea.

New Moore was an accidental island but it was also a product of nature. The story of its short life shows us that, for many of the new islands that suddenly appear on the shores of our crowded continents, untangling what is natural and unnatural has become impossible.

HUNGA TONGA-HUNGA HAʻAPAI, TONGA

Over the last 150 years there have been only three vol-canic islands of any size that have sprung from the sea and survived more than a few months. One is Anak Krakatau ('Child of Krakatoa'), which had been growing since 1927 between Sumatra and Java until, in December 2018, an erup-tion caused two-thirds of the island to shear off into the sea. The second is Surtsey, south of Iceland. The third, since December 2014, is Hunga Tonga-Hunga Haʻapai.

In their early phase, volcanic islands don't just rise, they *writhe*; shorelines and hillsides spasm and flex with every passing week. There is an awful struggle to be born that is accompanied by shrieks and subterranean booms. Hunga Tonga-Hunga Haʻapai lies on the western fringe of the Pacific archipelago of Tonga, an ancient kingdom that comprises 169 small islands and sits just west of the interna-tional dateline. Tonga straddles a western arm of the Pacific Ring of Fire, one of the world's most volcanically lively and earthquake-prone tectonic collision zones.

On 19 December 2014 an undersea eruption began 45 kilometres north of the Tongan capital, Nukuʻalofa. Early in the new year of 2015 a new volcanic island was sighted. Today the island is about 2 kilometres square and looks something like a fat bat, with two rocky wings and a pen-dulous belly in which reposes a round crater lake. The wings of the bat are two pre-existing, remote, uninhabited and (for the Tongans) famously earthquake-prone islands: Hunga Tonga to the east and Hunga Ha'apai to the west. The first signs of the new island formed in the sea between these two protecting arms. Eventually it grew so large that it sprawled over and connected them up. It still has no official name, though the scientific community has taken to labelling it Hunga Tonga-Hunga Ha'apai.

I'm cocooned up in a beachside bungalow in Nuku'alofa with the first person to land on Hunga Tonga-Hunga Ha'apai, the fabulously tattooed and sinewy Pacific mariner and rum distiller, Branko Sugar. Outside, a warm wind is making the long hard leaves of the coconut and palm trees clack: Cyclone Keni is on its way, arriving just a few months after Cyclone Gita tore roofs off across the country.

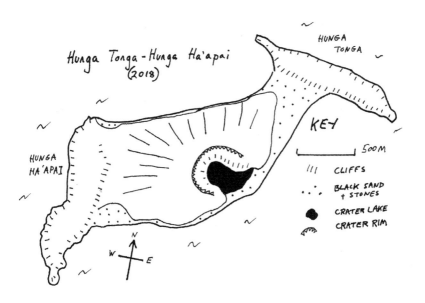

I've been told there will be a short lull, a window of maybe twenty-four hours or so, in which it will be safe to sail to the world's newest volcanic island. That's tomorrow. For the time being I'm happy to be held captive by Branko's stories about what we can expect when we arrive on what he calls 'Hunga Tonga' (this is the name Hunga Tonga-Hunga Ha'apai goes by in Tonga so, from now on, I'll use it too).

The way Branko tells it, Hunga Tonga is a prismatic and strange place and not as terrifying as I'd feared. His voice carries many journeys: a strongly flavoured, fifty-eight-year-old, Croatian-Italian-Swedish-Tongan brew. 'We were the first to come there,' he tells me. 'When we came back I got phone calls from New York, ABC, NBC and god knows what. I freak out and just hung up the phone.'

Branko begins to explain, not for the first time, that to get onto Hunga Tonga we'll have to moor 10 metres offshore and swim the rest of the way. He turns a wary, weather-wrinkled eye my way and is clearly wondering if I'm even capable of getting off the sofa. Unsure how to prove my athleticism, I proudly show off the little Tupperware tub that, for weeks now, I have practised cramming with my essentials (phone, camera, water bottle) and will loop round my waist: just so!

'Yeah, sure. Fine, fine.' This is not a man who does Tupperware. It's the island that matters. 'Ah, that lake! Where ground zero was!' Branko makes a cannon noise and continues: 'It's a green colour; it smells a bit green like

green paint, and the ocean is deep blue so you can stand'
– now he leaps up, filling my small room – 'Yes! With the
deep-blue ocean on this side and the green, green lake on
the other.' It's glorious. I'm a wide-eyed child as the island
is conjured before me. 'Plants? Yes, yes, plants is already
growing. We planted six coconuts and I saw them last week
and they are growing. But normal trees, grass have started
growing. There is thousands of birds, eggs, little chicks.
Everywhere, everywhere on the ground. You can see it from
the boat, it's green.'

We scroll through some of Branko's photographs. Many
of them show the ground turning to thin scrub and littered
with simple nests and a big blue sky, full of gulls.

In brooding retrospect, I realize that the fierce glamour
of new volcanic islands has been beckoning me for a long
time. I was born a year after Surtsey, the most filmed and
famous one of the twentieth century, broke through the
North Atlantic in 1963. Named after Surtr, a fire demon
from Norse mythology, Surtsey was a visual sensation.
Unforgettable films showed burning red entrails of lava.
Some of these molten streams were not red but black and
crusted and torn with terrible golden wounds. They spewed
quickly seawards, exploding into white steam. It was horrible and beautiful, elementally powerful and disorientating.
To *see* that I shared a planet with this otherworldly entity
made the suburban streets around me feel fragile and unreal.
The taming of Surtsey by plants and animals had its own

primitive allure, like bringing first life to a dead planet. The island's first plant, a sea rocket, sprouted in 1965; its first bird's-nest was found in 1970. Today, Surtsey is a plump, naan-bread-shaped island with swathes of green scrub-land and thriving bird and seal colonies. Surtsey is protected from humans. No visitors are allowed, other than authorized scientists. Used as a laboratory for the study of natural colonization, the island is sealed from contamination. A website devoted to its study primly reports that 'It is believed that some young boys tried to introduce potatoes, which were promptly dug up once discovered.' Still more shocking: 'An improperly handled human defecation resulted in a tomato plant taking root which was also destroyed.'

There is no chance of such consideration being extended to Hunga Tonga. Human defecation – or Branko's coconut-planting activities – are the least of its worries. Tonga sits on a trans-Pacific drug route, and I've been told that packages of cocaine and other narcotics regularly litter the beaches of its numerous remote islands.

Hunga Tonga was visited by NASA scientists six months after my trip with Branko. The story got quite a bit of press coverage. I couldn't help noticing the huge size of the yacht that took them there. Since the island's first appearance, the international geological community has been using satellite imagery to trace its growth. The evolution of Hunga Tonga is even providing a rare glimpse into volcanism on other planets. For example, it has been used to model 'small kilometre-scale hydro-volcanic edifices in the north plains of Mars', to quote one scientific paper lead-authored by NASA researchers.

Hunga Tonga sits on the rim of an underwater volcano that rises 1400 metres from the sea floor. The last major eruption here was in 2009, an event that also saw lava shoot up to the surface, adding a new shore to the island of Hunga Ha'apai. Since it is made mostly of ash, early predictions were that the new island of Hunga Tonga would soon be washed away. This hasn't happened. Although it is being eroded at about five times the rate of Surtsey, some of its mounds of ash appear to have mineralized and hardened. Hunga Tonga is far more robust than once thought and its predicted life is now a guessing game, with estimates of anywhere from seven to forty-two years.

Into the new year of 2015 Hunga Tonga was still vigorously pouring out clouds of fine debris, a spectacle easily visible from Tonga's capital. The Tongan newspaper *Matangi* reported a series of natural wonders: the sea was turned 'frothy white, chocolate and red while the sun shone through a champagne sky'. 'Pretty bizarre out here this morning,' commented one beachside resident to a *Matangi* reporter: it 'started out ordinary enough then the beach misted over with a brown haze and the ash cloud created rings around the sun'. That the sea turned red was reported by multiple sources and remains an enigma, though it is widely thought to have been caused by algae responding to high water temperatures.

The first vessel to report a sighting of the new island was a ship of the Tongan Royal Naval, on 14 January 2015. The captain also noted that the volcano, now above the surface, was erupting every five minutes. The first few months of Hunga Tonga's infant life saw it morph in size and shape. After a period of rapid expansion, when it latched on to its western neighbour, it began to shrink. In May 2015 waves washed away the bar of material separating the island's crater from the ocean. However, this debris did not all disappear off into the ocean; a lot of it was carried eastward, joining the island to its eastern neighbour. Branko saw the transition unfold. 'When the eruption died out and we went there,' he told me, 'the new island was connected to just one other island, so there was still a little water between it and the other one. The next time we came, four weeks later, that little channel was now land and it's still like that now.'

Photographs taken on Hunga Tonga in 2015 show an ash-grey and black lunar landscape. Anything living on the two rocky islands it swallowed up had been burned away. The landscape was colourless, with sweeping charcoal hills caked with lines of ragged gullies. Walking on the broken surface was very difficult and some experts warned against venturing onto the island at all in case the crust collapsed.

The world's news media has an unslakable thirst for extraordinary images that keep as many internet surfers as possible clicking through. Dramatic volcanoes come with a guaranteed income stream. Even small, ephemeral volcanic islands are shoved onto the geological catwalk. In 2018 one a mere 8 or so metres across, just off the coast of Hawaii, was being splashed as news. A journalist from the *Washington Post* emailed me with a list of questions, such as: 'Are we likely to see more and more new islands forming?' With the profusion of visual proof of nature's extreme events, people have become willing to believe that volcanoes are chucking up more land and getting more active. Some scientists have suggested something of the kind. The theory is that the retreat of ice cover depressurizes and thus expands the Earth's magma belt, allowing more molten rock to be created and more eruptions to occur. Writing in *Scientific American*, one of the progenitors of this theory, Dr Graeme Swindles (a physical geographer at the University of Leeds) said, 'I think we can predict we're probably going to see a lot more volcanic activity in areas of the world where glaciers and volcanoes interact.'

It's not a prospect that would impact anywhere near Tonga and, talking to another eminent volcanologist, Dr Nick Cutler whose office is a convenient ten steps from my own at Newcastle University, I hear that the 'increase in volcanism' theory remains controversial. Nick's got some fascinating insights into the global significance of volcanic eruptions. The one that knocked me sideways is that 'the biggest eruption of the twentieth century was Mount Pinatubo in 1991, and the cooling effect of that, over a couple of years, was almost the same as the anthropogenic warming effect over the whole twentieth century.' The 15 million tonnes of sulphur dioxide that this one Philippine volcano released reacted with water in the stratosphere to form particles that scattered and absorbed incoming sunlight, thus cooling the Earth. Drawing on recent ice-core research from Greenland, Nick went on to explain that what he calls the 'volcanic forcing' of global climate change happens far more often than scientists once thought: climate change is 'forced' by 'fairly run-of-the-mill, two or three times a century type eruptions'.

It's a complicating factor: anthropogenic warming of the planet is interacting with a range of currently unpredictable natural processes and events. Nick is a wry observer of the human need to find patterns and predictability in nature. The mismatch between our mayfly-like life spans and geological time makes it hard to grasp that events like new volcanic islands, which seem extraordinary to us, start to look continuous when viewed in geological time. 'In terms of a human lifetime, you may not see magma emitted to make islands,' Nick tells me, 'but across millions of years you'd see them popping up all the time.' We know roughly where new islands will appear on the boundaries between plates (subduction zones) and in places where magma is burning through the crust (hot spots): 'Places like Iceland and particularly Hawaii and other Pacific island chains are going to get continual creation of islands.' But that's as far as he will go: 'When it will happen and how quickly and precisely where – that's much harder to predict.'

Could such island creations have planet-changing consequences? Nick explains that generally, while volcanic activity certainly could and does, island-creation events tend to be less destructive. He has to go back two million years or so to find a counter-example, namely the supervolcano of Toba in Indonesia: 'a sizeable island which then more or less totally blew to pieces' (and today is the site of Lake Toba). This event caused widespread cooling in the atmosphere, and it has been speculated that it nearly extinguished human life on Earth.

For scientists the importance of new volcanic islands is not really to do with their planet-changing potential. It's how they allow us to study, from a blank slate, the formation of soil, of plants, of life. In truth, that is what I am most looking forward to seeing when I finally get to swim ashore and step foot on Hunga Tonga.

Saturday: the day of my journey. Another hot and humid morning. A battered pick-up grinds into view and soon I'm bouncing along Nuku'alofa's seafront with one of Branko's sons, a large, tattooed and quiet young man who has also brought a stack of 'meat sandwiches'. On the dockside Branko, in his trademark and faded 'Drink Beer' t-shirt, is busy and ready. The launch, which is about 12 metres long, has two big outboards; amid their overwhelming din, we are soon thumping straight out, past sand-bars and islets, towards darker water. We're in good spirits and I catch stories of other Tongan islands, such as the mysterious Falcon Island, an ephemeral and actively volcanic island way out to sea that last emerged in 1987. Today it is underwater but it is expected to return. Like the weather, it comes and it goes.

I wedge myself down and cling on. After half an hour I chew down a meat sandwich and risk a peek ahead. I can tell Branko and his son are getting worried – not by the water under us but by what they see ahead. Branko turns and shouts in my ear: 'It's big sea. Doesn't look good.' He points my gaze towards a forward zone in the water, beyond which white caps are lined up in military ranks. I want to keep going: 'Let's just see,' I keep saying. We lunge onwards. At some point, our relationship to the boat changes. Yawning valleys open out between sickeningly high water and the boat rushes down into them. Each time Branko and his son wrestle us out, powering the engines along and up the gentlest slope they can find. But it's getting hard: the outboards shriek indignantly; the boat is beginning to roll and turn on itself. It's time to go.

Back in the harbour Branko is apologetic, his son even more so. They refuse my offer of money for the spent diesel or for the sandwiches. Another time, perhaps. But I guess they know that, for me, this was a once-in-a-lifetime opportunity. I ask Branko to pose for a final photo. He is as accommodating as ever, someone I got to know and like, but his usual jauntiness has collapsed.

At least I have his stories. His adventures since arriving in Tonga at the age of twenty-five could fill any seafaring novel. One I remember concerns the time he sailed to a volcanic island with what he calls 'the Google man – founder and owner of Googles'. With an appalled grin he tells me, 'He came in a private jet; his secretary called me up: "Oh, we want to go the volcano."' A cyclone hampered that trip too. Once they had reached the uninhabited island, the wind picked up and Branko explained they couldn't get back until tomorrow. In response his customer 'picked up a phone and he called Houston. I just looked at him, thinking "who is this guy?"' Branko imitates the commanding boom of 'the Google man': '"Hello, Charlie. Can you give me weather prediction for …" – and he look at me – "What's our position?"' Houston's advice was to 'get the fuck out of there, there's a cyclone coming'. They hunkered down and made it back the next morning: '8-metre waves, six hours home'.

Whatever the height of the waves or the time taken, islands have a magnetic pull. When they rise up out of the sea, it's an act of creation – at least for land-bound creatures like us. No wonder so many creation myths start with island-building. That's certainly true in Tonga. It's a speckle of low, small islands that are next door to nothing. It's 2000 kilometres to the nearest large land-mass, New Zealand. Stories of island creation are still handed down through the generations. Tongan legend has it that, in the beginning, there was nothing but sea. The ruler of the sky and god of carpenters, Old Tangaloa, became tired of the emptiness beneath him so sent down one of his offspring, in the form of a plover, to see if he could find land. When this mission failed, Old Tangaloa demanded that his son take shavings from the wood carving he was working on and pile them up in the sea. And so the first islands of Tonga were stacked up, the gift of the gods.

The Tongans have also learned that islands come and go. Hunga Tonga burst into the world, and it grew, but one day it will disappear. The sand-bar protecting its crater lake has now returned but it is again being whittled down; once it goes, the ocean will pour in, eating away at the island and hollowing it out, returning Hunga Tonga and Hunga Ha'apai to their former separate selves. But then – it could be tomorrow or in a hundred years – another new volcanic island will just as suddenly cleave the seas. As yet these dramatic births are well beyond our powers of prediction. Volcanic eruptions are hard to call; they may be minor events or be planet-changing – remote and beautiful spectacles or the cause of the end of all life. Our human mastery of the planet, even our much-heralded Anthropocene, is only skin deep.

It's time for my early flight out of Tonga. The black dawn begins to lift, and through the plane window I scan the sea, hoping to catch a glimpse of the island I came so far to see. Maybe I did. There are a few lumps down there, just shavings in the sea. I look again and they have vanished.

THE ACCIDENTAL ISLANDS OF
PEBBLE LAKE, HUNGARY

Why am I hunting for islands in landlocked Hungary? The nation's capital, Budapest, is 542 kilometres from the nearest salt water but I'm intrigued by pictures of a flooded gravel quarry in a southern suburb. It is dotted with islands and has been given the name Pebble Lake. Aerial photographs show the islands have a central green space and a circumference clotted with tiny self-built houses; from the air they look like eccentrically arranged but complete sets of teeth gnashing at the water.

Pebble Lake is an example of a distinct category of artificial island: the accidental island – a side effect of human activity. Like many quarries, this one was only partially dug out. Tall pillars of rock were left standing. It was then abandoned and, because it's deeper than the local water table, it filled with water. The result was a scatter of islands encircled by deep cold water.

The planet's biggest example of an accidental island is René-Levasseur Island. If you type that name into Google Earth you may be in for a surprise. At 72 kilometres wide, it is a very large – and, from high up, very circular – island that looks like a big button dropped on Quebec's northern expanses. One of the biggest objects ever created by *Homo sapiens*, René-Levasseur was an unintended consequence of the flooding of its surrounding land in order to make a reservoir. It is on the opposite end of the scale to Pebble Lake but they are distant cousins and I'm hoping my visit to Kavicsos-tó (the Hungarian for 'Pebble Lake') could be a gateway into this intriguing subspecies of island.

Pebble Lake is a thirty-minute drive from the centre of Budapest. I put the co-ordinates into the satnav and it doesn't take long for the affluent city of palaces and pavement jazz musicians to slide away into a dusty edge-land of grey blocks and car fumes. I steer across an arm of the divided Danube onto Csepel Island. Somewhere at its northern end is Pebble Lake. At 48 kilometres long, Csepel is one of the Danube's largest islands (the biggest is in Slovakia and stretches 84 kilometres) and was once the heartland of Hungarian heavy industry. From what I can see through my increasingly dirty windshield, Csepel is now a post-industrial dumping ground, a sprawling mix of anonymous housing blocks and semi-derelict areas. Perhaps I am prejudiced by the grisly news item I clicked on a few nights before, which named Csepel as the place mobsters and paramilitaries bury their victims alive. In 2011 four bodies were unearthed, all of whom had met this end. It is suspected that the island is the lonely resting place of others. It feels a long way from Budapest's most famous island, Margaret Island, a beautiful park that lies in an affluent reach of the river. I was walking there only yesterday: happy in the hot July sunshine, enjoying the good-natured crowds, the carefully clipped flowerbeds and a delicate cone of lemon sorbet.

Pylons and power lines grid the blue sky as my satnav signals a curt right. It takes me along a straight, potholed dirt road and, with each passing vehicle, clouds of yellow dust choke the breezeless summer air. The radio station is playing 'Hotel California'. I won't be able to shake that tune out of my ears. I'm also remembering from my late-night research that the Pebble Lake community is disputatious and values its privacy. The 166-hectare site (106 hectares of which is water) is privately owned and there is no public right of access. After the quarry was abandoned it started to fill with groundwater and its shores were quickly colonized by weeds, trees and bird life. Within a few years it was a verdant green oasis. Only the fish, of which the lake is famously full, are artificial introductions.

A few turns later and I'm thumping slowly along a twisting peninsula that bends into the heart of the lake. Weekend shacks are irregularly spaced anywhere and everywhere and it feels like I've sneaked into an idiosyncratic and private club. I'm not betting on a friendly invite over to one of the lake's five settled islands. So far, I've seen no one. Seventy families are said to live here year round but, if so, they keep a low profile. The self-built homes are modest but well-cared for in a pleasantly ramshackle way but they all have high fences. It's time to park the car and start walking.

It's mercilessly hot and I'm soon distracted by fat coal-black bees that bounce drunkenly between trumpet-shaped flowers and by a chalk-white moth that makes slow, unsteady steps along my forearm. Near the water's edge I take photographs of the little houses. Some are brightly painted and have manicured gardens and shady porches where rocking chairs wait out the day. Nearly all of them have a small floating pontoon, designed for idling and nursing a cold beer.

My first sight of human life is a tubby swimmer in tight Speedos. Somewhere in his retirement years, he plods heavily down a private jetty 10 metres in front of me and slaps into the water. Suddenly conscious of my unseemly lurking, I make a hasty retreat and scrabble up a steep ridge, past piles of dumped building material, to gain a view over the whole lake. Despite the prosaic names given to them by their residents, such as Bare Island and Small Bald Island, the islands are effortlessly cute. They have no shoreline. There is a vertiginous drop into the depthless waters. However, there are signs of shallow sunken structures that project just under the water – ghostly forms indicating that the waterline has risen since settlement began, covering terraces and pathways. On this high ridge, the grey hinterland of Pebble Lake is visible from every angle. You can hear it too: the grinding of the big city punctuated by periodic shrieks of aeroplanes or train brakes. Amid all this, Pebble Lake looks unreal, as if it has been dropped from another, better planet – a beautiful alien abandoned on a hostile world.

My reverie is terminated by another middle-aged man in Speedos. A more gamey and athletic type, he rushes out from what I took to be an empty house to repeatedly bellow the word 'Finish!' Throughout the years I've spent researching islands, I've been told to 'go away' many times and in many different languages. Waterfront exclusivity is eagerly guarded; it has a hair-trigger intolerance of outsiders. My feelings of admiration flip into resentment at being shut out and shouted at. I'm reminded that Pebble Lake regards itself as a private place, acquired by 664 anglers who joined together to pay the purchase price. Disputes over ownership and access continue to rumble on, with residents siding with one faction or another. On a Budapest news site journalist Janice Kata reports that 'everyone is suspicious of the other'. Talking to 'the elder of the lake system', an octogenarian called József Antal who spends much of the year here, she discovers that thieves have twice ransacked his home; they 'took the gas bottle, even his pile of aluminium cans'. The recent arrival of electricity is heralded by the Pebble Lakers because it has finally allowed them to fulfil a long-held dream: to fit burglar alarms.

Despite its jealously guarded desirability, Pebble Lake was the product of accident not design. Many of the world's 'side-effect islands' share this paradox: unplanned by-products that have come to be seen as desirable addresses. Sometimes the meaning of this value is a source of conflict.

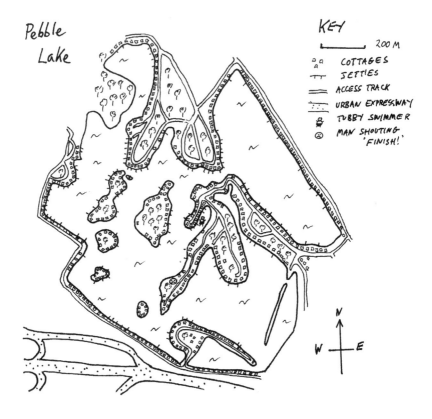

Pebble Lake

KEY

200 M
COTTAGES
JETTIES
ACCESS TRACK
URBAN EXPRESSWAY
TUBBY SWIMMER
MAN SHOUTING 'FINISH!'

René-Levasseur Island is, at one and the same time, a logging resource, a sanctuary for undisturbed nature and a protected slice of native land. It was formed in 1970 when two existing lakes were joined, flooding a continuous loop of land to create a reservoir that is used to power hydroelectric generating stations. The circular shape of both the reservoir and its island is a telltale sign that this landscape was created by a 'falling star'. It was here, 214 million years ago, that a meteorite 5 kilometres long struck the planet. It was the fourth-biggest impact Earth has experienced, forming a crater 100 kilometres wide. What geologists describe as 'post-impact rebound' appears to have been responsible for the centre of the crater rising up to form Mount Babel, the island's 1000-metre mountain.

Although a by-product of Quebec's pursuit of hydroelectricity, the island was soon being thought of as a significant and important place. A portion of the island was set aside for the Louis-Babel Ecological Reserve, and activists began campaigning for the entire island to be protected. In 2003 a coalition called 'Sauvons l'île René-Levasseur' (since renamed 'SOS Levasseur') began lobbying to save what they call 'the integral ecosystem of René-Levasseur Island'. The logging roads that criss-cross the island demonstrate the threat posed and SOS Levasseur's website declares that the island is a threatened natural paradise, home to caribou and golden eagles. Their heartfelt *cri de coeur* is addressed to every 'forest lover and animal protector'. René-Levasseur has no permanent residents, just fifty or so cabins occupied by seasonal hunters. Another 'stakeholder', apart from the logging and mineral rights companies, is the local native population, the Innu. They too have been campaigning to stop all logging activities on the island, which is part of their ancestral land. The campaigners make similar claims for the great forests that extend in all directions around René-Levasseur but the island has come to provide a focus for these concerns *because* it is an island and, hence, special.

A similar story can be told of the islands formed at the start of the last century, thousands of kilometres to the south of René-Levasseur, when Gatun Lake was created in Panama. A network of flooded valleys, the lake is a key component of the Panama Canal, providing headwater to fill the locks. Every ship that transits the canal uses 202,000 cubic metres of water from the lake – water that then flows out into the Atlantic or Pacific. Over the years, the verdant, tropical islands created as a by-product of the creation of Gatun Lake have come to be valued as wildlife sanctuaries and eco-tourist attractions. The world's most famous and oldest artificial 'eco-island' is here: Barro Colorado Island, which was established as a nature reserve in 1923. The island is home to the Smithsonian Tropical Research Institute and is considered one of the few places on the planet where an untouched tropical ecosystem can be studied.

Modern industry requires continuous gouging of the Earth's surface: mining, drilling, building, dredging. A lot of debris is created and it has to go somewhere. Often it gets washed downstream. In some places the accidental islands that result are places of reprieve, the silver lining in an age of ugliness. This redemptive quality is certainly to the fore in Florida's Spoil Island Project. If you look closely at satellite images of the east coast of Florida you'll see them dotting coastal lagoons. There are 137 spoil islands in the Spoil Island Project: industrial by-products that over the past few decades have been reclaimed as environmental reserves and eco-tourist destinations. Colonized by sea grasses and mangroves, the islands are managed by Florida's Department of Environmental Protection. They designate some as 'conservation islands' and others as 'recreation islands', with the latter offering very basic camping sites with picnic tables and fire rings. The Florida Spoil Islands are an encouraging example of how by-products of human industry do not always have to be places of abjection. For some, even the words 'spoil island' may send a shudder down the spine. They could have been relabelled and a lie told – branded as 'paradise beaches' – but I think the Florida project has got it absolutely right: they call them what they are.

Despite having been told to 'Finish!', I'm still mooching about the byways of this densely settled former quarry, enjoying some of the quirky 'art' its residents have assembled from advertising hoardings and assorted junk. It's a hive of private individuality. It has certainly satisfied my feeling that the lure of islands is not confined to countries with shorelines. 'Landlocked' is an unfortunate, graceless kind of label. There is no more reason to cast 'landlocked' Hungary into a dungeon of topographic isolation than salty, seafaring, 'sea-locked' Britain. In Hungary too, in a low-key kind of way, it is the age of islands.

I'm back in my mud-splattered hire car; it's time to leave this green refuge. On the interminable dirt road out of Pebble Lake I edge past yet another middle-aged man wearing only a small pair of Speedos and flip-flops. It must be a Hungarian thing. He has a long walk in front of him; perhaps I should give him a lift. I slow down but he curtly waves me on; like other Pebble Lakers, he is gruffly self-sufficient. As with other private islands – accidental or not, owned by millionaires or, like these, by ordinary people – the default gesture is a wave of the hand, not as a signal of welcome but to tell the outside world to go away.

TRASH ISLANDS

Deep into the future, a geologist traces a finger along a thin, darkly resinous deposit in the strata and, before moving on to more substantial layers, mumbles something about 'the plastic age'. It's not an implausible vision. A defining feature of the modern world is its waste: rubbish is being produced in such abundance and from materials of such durability that it is forcing us to rethink geology. I want to take another step in this conceptual revolution and make the case that it is also changing the way we think about islands. Trash islands form a global archipelago that reaches from the smallest floating clot far upstream to the unimaginable expanses of the Pacific Trash Vortex.

One hot morning a few years ago I took a long and bumpy taxi ride to visit Cairo's 'Garbage City'. The Coptic Christians who call it home make a meagre living by recycling as much of Cairo's rubbish as they can, which is pulled in by donkey carts and little vans and sorted in noisy household workshops into different types of metals, plastics and paper. Six hours later I was downtown: invited by a wealthy Cairo resident, a friend of a friend, to a swanky bar high above the Nile. As we walked on the rooftop terrace, admiring the glitzy panorama as ice cubes jingled in our G&Ts, I tried to make a joke about being a million miles from 'Garbage City'. My new pal grinned sardonically and pointed down to the river. In small boats would-be fishermen were pushing their way through dense mats of floating trash. Elegant white egrets picked their way across the ugly surface as the plastic waste sealed up each boat's wake.

Plastic takes between 500 and 1000 years to degrade and we make hundreds of millions of tonnes of it every year. Every decade production of plastic more than doubles. Little of it is being recycled; most is burned, buried or just tipped into rivers, eventually washing far out to sea. The thickest and most common trash islands can be seen along coasts and in rivers in Africa, Asia and much of the Americas. Recently news websites like Newsflare, which allow anyone with a smartphone to upload video of local stories, have provided the most urgent and grim testimony of the ubiquity of trash islands. Filmed in October 2107: 'Shocking scenes of vast quantities of plastic waste floating along a river in Mexico's southern Chiapas state'. Filmed in September 2018: 'Rivers of plastic flowing in the [Spanish] province of Almería'.

Filmed in January 2018 in Bukittinggi, Indonesia: 'Water for human living and irrigation has been polluted by plastics and rubbish'. In some of these rivers, fishing has become impossible and what fishermen are left have swapped profession, turning their boats into trash-breakers and thrusting through the flotsam to look for saleable waste.

Once offshore, trash islands usually break up, which makes clearing up their toxic cargo all the more difficult. It is only when they stick together – because of some whim or habit of the current – that people take much notice. The 'garbage island', about a kilometre long and weighing about 100 tonnes, that formed in the Gulf of Thailand in 2017 was soon spotted and branded as an unsightly disgrace by the local media. Swift action followed: speedboats with fishing nets were sent out to scoop it up. Unfortunately, this kind of prompt response is the exception rather than the rule. Even when it does happen, much of the debris will already have been missed. Plastics that are dispersed, broken up and sunk are out of sight and out of mind. Many of the commonest plastics, such as Polyethylene terephthalate (PET, which is used to make drinks bottles) and polyester, are relatively heavy and quickly sink.

Another thick plastic agglomeration that occurred in 2017, this time off the coast of Honduras, shows how dealing with the problem, even when it is within easy reach, is rarely straightforward. The mayor of Omoa, the nearest town, complained that the clean-up effort was beyond his resources: 'On Friday, we filled twenty dump trucks of thirteen cubic meters each, and it made almost no difference.' The Hondurans claim, not unreasonably, that the waste was created upstream. They blame the Guatemalans. The local tourism chief drove the point home by taking journalists on a tour to show off the Guatemalan labels on the plastic bottles scooped from the sea.

Responsibility for the pollution of water can be impossible to pin down, with different regional and national authorities all pointing at each other and arguing that the real source of the problem is further upriver. The biggest rivers are the biggest carriers of waste and they often traverse a number of countries. It is now thought that much of the plastic waste found in the world's oceans comes from just ten rivers, eight of which are in Asia. One of them is the Mekong, which travels through China, Myanmar, Thailand, Laos and Cambodia before disgorging its load in Vietnam – at which point blame has become almost as thoroughly dispersed as the plastic itself.

Some of the plastic that feeds the garbage patches forming in the middle of the large-scale circulation patterns, or gyres, of our oceans has been thrown off ships but most has arrived from beaches or rivers. Footballs, kayaks and Lego blocks have all been spotted, along with the usual mass of plastic bottles and fishing net. Most of the plastic has broken up into fragments. The oceans' garbage patches do not exist as a single entity but a soup or galaxy of rubbish, most of which has sunk to the ocean floor or floats just below the top and sometimes gloops together on the surface. Oceanographer Curtis Ebbesmeyer has argued that these patches 'move around like a big animal without a leash', and every so often they find a shore and cough up plastic all over the beach. Ebbesmeyer puts it in suitably grotesque language: 'The garbage patch barfs, and you get a beach covered with this confetti of plastic.'

All oceans have circulating currents and, since rubbish is being picked up by such currents around the world, so trash vortices are forming in every ocean. In fact, the Pacific has two: an Eastern and Western Patch. Intimations of a North Atlantic Garbage Patch came in 1972 when oceanographers discovered plastic pieces in the Sargasso Sea. The North Atlantic's debris zone moves seasonally, drifting 1600 kilometres north and south each year. Photos of the North Atlantic Patch, taken by the research vessel *Sea Dragon*,

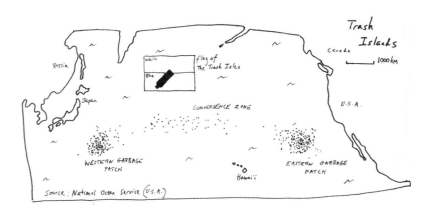

which since 2010 has been studying trash vortices all over the globe, show a mass of floating debris on rough sea.

Estimates of the size of the oceans' various trash vortices vary hugely. The Pacific Trash Vortex, which is the one that gets all the attention, has been measured as 670,000 square kilometres but also as 1,500,000 square kilometres. However large it is, it is clearly highly contaminated. It has been estimated that at its centre every square kilometre contains 480,000 pieces of plastic. Animals are ingesting this fragmenting debris and so taking in toxic pollutants. In one 2018 study, marine scientists from the National University of Ireland found plastic in 73 per cent of the deep-sea fish collected from the Atlantic. It's not just marine life that is impacted by the dispersal of plastic; a review conducted by the World Health Organization in 2018 found microplastics in 90 per cent of bottled water.

The Pacific Vortex was discovered by yachtsman Charles Moore in 1997 on his way back to Los Angeles from Hawaii. He decided to take his yacht into a part of the ocean usually avoided by sailors because of its slow currents and lack of wind. To his astonishment, he found himself sailing into a sea of gunk: 'Every time I came on deck, there was trash floating by.' Moore, who has since devoted himself to cleaning the oceans, says of the Pacific Garbage Patch that it is 'just absolutely gross – a truly disgusting plastic cesspool' and that it 'has to be burned into the consciousness of humanity that the ocean is now a plastic wasteland'.

More recently, some scientists have been using the term 'plastisphere' to think about the new kind of ecosystem that all this debris is creating. Plastic is quickly colonized by a diverse array of microbial life. One of the marine biologists who came up with the term, Linda Amaral-Zettler of the Royal Netherlands Institute for Sea Research, points out that the plastisphere 'is really quite a little zoo'. Larger organisms are also making use of marine plastic, such as marine worms who researchers at the Korea Institute of Ocean Science and Technology have discovered are eating plastic and excreting microplastics.

Some scientists have recently been taking a sceptical tone about 'trash islands'. In a piece published on the science blog io9 titled 'Lies You've Been Told About the Pacific Garbage Patch', tech journalist Annalee Newitz lays into the 'myth' that 'There is a giant island of solid garbage floating in the Pacific.' Another counter-blast came in 'The Dirt on Ocean Garbage Patches', published in *Science*, where Jocelyn Kaiser tells us that 'Their biological impact is uncertain and their makeup, misunderstood.' This myth-busting shtick makes for arresting headlines but rather misses the point. Of course the Pacific Garbage Patch is not a solid island where you can build a house or park your car. No serious report on it has ever suggested anything of the kind. The Pacific Garbage Patch is one end of a spectrum, along which a diverse flotilla of trash islands can be arranged – from the soup-like to the immobile and metres thick. Each is an evolving, changing form; even the most stuck and solid-seeming river trash eventually gets washed downstream, while the liquid ocean 'vortices' will get thicker and more lumpy as more ingredients are poured into them.

Much of the impetus for thinking about the Pacific Garbage Patch as a new island is rooted in environmentalists trying to make people care. They are asking us to shift our ideas. It's a geographical reboot, a necessary shake-up. The plan to ask the UN to accept the Trash Isles as a new country was dreamed up by two environmentalists and advertising creatives, Michael Hughes and Dalatando Almeida. Talking to an advertising trade magazine, *Creative Review*, they explain: 'We wanted to come up with a way to ensure world leaders can't ignore it anymore, a way to stick it under their noses, literally.' They were struck by the fact that the Pacific Garbage Patch covers a country-sized area, and so 'With no one paying attention to this catastrophe' they submitted a Declaration of Independence to the United Nations.

If we become a country and a member of the UN, we are protected by the UN's Environmental Charters, which state ... 'All members shall co-operate in a spirit of global partnership to conserve, protect and restore the health and integrity of the earth's ecosystem'. Which in a nutshell means that by becoming a country, other countries are obliged to clean us up.

The Trash Isles campaign has been slick but playful, with the would-be country's flag, passports, official stamps and a currency (twenty-, fifty- and hundred-Debris notes) all splashed with artful portraits of both the rubbish and its victims. On the twenty-Debris note there is a turtle, its waist girdled by plastic. The Trash Isles established a monarchy and appointed Dame Judi Dench as its queen. At the last count 132,000 people have asked to be citizens, the first being former US vice president Al Gore. A spokesman for the UN's Secretary General declared that the Trash Isles campaign was 'creative and innovative. But the chances of it being accepted are fairly nil.'

The Trash Isles bid to the UN was prefigured a few years earlier by the Italian artist Maria Cristina Finucci, whose Federal State of Garbage Patch was declared to be a nation on 11 April 2013 at UNESCO Headquarters in Paris. This rival state's territorial claim encompasses five garbage patches as a 'federal state with a "population" of 36,939 tons of garbage' and a total area of 15,915,933 square kilometres.

These two nation-making projects have overlapping territorial claims but appear to be ignorant of each other's existence. Our polluted seas are provoking a growing community of artist-activists, with much of the resultant work playing with images of islands or going one step further and actually building islands out of plastic. The éminence grise of such enterprises is the British-born eco-artist Richart Sowa, who has been building and living on tiny islands made of plastic bottles off the Mexican coast since 1997. The latest version, Joysxee island, is 25 metres wide and 30 metres long, floating on approximately 150,000 plastic bottles. On his website Sowa says: 'I AM LIVING on a Franchiseable Prototype FLOATING ECO/ISLAND which SOLVES the PROBLEMS of,,,, INCREASING TRASH, by preserving it in net bags under used shipping palettes to provide a floating form for humans, animals, marine life and a garden to flourish on.'

In 2018 Rotterdam-based Recycled Island Foundation launched their floating Recycled Park. Plastic waste recovered from the busy harbour has been shaped into a series of hexagonal platforms that are used as refuges for plants and small animals. It's a modest endeavour but points the way. After all, just clearing up the plastic is only part of the problem; we also need to figure out what to do with it. Another Dutch initiative is scaling up Rotterdam's idea. Dutch company WHIM Architecture has outlined a plan for a floating city of half a million people living on an island made up of waste recycled from the Pacific Garbage Patch. 'The proposal has three main aims,' they declare, 'cleaning our oceans from a gigantic amount of plastic waste, creating new land and constructing a sustainable habitat.'

In 2018 yet another Dutch scheme, Ocean Cleanup, pro-totyped a marine 'sweep', a long boom that captures refuse which is then picked by boat. Ocean Cleanup claim that 'A full-scale system roll-out could clean up 50% of the Great

Pacific Garbage Patch in just five years.' Others have been less impressed, warning that the system will catch only the most visible fraction of plastic pollution while killing creatures such as turtles and floating plankton. Another scheme that is attracting attention is the deployment of plastic-eating bacteria. A Japanese research team sifted through hundreds of samples of discarded PET plastic before finding a colony of organisms using the plastic as a food source. But the researchers are cautious: Professor Kenji Miyamoto from Keio University noted that there are 'many issues' still unresolved and that 'it takes a long time'. Since this bacteria only works on PET plastics, which are already 100 per cent recyclable, it is unlikely to be the breakthrough that is desperately hoped for.

It's a modern conceit to imagine that – having filled our rivers, oceans and indeed our lives with plastic junk – some clever scientist will invent a gizmo and clear it all away. It allows us to sidestep the fact that the scale and spread of plastic entering our seas and rivers – and hence the scale and spread of trash islands – is increasing at an alarming pace. It's this that must be tackled.

Deep into the future, the geologist has made an exciting find. All that remains from the plastic age is now reduced to microparticles, a permanent geological feature since it cannot be broken down by micro-organisms. But every blue moon you can strike lucky. And here, unbelievably, revealed from deep history, is a fragile bluish fragment of plastic fabric hanging delicately from a crumbly black layer. What a find! A museum piece, of course – a rare relic from a period in which (so the current theory goes) *Homo sapiens* both drank and swam in solutions of toxic plastic because they thought it would cure their ailments and stave off death. That's the current theory; in truth, no one is at all sure what they were thinking.

VTOPIAE INSVLAE FIGVRA

The new island of Utopia: illustration from the 1516 first edition of *De optimo rei publicae statu, deque nova insula Utopia* (Of a Republic's Best State and of the New Island Utopia) by Thomas More (*Lebrecht Music & Arts / Alamy Stock Photo*).

Early phase of Chinese building activity on Johnson South Reef (*Kyodo News/Getty Images*).

A number of the Solomon Islands have disappeared or are soon to disappear. This photograph shows the Russell Islands (which lie in the middle of the archipelago), where shorelines are rapidly retreating (*robertharding / Alamy Stock Photo*).

My row boat, unnamed island, Loch Awe.

Snack food packaging, fishing lines and broken glass found on the shore of an unnamed island, Loch Awe.

Multiple cranes slotting together the Kleindienst Group's 'Heart of Europe', as seen from 'Lebanon', 'The World', Dubai.

The islands of 'Palestine', 'Jordan' and 'Saudi Arabia' as seen from 'Lebanon'. In the distance: downtown Dubai with the hazy pinnacle of the Burj Khalifa.

In front of the *Nieuw Land* museum, Flevopolder. A white head rises from a bright blue rectangle representing the sea, with a life-size Cornelis Lely standing on top, punching the air.

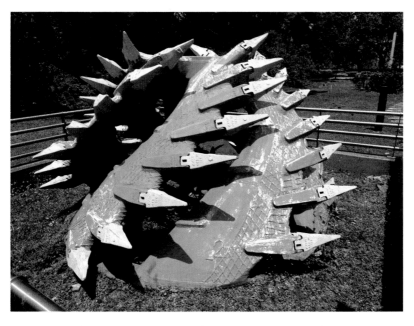

Chek Lap Kok, Hong Kong. Walkers' finger post, pointing the way to 'Ancient Kiln' and 'Historical Garden', with Hong Kong-Macau bridge in distance.

Cutter head from a 'cutter-suction dredger', Chek Lap Kok, Hong Kong.

Cable car on Lantau Island, with Chek Lap Kok International Airport in the distance.

Students sitting on the tiled plaza beneath HSBC headquarters, Hong Kong. A security guard has just arrived and is telling Michael that this is not allowed.

Sanya Bay. The inset of the South China Sea as it appears on the Hainan tourist map. The thick dotted line delivers almost the entire sea to China. The squiggles in the centre are the Spratly and Paracel islands.

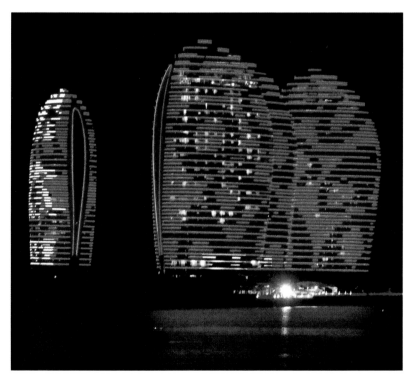

Phoenix Island's towers pulsing with multicoloured patterns. Sanya, Hainan.

Screenshot of graphic showing the 'Ocean Flower', Hainan, taken from developer's promotional film. Translation: 'Sea Flower Island. Filmed March 2019' (*Evergrande Group*).

Ocean Reef, Panama City. Isla II is on the right connected to Isla I by a bridge. Behind Isla I are the towers of Punta Pacifica.

Gated entry onto the private bridge that leads over to the Ocean Reef islands, Panama City.

Early growth and nesting birds on Hunga Tonga-Hunga Ha'apai (*Photograph by Branko Sugar*).

Branko back in
port after our
unsuccessful trip.

Pebble Lake, Budapest. Small floating pontoon, designed for idling and nursing a cold beer.

One of the islands of Pebble Lake.

San Blas Islands. A typical small inhabited island.

A typical San
Blas shoreline.

Tupsuit Dummat. *Ulu* canoe and artificial island just offshore.

Toilets poking out from Tupsuit Dummat.

Bernado building up his artificial island, Tupsuit Dummat.

Fafa, Tonga. Its southern shore is an obstacle course of palms and wooden posts felled by the surging waters.

Tongatapu, Tonga. Boulder sea defences on the north coast.

Storm damaged house, Tongatapu, Tonga.

Rising seas in
Hugh Town
harbour, St Mary's.

Iron Age village of Halangy, St Mary's.

Aphra on top of a coastal burial cairn, St Mary's.

Another, even smaller, unnamed island in Loch Awe.

PART TWO

DISAPPEARING

Disappearing Islands

ISAPPEARING ISLANDS ARE the star exhibit of sea-level rise. This is perverse. Most of the world's coastlines are at risk from sea-level rise. By far the greatest impact will be on low-lying coastal plains crowded with cities, where hundreds of millions of people now live. Along the eastern seaboard of the USA, or the densely settled coasts of South East Asia, surging waters will create more islands than they destroy, turning landscapes of valleys and hills into archipelagos.

Yet the image of the inundated island remains compelling. And urgent: they are disappearing right now, especially low-lying islands in the tropics. What is happening to them is an early warning to the rest of the planet. There are less rational reasons why vanishing islands touch us. To see a whole place – often an ancient one where people have lived for hundreds or even thousands of years – erased from the horizon is painful in a way that, for the moment, forecasts of the flooding and subsequent 'break-up' of continental seaboards are not.

On the next part of my island adventures I will travel to islands threatened by sea-level rise. The three island groups I will be exploring could scarcely be less similar. They are certainly far apart: one lot are in the Caribbean (the San Blas Islands of Guna Yala), another in the North Atlantic (the Isles of Scilly), and the third are in the South Pacific (Tongatapu and Fafa).

Like a number of other low-lying tropical islands, the San Blas, which belong to Panama, are facing imminent evacuation. That is not true of Fafa and Tongatapu, which are in Tonga. Not yet, although many problems are being thrown at this redoubtable kingdom: it is facing environmental, social and economic crises that interlink and feed on each other. England's Isles of Scilly are, by contrast, affluent and appear very content. But the sea is a great leveller and the sea is rising here too. The Isles of Scilly – the most westerly point of England – intrigue me in other ways. For you can see on many of them clear evidence that sea level has been rising here for a very long time.

These three island groups don't exhaust the ways that islands vanish. Islands subside and erode, and volcanic and tectonic forces can destroy islands just as easily as they create them. There also is a darker story to tell about the death of islands. Intense forms of human exploitation, such as mining or nuclear testing, have left the world with a sad profusion of destroyed islands.

Rising seas

Small flat islands, especially those in warmer latitudes, are very vulnerable to sea-level rise. It's odd, then, that building small flat islands in warmer latitudes is such big business. One day the dots will join. Without the installation of pumping equipment and stout walls, many of our 'age of islands' newest creations will not have a long life.

News stories about disappearing islands can be alarmingly short-sighted. Sometimes tagged as 'breath-taking places to visit before they disappear', they often leave the impression that sea-level rise is a problem confined to remote, unpronounceable, Pacific atolls. Hand-wringing about 'the plight of the Kiribatians' translates a global, universal crisis into something comfortingly far away, affecting a reassuringly tiny group of people.

The Pacific *has* seen more than its fair share of losses, however. Since 2007 the islands of Laiap, Nahtik, Ros, Kepidau en Pehleng and Nahlapenlohd, which were all once part of the Federated States of Micronesia, have gone. Five of the Solomon Islands have also been lost. Unlike most island disappearances, these losses have been widely reported, often accompanied by a link to other stories on places that will go the same way. The Maldives, Palau, Fiji, Tuvalu, Seychelles, Kiribati, the Cook Islands and French Polynesia all regularly appear on lists of vanishing countries.

It is revealing that the journalist I cribbed that roll-call from finishes her article with an incredulous footnote: 'Even the United States is affected by rising sea levels.' The idea that sea-level rise impacts *us* has not quite sunk in. She cites the best-known American example: the islands of Chesapeake Bay, an estuary that separates Maryland and Virginia. But let's not get too worried. President Trump called the mayor of one of the Chesapeake islands, Tangier, telling him he shouldn't worry about sea-level rise – it is, Trump says, fake news. Those looking for a more sober witness can find it in William Cronin's island biography, *The Disappearing Islands of the Chesapeake*.

Globally, sea and air temperatures are higher today than at any time since records began. However, it is not getting hotter at the same rate everywhere and nor are sea levels rising uniformly. The rate of rise is determined by a complex mixture of sea currents, the gravitational pull of the polar ice sheets (the thinner they are, the less they pull water away from lower latitudes), the fact that warm water expands, post-glacial 'bounce-back', and local factors such as land subsidence. Even within the same country there is huge variation. In the Philippines the sea is rising 14 millimetres each year in Manila, the country's capital, but go a few hundred kilometres to the south, on the island of Cebu, and the rise is much less: 0.9 millimetres per year.

The range of predicted rise, averaged across the world, is also considerable, from just 26 centimetres to nearly 3 metres by the end of the century. The estimates vary but all these predictions point to an accelerating trend: increases that are now 'locked in' will continue to grow. Moreover, these predictions do not take threshold breaks into consideration; tipping points when what we have seen so far (slow-building acceleration) will shift into another gear. One of these thresholds is the point at which the polar regions get too warm to sustain their ice sheets. The ice sheets that cover Greenland and the Antarctic hold enough water to raise sea levels by about 65 metres, which is the height of the Sydney Opera House. The important point is that ice-sheet melt has not *yet* made a substantial contribution to sea-level rise. Most of the rise we have experienced has been from the thermal expansion of the sea, with a smaller portion due to melting glaciers. If temperatures continue to rise, the ice sheets *will* melt in a big way and that will change everything. In early 2019 the ominous news came that the Greenland ice sheet is melting four times faster than previously thought. 'This is going to cause additional sea-level rise,' says the report's lead author, Michael Bevis, a Professor of Geodynamics at Ohio State University, adding, 'We are watching the ice sheet hit a tipping point.' Bevis is sombre: 'The only thing we can do is adapt and mitigate further warming – it's too late for there to be no effect.'

We are headed into the unknown but not the unforewarned. Some, but not all, disappearing islands can be defended. We should not assume that to 'adapt and mitigate' always means having to evacuate or that what we will be witnessing over the coming centuries will be a straightforward universal drowning. Just as islands can be artificially built, so they can be artificially protected – sometimes aided by nature herself. In a recent study of Tuvalu's atolls and reef islands, Professor Paul Kench of the University of Auckland found plenty of evidence of sea-level rise but also of island growth caused by sediment deposited by storms. Overall Tuvalu's total land area actually got bigger between 1971 and 2014 by 2.9 per cent. It's not much of a counter-trend, however, and bulked-out beaches will be no match against remorseless sea-level rise. But Kench is right to counsel against the idea that, at least in the short term, the disappearance of low-lying islands is inevitable and that they should all be abandoned. The crisis is a real one and the long-term outlook is not good, but the complexity of the processes reshaping islands coupled with human ingenuity suggests that mass relocation should not be the first solution we consider.

Eroding and exploding islands

The island of Esanbe Hanakita Kojima was only named in 2014 and the next time people looked for it, off the far north shore of Japan, it was gone. The Japanese government named it, along with 158 other uninhabited islands, in order to shore up territorial claims on its northern seas.

But the stormy wind and ice flows that barrel along this forbidding stretch of coast had other ideas and, after scraping and blowing away the island's surface, they removed it from the map. These are natural processes that, many times every year, remove islands. Esanbe Hanakita Kojima went under in 2018, the same year that East Island in Hawaii was reported missing. At 800 metres long and 120 metres wide, East Island was a wildlife haven for seals, turtles and albatrosses but a hurricane rattled by and it was dashed to bits.

Separating the natural from the unnatural is getting tricky. Since global warming is making storms more frequent and harsher, more islands are probably being washed away. Ice melt in the high north also makes islands more vulnerable. In 2008 the population of the Alaskan island of Kivalina, who will soon need to start new lives on the mainland, filed a lawsuit against ExxonMobil. They were suing for their relocation costs but the case was thrown out of court on the basis that doing something about greenhouse gases was not the responsibility of oil companies.

The interaction of the natural and the unnatural can also be seen in land subsidence. Along many coasts the land is falling at a faster rate than the sea is rising. It's a particular problem in South Asian cities, like Jakarta, Ho Chi Minh City and Bangkok, where huge quantities of water for human and farm use have been pumped out of the ground. The impact of subsidence on islands is especially alarming in deltas because so many people live on them: about

500 million people today. But they are sinking fast. Three-quarters of the Ganges delta – home to 130 million people – faces inundation. China's Yellow River delta is currently dropping so fast that local sea levels are rising by up to 25 centimetres per year. In some places, the Mekong River delta has been found to be falling by 70 centimetres a year and it is projected to carry on falling by 80 to 150 centimetres within the next two decades. These are colossal numbers and, while some of the causes are purely natural, some are not. Groundwater extraction – much of it to feed the aquafarming of fish, shellfish and suchlike – acerbates subsidence. The coast is also threatened by cutting down coastal mangrove forests and upstream river damming. Dams have all but halted the arrival of new sediment to the deltas of the Nile, Indus and Yellow rivers. This means new islands are not formed and old ones are washed away by floods. Although in some places, like Bangladesh, polder-building is helping to create new farming islands, the prospects of hundreds of millions of delta-dwellers are not bright.

Volcanoes and earthquakes can destroy islands as well as create them. Two-thirds of Krakatoa Island was obliterated by the 1883 eruption. The explosion was heard 4800 kilometres away, and killed about 37,000 people, and the amount of ash released caused global temperatures to fall by as much as 1.2 degrees Celsius. The death of islands can be world-changing. But islands have a rhythm; they come and go and come again. The curious story of Graham Island, which lies in a region of underwater volcanoes between Sicily and Tunisia, is a case in point. After a series of earthquakes, it was spotted on 19 July 1831 and described by a British naval officer as 'a small hillock of a dark colour a few feet above the sea'. Within a month the island was 65 metres high and had a circumference of 3.5 kilometres. Like flies to honey, competing territorial claims soon descended on this grey heap. A Union Jack was planted on 2 August 1831 and the island named after Sir James Graham, First Lord of the Admiralty. It was then named Ferdinandea and claimed on behalf of Ferdinand II by the Kingdom of the Two Sicilies, recently formed by the unification of the Kingdom of Sicily and the Kingdom of Naples. Then the French tricolour was raised on the island. Its French discoverer named the island Julia, in honour of the month it first appeared. However, like most new volcanic islands, Julia was made of ash and light rock and quickly began to disappear. By December the island was nothing but a low reef. The Italian volcanologist and Catholic priest Giuseppe Mercalli wryly observed, 'All that remained of Julia Island were the many names imposed upon it by travellers of various nations who had the good fortune to witness the spectacle of its formation and disappearance.' The story is, of course, not over. The island has been active again, and in 2002 Italian divers planted an Italian flag on the top of its underwater summit, getting in their nation's claim in good time before Graham/Ferdinandea/Julia's next appearance.

Islands we have destroyed

Arguably the world's most frightening island is Runit Island. It is a tiny Pacific island inhabited by a monster. A vast concrete dome called 'The Tomb' sits at one end, packed with nuclear waste and occupying about a quarter of the whole island. Many of the Marshall Islands became uninhabitable, including Runit, after the US conducted sixty-seven nuclear tests across the archipelago between 1946 and 1958. The Tomb was supposed to be part of the solution; it was built in 1979 as a repository for 73,000 cubic metres of radioactive waste. Unfortunately, rising sea levels mean that water has leaked into the dome. A 2013 US Department of Energy report on Runit is a litany of alarming descriptions of deformations, cracks and leaks in the concrete shell.

The Marshall Islands is also where we find the most famous casualty of the USA's nuclear testing programme, Bikini Atoll. Some of the devices tested were colossal: one bomb dropped in 1954 had an impact 1100 times larger than the one dropped on Hiroshima. During these years, Runit and Bikini accounted for more than 50 per cent of the world's nuclear fallout.

Islands that have been used as nuclear test sites are, of course, best avoided: the water cannot be drunk, seafood cannot be eaten, and plants cannot be farmed. But small islands have also been the site of biological weapons tests. Gruinard Island off the west coast of Scotland became 'Anthrax island' when, in 1942, Britain started to test anthrax on the island's sheep. Gruinard was decontaminated in 1990. The Soviet Union constructed a biological weapons test site, called Aralsk-7, in 1954 on Vozrozhdeniya Island ('Renaissance Island') and neighbouring Komsomolskiy Island in the Aral Sea. The islands were also used to develop new bioweapons that were reportedly tested on prisoners. Dubbed the 'Island of Death', Aralsk-7 saw a series of accidents and scandals, such as an incident in 1971 during which smallpox was accidentally released, killing at least three people. Abandoned in 1991, the islands continue to store containers full of an unknown variety of biological weapons. The containers are not maintained and it is said they are leaking. Since irrigation schemes have drained the Aral Sea, turning Vozrozhdeniya Island into a peninsula, the worry is that whatever bioweapons were developed there may find their way out to the wider world.

Another form of destruction inflicted on islands is mining. One of the most spectacular examples is Japan's Hashima Island ('Battleship Island'), which in 1887 began to be covered with buildings that eventually grew into high-rises housing thousands of coal miners and their families. By 1974 the undersea coal seams were exhausted and Hashima was abandoned, though it has had an interesting afterlife. Resembling a collapsing industrial castle, Hashima has a dystopian appeal and today attracts filmmakers and tourists.

This unlikely upside of despoliation will not save Nauru, a 21-square-kilometre nation in the South Pacific once covered in valuable phosphate deposits. Over the last hundred years the entire island has been strip-mined – first by European powers and then, since 1968, by its own government. Once one of the world's wealthiest nations, Nauru is now a wasteland where little can grow. Today its few sources of income include selling passports to foreigners and hosting refugees refused by other countries.

These islands have been destroyed by human activity but they are still on the map. Over the past two decades numerous islands were completely eradicated by mining. The global demand for sand, fuelled by Asia's building boom, is the main cause. Journalist Vince Beiser, who has spent years investigating the global sand trade, reports that in Indonesia alone about two dozen small sandy islands have been dug out and are now below sea level.

Islands are under threat from the South Pacific to the North Atlantic. For islanders these are anxious times.

THE SAN BLAS ISLANDS OF GUNA YALA, PANAMA

Justino chops a leathery hand against one knee: 'In December the water comes here.' He is a Kuna, one of Panama's indigenous communities. Although he's grinning, worry lines bind his forehead as he tells me about sea rise on his home island. It is one of about fifty inhabited by the Kuna in the San Blas archipelago of Guna Yala ('Kuna land'). The whole group consists of 365 islands and stretches for over 200 kilometres on the Caribbean side of Panama.

We're 70 kilometres but a planet away from the high-rises of Panama City. The Kuna are poor and their islands are minuscule – often just a football pitch in size and a few centimetres above sea level. From the shore or sailing past, all you see of many of the islands are some palm trees and a few huts fashioned from palm fronds. The Kuna came to live on these scattered sandy islets about two hundred years ago. The islands were free of the insects and wild animals that plagued – and still plague – the thickly forested mainland. They also offered protection from other hostile tribes. The islands were sanctuaries: with few pests, surrounded by fish, crabs and lobsters but close enough to the mainland to have easy access to farmland, firewood and fresh water.

Justino tells his story in the old but spotless 40-foot yacht on which I have rented a berth and which is captained by his friend, a softly spoken sixty-year-old: a Majorca-born mariner called Toni. This archipelago and this cramped boat are Toni's home and he is keen to point out the islands that have disappeared. 'Over there, that was an island,' or: 'We are passing straight over another island,' or: 'Again, again, all gone.' In every direction Toni jabs his finger at yesterday's islands. What remains are shallows, sometimes marked by a few sticks and a cresting wave.

A battered copy of *The Panama Cruising Guide* by Eric Bauhaus lies below deck. Its detailed maps make it indispensable for the small yachting community who anchor in convivial packs. Toni's copy is so well thumbed that it is now a spineless wad of weathered pages. During my few days in San Blas, and with little else to do once it got dark, I transcribed its maps and local lore. Bauhaus is clear: 'Every time I do a survey after being away for some time, I have to take islands off the maps that are now nothing but shoals.'

Justino gestures to the mainland: a green mass, alive with mosquitoes and crawling with snakes and not a few crocodiles, just a kilometre or so away: 'We have to go there,' he says, running his hands through his hair. 'My head whirls with problems.' He's expecting that, sometime soon, everyone on the seven islands that make up the Robeson group where he now lives will have to relocate. The Robesons lie at the northernmost fringe of San Blas and are so remote that they don't even show up on Google Earth. It seems that different island groups will head off in different directions and see what happens: 'They go there; we go here – all different.' Justino's smile is fading again. It's a chaotic scenario and what the future will bring is uncertain for him and his extended family. But on only one point he is clear: 'We leave, all go.'

There have been fitful plans for an ordered evacuation. I have brought with me a report by an NGO called Displacement Solutions, which runs through the travails of a central government-funded scheme for the relocation of the relatively large and densely settled Kuna island that everyone here calls Carti. The rough track to the San Blas coast takes you past the empty, half-finished and overgrown accommodation blocks that one day, supposedly, are still going to provide homes for the Carti islanders. Government funding was pulled some time ago and the 'relocation village' is disappearing into the jungle. At the moment it looks like the Kuna's 'displacement solutions' will be ad hoc and unassisted.

The San Blas islands continue to be presented in tourist brochures as shimmering flecks of paradise. On the surface, it is easy to see why. They are tropical, palm-fringed and flung across a warm and usually calm sea. The wide availability of cannabis and cocaine (I am told cocaine on the islands is cheaper than Coca-Cola) adds to the intoxicating atmosphere and pulls in Panamanian partiers and backpackers.

A few Kuna actively provide for the tourist drug trade but others scorn it. Separate islands are under the control of elders called Sahilas and it is they who decide what is permissible. The Robesons are one of the more traditional areas and even beer is banned. Justino lives on the most populated of the Islas Robeson, Tupsuit Dummat. It is a hugger-mugger labyrinth of sandy lanes and running, laughing children. It's happy and well cared for. Weaving around the palm-leaf huts, I pass a neatly painted blue school and the dark entrance of a stoutly built 'congress hall', where the Sahilas issue their edicts, traditionally by singing long sacred songs. Over on Carti, which is regularly overrun with visitors and more plugged in to the modern world, modern manners prevail: the locals tend to be brisk, unsmiling and commercially savvy. But on Tupsuit Dummat there is warmth in the smiles and a sense of excitement that visitors have come. Like nearly all Kuna women, those on Tupsuit Dummat are dressed in colourful handmade shawls decorated with 'mola' – complex embroidery designs that are Panama's most famous handicraft – and plenty of leg bangles. Some also have golden nose plugs and henna tattoos on their faces. Offshore, men and women can be seen paddling in the Kuna's elegant dug-out canoes called *ulus*, bringing sugar cane and fruit as well as firewood and water from the mainland.

It's an idyllic scene but there is a sense of uncertainty in every conversation. Life is getting harder. Interviews collected by Greta Rybus, an American photojournalist, on a Kuna island called Coetupo about 160 kilometres south of the Robesons provide a vivid portrait of the many problems people face. With climate change have come higher tides but also warmer waters and this has led to a decline in the fish catch. 'Now the sea can't heal the way it used to,' a

Coetupo elder told Rybus, explaining that, 'It is too hot [so] nowadays there is not much fish. Before, there were a lot of coconuts and bananas. But not now, because of the changes with the sun.' A teacher who lives on Coetupo described how some of the measures the islanders have used to protect their shore have only made matters worse. 'When people realized the sea level was rising,' the teacher told Greta Rybus, 'they started to destroy and use corals to build a kind of wall, which is very damaging.' This local educator went on to identify one of the key problems with ad hoc, uncoordinated relocation plans: 'About five years ago, we tried to start a project to relocate to the mainland, but there were disputes within the community. The land on the continent is already distributed; it has owners. And these owners don't want to give their land to other people.'

Back on Tupsuit Dummat, I've been invited inside Justino's family hut. Thin sunshine patterns the mud floor with slips of yellow light, pitted and smoothed by last winter's flood. Occupied hammocks swing from every roof beam. At the back is Justino's grandmother, too sick to raise her head. She is relying on traditional remedies but they are not working. A shivering fever has taken grip of the whole island. So many are ill that the usual festivities marking the start of November (a month full of pageants in Panama) have been abandoned. Later, captain Toni slips Justino two ibuprofen tablets: it's the sum total of the modern medical help his grandmother is going to get.

It's no surprise so many are unwell on the Robesons. Levels of sanitation, as on all the San Blas islands, are basic. Arriving at any of the larger inhabited islands, what you see are dozens of latrines perched on the end of rickety jetties poking out in all directions. The houses face inwards, away from the sea, which is the Kuna's sole source of protein but also a giant toilet. I realized the limpid waters were not a great place to swim on my first morning when, after a few hearty strokes, I found myself trying to negotiate some serious-sized turds.

A crowd of children tumble into Justino's compound, including a girl with a shock of blonde hair and very white skin. Albinism is common among the Kuna and such children are considered lucky. Toni asks the children why they think the island keeps getting flooded. They giggle and push each other; they don't know. It turns out none of them – not even the older teenagers – has ever heard of sea-level rise or climate change or global warming.

Maybe from their point of view things don't look so straightforward. They see the islands inundated but also actively defended. As those interviews on Coetupo suggest, some of the techniques used by the Kuna to protect the islands are of dubious value. I came across an even less likely practice a couple of hours' sail south of the Robesons, on Chichime island. Here the elders had advised that sea rise could be stopped if a particular mixture of sand – with equal parts from different parts of the island – was banked up. The sand was soon washed away, and later I picked my way along Chichime's fast-eroding shore, over scattered plastic waste and the dying black roots of palm trees that were once inland.

Ill-conceived responses like this may be more the exception than the rule. Other Kuna techniques do work, at least for a while. On Tupsuit Dummat I listen to the account of Armando who is taking a rest from unloading sand that he has collected from the mainland in his *ulu*. He uses the sand to reclaim land. Even with a mechanical digger it would be a big job, but all he has is a dug-out canoe, a bucket and a spade. Armando looks weary and is frighteningly thin but the work, he says, must continue, for the land will be used for a new hut for visiting doctors, allowing them to stay on the island for longer periods, perhaps even overnight.

Turning around, I spot another man a little way out to sea, building up land. He is taking gravel and coral out of his *ulu* to make a new island, fetching up rocks from his canoe as he has been doing every day for months. This is Bernado and when he paddles back he tells me about his big plan. The island he is constructing will be used to build rented accommodation and is part of his scheme to lure back his children who, like many other Kuna, have gone to live in Panama City. Bernado's efforts are not unique: the Robesons have other tiny, self-built islets. The Kuna don't just live on islands; they make them.

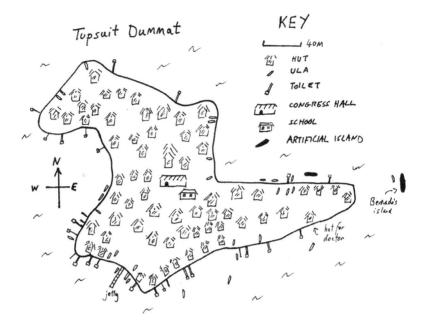

Given the doom-laden scenarios that surround San Blas, such efforts might appear futile. But they might also make us question the way these islanders' 'displacement' is talked about as inevitable, almost natural. If the Kuna had access to the resources that the Dutch are using to build Ocean Reef in Panama City, they would not have to leave. It wouldn't be complicated: these are usually calm waters, and bulking out the top and sides of these islands with rock would not be rocket science. It's not going to happen because the Kuna are poor. Not only that, they have an uneasy relationship with the rest of the country.

In order to understand the Kuna's isolation we need to delve a little into their history. In many ways the Kuna are a rare example of indigenous survival. Not only are they still here but their language and culture have flourished. Some aspects of their culture are surprisingly liberal. When men marry they move into the wife's compound and it is women who control all the money in Kuna households. It is also common to see transgender men who live and dress as women in the islands. Apparently the youngest son in a family is assigned a female role if there aren't any daughters.

Anthropologist James Howe's *A People Who Would Not Kneel* is the telling title of the most comprehensive history of the modern Kuna. An indication of what the Kuna were up against is Panama's 1912 law on 'indigenous civilization'. It opens with the proclamation that 'The Executive Power shall seek, by all possible peaceful means, the reduction to civilized life of the barbarian, semi-barbarous and savage tribes that exist in the country.' Kuna clothes, beads and nose rings were forcibly removed, while the Kuna language was repressed. The 1920s saw stand-offs and violence between the police and Kuna armed with machetes. It was a confusing time and the call for Kuna independence also reflected the activities of outsiders, most famously Richard Marsh, an American explorer sympathetic to the Kuna. Marsh wrote and circulated the 1925 'Declaration' of Kuna independence that led to the brief existence of the Republic of Tule. This would-be state was soon reunited with Panama following the mediation of the United States.

Whatever Marsh's role, the events of those years are remembered and re-enacted across Guna Yala every year and referred to as the Kuna Revolution, a proud moment of defiance and a living legacy of resistance. Rather alarmingly (though misleadingly), the flag of the 'revolution' was a bright swastika and is still a common sight in the islands. The flag has no connection with the Nazi symbol, although I was unsettled to read Eric Bauhaus's claim that the revolution was accompanied by a 'Holocausto de las Razas' in which people of mixed parentage were murdered. While James Howe acknowledges 'ugly killings of non-Indians', his account suggests a total death toll of only thirty, so the word 'holocaust' hardly seems fair. Nevertheless, a profound dislike of 'mixing' is still very much alive. I was told repeatedly by Kuna and non-Kuna alike that it is forbidden for Kuna to have relationships with non-Kuna.

Panama won the Kuna back after their revolution – as they have several times since – with promises of autonomy. 'Autonomy' sounds like a good thing and today the Kuna pretty much govern themselves. Yet, in an age of global crisis, this kind of freedom comes with a sting in the tail. Unlike other 'sinking' and fully sovereign islands such as the Solomons or Maldives, the Kuna's plight is invisible. They have no voice at any international table. Small islands like these, without independence, have a problem: few have heard of them, and their concerns mean very little to the outside world. The problem is made worse when they are inhabited by an impoverished minority in a country where environmentalism has made few inroads. In my experience, in Panama – as in so many other countries – concerns about damage to the environment are met with a shrug. The political autonomy of the Kuna makes this shrug more certain and more dismissive. At best the Panamanian attitude to the Kuna is a form of benign neglect, but it is frequently clouded with irritation – even anger – at the Kuna's stubborn refusal to join the modern world.

The Kuna's hard-won autonomy has an impact on those wanting to visit San Blas. Tourist provision is haphazard and it isn't an easy place to get to. Travellers need to show their passport at the border of Kuna territory to listless armed police; after that it's often unclear who, if anyone, is in charge. My visit coincided with a breakdown in Panama–Kuna relations. The Kuna have long been annoyed that outsiders – particularly the yacht-owners – are taking tourist dollars. Since there aren't any hotels, a lot of people stay on boats and they are all owned by non-Kuna. In Panama City I got panicky WhatsApp messages from Toni and his confederates, explaining that the Kuna Congress had made my berth on his yacht illegal. I was bewildered. Tapping my smartphone into the small hours, I ended up agreeing to a cloak-and-dagger arrangement that involved taking a taxi from my hotel at 4 a.m. but not divulging to the driver where I was going: 'If anyone ask you, say you're going to David's place, OK?' It was the strangest taxi ride of my life. I had no idea where I was going (except that I needed to meet a man called Toni), yet I was forbidden from announcing my destination. The journey was four hours long, cost $70 in cash ('Give me the money now, please') and took place in an ancient Jeep that wheezed and juddered on ever smaller and more potholed roads. Eventually, I found myself in what I was told was a port but was, in fact, a clearing by a bend on a muddy river. After a long wait in the blistering sun, I was directed into a small boat equipped with two fat outboards. It powered upriver and then into the open sea. The rain began to pour as it arrived at our destination, which I later learned was the island of Chichime. Toni emerged, padding across the sand in a bright cagoule. There followed a mystifying stand-off between him and a few Chichime Kuna, which was resolved by me handing over $75 in return for a lobster dinner. I'm pleased to say my self-pity cleared up as the rain stopped and soon I was making a cosy bunk below deck on Toni's boat.

Having read about the Kuna in the international press, I was expecting confirmation of a now-familiar narrative: that the Kuna are doughty, plucky natives who are choosing to leave their islands on their own terms. It's a nice idea but it's wishful thinking. The impression I came away with was very different, less hopeful and far more chaotic. What is going on here is slow-motion panic. The Kuna are being left to fend for themselves and to make their way through a calamity that is not of their making but that is turning their way of life upside down and inside out.

The modern, industrial world is destroying these islands. Yet they fascinate the industrial world's restless and beauty-starved citizens. Each island is unique, enchanting. It's no surprise that the San Blas islands draw in tourists and outsiders like me, searching for paradise. We circle round, always looking for another lovely thing, another photo opportunity, around and around, waving and smiling, as everything disappears from sight.

TONGATAPU AND FAFA, TONGA

'Islands come and go. Some parts grow bigger, other parts disappear. It's not humans that make it happen.' We're the only customers at the island's only bar. Tom orders another large glass of red wine, takes a thick slurp and becomes adamant that 'There are no signs of anthropogenic sea-level rise but that's all people want to hear.' I wince. He's got me in his sights. A slight and rather weary young German, Tom is goading but also confounding me: he's a marine biologist, an expert and he's self-consciously dismissive of the tide of received opinion.

Tom lives on Fafa, a *very* small square island – it's about 450 metres across – and 'off-grid' eco-resort. He studies its corals and has told me he also serves as the island's doctor, which confuses me. Fafa has just thirteen newly built, traditional-looking, coconut-thatch huts for its well-heeled visitors, each standing in a clearing of palms and tropical flowers, and it's only 6 kilometres from Tonga's capital. What would be the point of a doctor? Perhaps I've misunderstood or misheard. At the moment I'm not feeling certain of anything. Some hours later I lurch into the darkness, my bare feet snouting along warm sandy paths to my own 'native' hut.

I try to fall asleep to the shush of cradling waves. There's little wind tonight to disturb the tropical air and the only other noise is the occasional squawk of a swamp hen, querulous long-legged birds that jealously patrol the island.

A tiny island can feel like a very soothing place – womblike and a world away from danger. Yet I'm restless, gnawing over that indigestible conversation. I should have challenged Tom: what natural process could cause so much rapid sea-

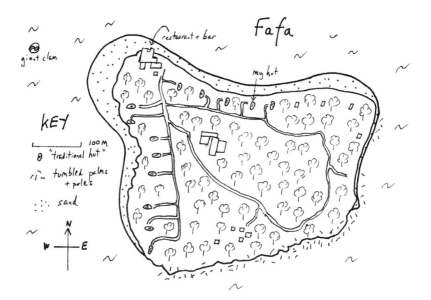

level rise? I should have said, 'Look, Tom, satellite data indicates that the sea level around Tonga has been rising every year. It's exceptional and dangerous, especially as it has been accompanied by more severe storms and cyclones.' Something like that.

On the bedside table my wristwatch is ticking. Loudly. I get up and smother it under some clothes. As the minutes drag by more rebuttals come to mind. All eighteen member states of the 2018 Pacific Islands Forum, including Tonga, have agreed that climate change is the 'single greatest threat' to the Pacific region. The plea of the Tongan government at the UN climate conference in Paris was stark: 'A lot of countries and governments are in Paris negotiating their economies – we're just asking for survival.' Just as telling was the response of the government's senior climate finance analyst, Sione Fulivai, when he was asked by journalists if a mass evacuation was being planned. 'Where would we go? We are tied to our land, to our culture,' said Fulivai. 'Without our lands who are we?'

I recall how I first heard of this place: a BBC television report from 2015, which featured an interview with Fafa's former manager and showed how the beach had retreated between 5 and 10 metres. 'We're already having to move the restaurant and bar area back,' the manager said, adding: 'We're fighting the inevitable.' The journalist asked if in a hundred years the island would still exist. The reply was simple: 'Absolutely not.'

Earlier, in bright sunshine, I'd tried to walk the island's sandy circumference and it was soon plain that this is a place under attack. Much of Fafa's southern shore is an obstacle course of palms felled by the surging waters. Attempts to stave off the rising waters are now part of the wreckage. Wooden posts, planted a few years ago to defend the shore, are now mostly at an angle or scattered and some are in the midst of water. On disappearing islands in the tropics you are often just a metre or so from storm-damaged and sea-broken trees and homes and a rapidly eroding shore – from over-whelming proof of sea-level rise and more turbulent weather.

Before I started visiting endangered islands I imagined that I'd be talking to angry people. So far, that hasn't happened. I guess if I sought out politicians or activists it would be very different. But I'm not picking or choosing; I'll talk to anyone. What I hear are sighs and shrugs – a very occasional denial that there is anything amiss – accompanied by the steady beat of waves on beaches. On the main island of Tongatapu, a guy in his sixties, who was waiting at the harbour-side, told me about the changes he'd witnessed: 'I can see the high water in the harbour; it's much higher now, so when it's high tide now it's coming over.' Then he sighed: 'I don't know if it's the sea rising or the land sinking. It doesn't matter which. Nothing I can do. Nothing I can do.'

'Nothing I can do.' We both stared out to the blue Pacific, an ocean larger than the land-mass of every single continent and every single island combined. 'Nothing I can do.'

'Nothing I can do' has begun to sound like humanity's agreed position and its solace. I'm in no position to scold or sound superior. Back in England, I recycle odds and ends, ride a bike, occasionally buy a local vegetable, things like that. It enables me to be part of the ongoing chat about being green and to think that I'm in some way 'doing my bit'. Out here, all that, it's just *nothing*. Among people who are living with the imminent disappearance of their homes – of everything – the psychology changes. It is truly overwhelming. And if any gesture captures this mood it is the shrug and the sigh, the body language of fatalism.

Perhaps I'd better check the time on my phone: 3 a.m. Still no sleep, yet I'm so tired, plagued by repetitions of half-sentences, of questions never asked or answered. Others soon bubble to the surface, such as why this glaring crisis doesn't make people jump up and down in the way other crises do. Is it because other challenges, like economic calamity or even war, are small scale by comparison and have quick fixes? This is different; it's on a different scale. Global environmental disaster is, indeed, overwhelming. It runs against some innate human feeling that nature is there for us – that everything, in the end, will be OK.

I did get to sleep; I must have as next morning I'm up early. No sign of Tom, my nemesis; I guess he won't be up for hours. The early sun has already warmed the sand and I've taken one of the resort's snorkels and am soon splashing into the water. The corals are soft and colourful, though not to be touched, and anyway I'm on the hunt for a local spectacle, the giant clam. The last time I saw one was in a comic – a monster of the deep trapping the leg of our hero. I wasn't convinced: *that* could not be real!

Through the clear shallows I make out a boulder, sand glinting on its flanks. I'm nearly over it and have become not scared but amazed: inside the long, wavy lines of its wide-open mouth is an enormous muscular siphon, pumping in and out, the black hole as wide as my fist. The clam is well over a metre long and probably getting on for a hundred years old. The world is still full of marvels.

I stumble up the beach, gleeful. I've discovered a giant! I have to remind myself that I was directed to it by one of the current managers of the resort. It is 'the clam': a survivor in waters where they used to be plentiful. Tonga still has enough giant clams to export them to aquariums across the world, but probably not for much longer. As sea temperatures rise, the shell of the clams thins and they become vulnerable to predators. Across Asia and the Pacific their numbers are in free-fall.

Before leaving Fafa I talk some more to the resort's managers, a married couple who are more guarded than their predecessor about the future of the island. A super-friendly and efficient Australian husband-and-wife team who have decades of experience managing island resorts, they point out (like Tom) that the island is shifting, building up in some places and eroding in others. Reassurance – we all want it: everything will be OK.

Fafa is an enchanting place. The mood is different on what Tongans call the 'mainland', the island of Tongatapu. It is home to 70 per cent of Tonga's 108,000 people. The remaining 30 per cent are scattered across thirty-five of the archipelago's 169 islands. Unlike multiracial Pacific nations like Hawaii, Fiji or Tahiti, Tongans are nearly all Polynesian and take considerable pride in never having been colonized. Tongatapu is 40 kilometres long and 20 kilometres wide; at its highest point, near the airport in the south-east, it rises to 65 metres. It is mostly much lower, especially on its northern shores where the capital, Nuku'alofa, sprawls along the seashore.

I pick up a hire car in Nuku'alofa and set off on a day-long trip round the island. The road I'm on is often banked up above the surrounding fields and it pretty much circles Tongatapu. There are sporadic sea defences: bits of the north coast have barrier walls or are lined with great white boulders. But it's the upgrading of this road – from a dirt track into a tarmac-covered and rigid earthwork – that has (albeit unintentionally) created the island's most significant sea-wall. It's not an unmixed blessing: the road is making storm floods worse as it blocks rainfall from draining into the sea.

The road is getting emptier as I head east, looping round Fanga'uta Lagoon; a marshy body of water that scoops out the middle of Tongatapu and provides an access route for the rising and stormy ocean to penetrate deep inland. My first stop is to see the fishing pigs of Talafoʻou. On the shoreline I pull up near a tourist information board that describes how local pigs love swimming and snuffling for seafood. But the pigs are nowhere to be seen. Maybe the tide is too high. Since they 'fish' as well as swim, they sound more worthy of fame than the more celebrated but lazier swimming pigs of the Bahamas and Bermuda.

A family in a pick-up – the vehicle of choice for many Tongans – slows down to stare at me. I get the feeling that tourists have become a rarer sight round here than swimming pigs. The absence of tourism was obvious almost as soon as I arrived in Tonga. The taxi driver who met me at the airport – a man vast in all directions – began with the question 'You an aid worker, yeah?'

The flight got in at midnight and the drive to the capital proved a sombre introduction to the country. We had to make several detours as police curfews were in force and many roads blocked off. After the last cyclone a night-time lockdown round the centre of town was thought necessary to prevent looting by what the taxi driver called 'bad boys'.

Tonga's problems are interlinked. Rising sea levels, more frequent and more damaging cyclones, a rise in crime and social discontent, large-scale emigration, a collapsing tourist industry ... they are an interlacing burden of worry. We can add other problems to this weighty chain, such as an agricultural crisis, the increasing need to import food, and an obesity epidemic. Worsening and more frequent storms batter farms, blowing away crops and killing the soil with salt water. The result is that very little fresh green produce is grown in Tonga. Today Tongans have the unfortunate international status – along with other Pacific nations who face similar challenges, such as the Cook Islands and Nauru – of being one of the world's fattest people. When you look around the food shops, which are full of packets and cans of imported food and none of which sells anything fresh, you can see why.

I drive down the east coast, passing through tranquil coconut groves, extraordinary ancient graveyards, a 'stone henge' called Ha'amonga 'a Maui, and long empty beaches. Tonga is a very old and special place, with a history reaching back some three thousand years. Before long I'm on the southern coast, which is rockier and safer from the impacts of cyclones and sea-level rise. If more islanders lived on this side, rather than on the shallow north side, lives and livelihoods would be saved. The rocks of the southern coast are perforated with hundreds of blowholes. I find a vantage point where, looking both east and west and for miles up and down the coast, you can see, hear and feel powerful white jets of sea water being gunned high up into the air.

Elsewhere the rocky nature of the beaches has another cause: all the sand has been stripped off for use in the construction industry. A further casualty of development has been the mangrove swamps that once protected Tonga's coasts from storms and tsunamis. The many problems facing Tonga have been made more intractable by the fact that all the land is owned by the Crown. In 2010 Tonga stopped being an absolute monarchy and is now described as a constitutional monarchy. However, King Tupou VI and the noble families that constitute his court still literally own the country and that has made it difficult to relocate farms and people away from the vulnerable, low-lying northern coast. Writing about the need for relocation inland, the climate-change scientists Patrick Nunn and Nobuo Mimura warned, over two decades ago, that 'If the King and his nobles are not prepared to release more land to commoners for settlement, trouble may arise.'

Trouble has arisen but not against the monarchy. Discontent has been displaced onto the great bogeyman of twenty-first-century Tonga: the Chinese. The rioters who destroyed about 70 per cent of the capital's central business district in 2006 targeted Chinese businesses. Resentment against Chinese loans and business ownership continues to seethe. If you go into any store in Tonga, you're likely to see a young Chinese woman staffing the till, while glum Tongan employees and their friends hang out some distance away. You can almost taste the hostility in the shop-worn air.

It was only in October 2018 that Tonga got a sea-level monitoring station, and detailed information on the scale of the problem remains in short supply. Most people appear to agree that flooding from sea level is a less pressing issue than cyclones and the threat of earthquakes and tsunamis. Every corner I turn brings fresh evidence of the destruction wrought by the last cyclone. A lot of Tongans live in houses of breeze-blocks and corrugated iron, which keep getting blown down. Some homeowners have slung plastic sheeting up to keep off the rain but others have moved out. The risk of flooding, tsunamis and earthquakes in Tonga is extreme. Not only does Tonga sit in one of the most cyclone-prone areas of the ocean but it is also in the middle of the 'Tonga Trench', the world's most active zone of tectonic movement. This is a landscape well used to disaster. The island of Tongatapu periodically is buckled and tilted by earthquakes, such as the one on Christmas Eve 1853 that caused the whole northern coast to subside and flood. If you want to see what tsunamis can do to the island, a visit to Tsunami Rock is instructive. It's a boulder the size of a large house. Covered in small trees, it squats incongruously in the middle of a field. It was thrown up, far from the coast, a thousand years ago by a massive wave that swept over the entire island.

Earthquake and tsunami drills and planning are a regular feature of life in Tongatapu. Smartly uniformed schoolchildren have afternoons set aside in which they practise running to what passes for high ground. The Tonga Meteorological Service has a network of seismic stations but relies on the Pacific Tsunami Warning Center in Hawaii to

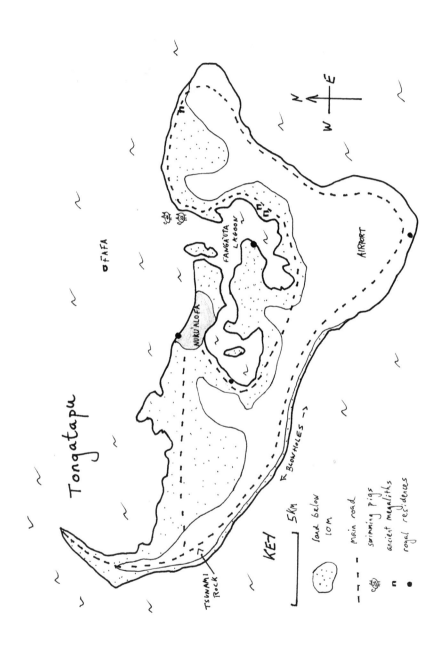

provide information that is early enough to save anyone. Tongans prepare for climatic and natural calamity on a daily basis. They have to. The problem is that they face a whole slew of interconnected issues – from salt-water intrusion to earthquakes, from crime to sea-level rise, from obesity to ethnic conflict. All thrown at a very remote and poor country of barely 100,000 people. In many ways, it's remarkable how well Tonga has coped. It hasn't fallen apart – not quite; it's still there. But the challenges are immense. The three-thousand-year history of Tongan civilization is slowly unspinning.

THE ISLES OF SCILLY, UK

It's a peculiarly warm and cloudless day in late February and I'm trying to take in all the rocky islands that freckle the small bay and the far horizon. My daughter and I are the only guests in a seafront guesthouse with a little balcony. Steve, the owner, has some helpful words of explanation.

'What you're looking at are the tops of mountains,' he tells us. For thousands of years the Isles of Scilly have been drowning. It's a flooded landscape, a vision from the past that is a fingerpost to the future. Leaving the balcony, we head to the holiday flat's kitchen, which has views over the Lower Moors: rough fields and reed beds that occupy a large wet chunk of the main island of St Mary's. There is a more urgent note in our host's voice: 'I'm hoping they will be there for a good while; that's the hope.' But later that day he produces a battered copy of the local council's 'Climate Change Strategy' plan, which includes a map in which the whole of the Lower Moors – and much else besides – is coloured in blue, given up to the Atlantic in what the document calls 'managed retreat'.

Since that plan was published in 2011, it has become clear that allowing the island's only freshwater bore-holes, which are on the Lower and Higher Moors of St Mary's, to be swallowed up by the sea might not be such a great idea. It's possible another fifty years could be bought for the Lower Moors with coastal 'rock armour' that will help reduce flooding during storm surges. For the time being at least, there is a determination to stay. This is, after all, a landscape that has been living with loss for a very long time.

The Isles of Scilly is an archipelago of 200 or so islets and islands, 43 kilometres west of England's western tip, and when the weather is kind – like today – you can understand why some call the Scillies the 'Fortunate Isles'. Its land-mass is tiny, just 16 square kilometres, but it feels less crowded than the mainland. The population of 2204 is small and stable. In fact, there are fewer residents today than in the early nineteenth century, when the population reached about 2500. There are five inhabited islands (St Mary's, St Martin's, Tresco, St Agnes and Bryher). Even the biggest, St Mary's, is easily walked round in a day. Not that you would want to rush: the entire island group has been designated an Area of Outstanding Natural Beauty. Many of its quiet roadside verges drip with succulents and shy pretty flowers and the Scillies has by far the greatest density of historic sites in the UK, with 239 ancient monuments and archaeological sites on land and many more lying uncounted under the waves.

Before the Scillies there was Ennor, Cornish for 'The Land'. Ennor was a big island whose higher peaks are now the main islands of Scilly. Ennor was always shrinking. St Agnes was a separate island by 3000 BC and it is estimated that in the 500 years between 2500 and 2000 BC Ennor lost over half of its area. The name 'Ennor' was still in use in the sixteenth century, and everywhere you look on the Scillies you can see its phantom traces. Ancient stone walls run into the sea; multiple tombs cluster on rock islets that used to be hill-tops; the ruins of the Iron Age village of Halangy sit on a low cliff, looking out over a seascape that would once have been farmed. From 1500 BC onwards most of this low-lying farmland turned into marsh. Charles Johns, from Cornwall's Council Archaeological Unit, explains that it would nevertheless 'have remained useful land, especially for grazing animal stock and would have been passable with ease almost all of the time'.

It took a long time for Ennor to completely fade from view. Charles Thomas, whose book *Exploration of a Drowned Landscape* is the definitive guide to the island's deep past, tells us that the final transition from Ennor to the Scillies 'took place between the seventh and thirteenth centuries, and that "from the viewpoint of people in small boats" the waters between the present islands would not have been navigable until Tudor times'.

Sea-level rise in the Scillies is a compound of two long-term processes and one recent one. The two long-term processes are an interglacial, warming period and post-glacial 'bounce-back' further north, which is tilting the southern half of Britain downwards (this 'isostatic adjustment' adds between 10 and 33 per cent on existing sea-level rise). The short-term process is modern, anthropogenic global warming, which is making a challenging problem not just worse but unpredictable.

It's not incremental rises that the islanders fear so much as storms and sea-surges, which regularly flood the island's capital (and only) town, Hugh Town, which straddles a sandy isthmus on St Mary's. The storms fling up salt water and boulders and eat away at coastlines, reducing the viability of the island's petite daffodil fields and threatening the tourist economy. The litany of recorded storms – from the Great Storm of 1744, through to the storms of 1962, 1989, 1994, 1995, 2004 and 2014 – suggests they may be becoming more regular. The last big one, in February 2014, ended up with the main street of Hugh Town covered in sand.

I've come to the Town Hall to talk to Julian Pearce, the council's Physical Assets and Natural Resources officer. The Town Hall is in the centre of Hugh Town and the hub of island life. There are posters inside and out, telling islanders to conserve water. The message could not be clearer: 'Water usage has reached an unsustainable level on St Mary's.' I have, though, a more lightweight message to deliver: Steve has told me to remind Julian about their badminton practice. They are both spry, middle-aged men so I can imagine it will be quite a workout. It's only later that I realize that my errand might be a clue to something important. It's no exaggeration to say that everyone here knows almost everyone else. 'Community' is an overworked word but in small islands it means something. The fact that there is a close-knit community explains why the Scillies, and other small islands, battle on. Julian tells me how 'the community still gets engaged', which in practical terms means that when there is just a few hours to prepare before an incoming surge tide, people get moving and start shifting sandbags.

To drive the point home he tells me a story about a meeting of a would-be flood-preparedness group that was called in Newquay in Cornwall, on the mainland. The assembled citizens were informed that seafront properties were in real danger of being swept away. 'It was supposed to be about getting the neighbourhood together,' says Julian, but 'the people living further back said: "So those houses are going to go? Fantastic! We can have seafront properties!"' Julian is clearly relishing the tale. Islanders know they are different and they define themselves against 'mainland' selfishness. Perhaps this also helps explain why, despite the dangers of sea-level rise, people want to move to islands and build islands: islands symbolize real community and the kind of values that so easily dissolve in the acidic anomie of mainland life.

There are some big decisions looming on the Scillies and they will test its sense of community. Julian is cagey about Hugh Town's longevity but he is clear that 'in x hundred years' it will be covered by sea-level rise. Yet 'managed retreat' is no longer a favoured phrase. Referring to the map with the big blue areas of 'retreat' that Steve showed me earlier, he cautions that 'that approach was based on defending property' and says today they need 'a better and more balanced viewpoint' that also considers essential infrastructure. Julian points out that the 2011 plan 'didn't look at water supply or access to airport or communication from town to up-country'. ('Up-country' is what people on St Mary's call the part of their island that isn't 'town', which is Hugh Town.)

Identifying problems with 'managed retreat' is one thing; coming up with an alternative is more tricky. Walling in the Scillies is not an option and, citing plunging sea depths round the archipelago, Julian is not keen on barrier islands. If the funding comes through, he is pinning his hopes on rock armour in parts of the north-west of St Mary's: 'That would give us another fifty years, say.'

I cast my mind back to the *Daily Telegraph* storyline that first attracted my attention to the Scillies: 'Scilly Isles could have to be abandoned because of global warming'. I also think back to the Skype call I had with Jan Petzold, who is a Science Officer for the Intergovernmental Panel on Climate Change, based in Bremen, and an expert on the Scillies. Petzold is concerned that all the attention on Pacific nations is giving people a false picture of climate change. 'We don't know much about islands in the north,' he says, even though 'we have a lot of islands in Europe and along the American coasts and people there are also vulnerable'.

The next day it's still hot enough for early summer (it will be confirmed later that this is the warmest February since records began) and I take the path to Old Town, a village that is overlooked by the ancient Ennor Castle, in order to meet up with Nikki and Darren from the Isles of Scilly Wildlife Trust. The Trust looks after 60 per cent of the Scillies. They have a ninety-nine-year lease from the ultimate power and landowner in these parts, the Duchy of Cornwall, the yearly payment for which is one daffodil. Under the Trust's care are all the uninhabited islands, the coasts of the inhabited ones (except for Tresco, which is leased to the Dorrien-Smith family), and St Mary's Lower and Higher Moors. Nikki and Darren are interested to know what Julian has told me and what his plan is. I am a little flustered to be imparting potentially important infor-mation – messages about badminton practice are more my style – and garble something about the errors of 'managed retreat', to which they readily agree. It seems I've come at a key time: old plans are being folded away but new ones have yet to be drawn up. Another complicating factor is that the Isles of Scilly Council is in the process of handing over responsibility for fresh water and sewage to a big supplier, South West Water. South West Water are promising to invest £40 million by 2030 but I doubt that protecting the islands from sea-level rise is part of their remit.

We walk beside a ditch that divides the Lower Moor. On one side are brackish water and an endemic species of sea rush; on the other are fresh water and common reed. Darren, the Trust's Head Ranger, is clad in waders; he's just come from chainsawing willows that are threatening to block the ditch. The Moor is hardly noticed by tourists keen to rush off to other islands but, for Darren and Nikki, this is a key landscape. We pass a concrete bunker where a fresh-water bore-hole draws up its precious resource. Keeping the Moor as wetland by controlling the water-level and managing its vegetation is essential not just for the human population but for many other species too. We hunch down on a walkway made of recycled plastic, and Darren draws up pond species found in few other places in the UK, such as Tubular Water-dropwort. Overhead he points out the black, gliding shape of a glossy ibis, a Mediterranean visitor which is becoming a more common sight as the climate warms. I can't help thinking that this is a Wildlife Trust like no other. It is working for both the human and non-human population and sees them as intimately connected.

During the tourist season the seas around St Mary's are full of chugging boats, ferrying visitors hither and thither. As soon as people land on one island they start thinking about another. Not many boats run in February and, anyway, I'm keen to get to Halangy and Bar Point, the northern sprig of St Mary's, which old maps show as offering a crossing point, a drowned road.

Julian tells me that, when his daughters were small, they would play at Halangy, calling it their fairy village. I'm here with my daughter, Aphra, who has moved on from her initial cynicism at the idea of my island adventures. I think she was hoping to join me on a more exotic destination but the Scillies do feel a world away, especially in this freakishly hot February. Aphra's too old to play fairies – in fact, I don't think she has *ever* played at fairies – but she's having fun leaping between the stones of the Iron Age village of Halangy. We drop down to the beach where signs of other ancient settlements have been found in the cliff face and have for many centuries been pulled apart and washed away by the rising sea. When we get to Bar Point there is plenty more evidence of prehistoric occupation, including a number of Bronze Age burial cairns. Aphra climbs on top of one that sits right on the coast. When built it would have been the summit of a hill surrounded by a broad valley laced with walled fields. The Scillies are so full of ancient graves that it has been speculated that important dead people from the mainland were rowed out here for burial. The landscape has so many layers of loss that, in quiet moments by the shore, it can feel a little odd that a tourist economy promising to deliver 'happy memories' has now been rolled out, smothering them all.

Back on the balcony of our holiday flat, my eye is drawn to the empty island of Samson. It has two low hills and is not inhabited nor much visited. For many thousands of years, however, it was home to untold generations, as testified by the many ancient sites and field walls scattered on it and around it in the sea. From the sixteenth century it was occupied and farmed by two large families, the Webbers and Woodcocks. The population was between thirty and forty by the end of the eighteenth century, though drought was common, meaning the island's small aquifer had to be supplemented by water brought from neighbouring islands. A Baptist minister called Bo'sun Smith (also known as the 'Seafarer's Apostle') visited in June 1818 and found a sorry scene. 'Two or three families are very poor, and have suffered much distress,' he reported, adding: 'their chief support has been limpets, as the immense piles of empty shells before their doors sufficiently testify.' The population was described as 'poor but industrious and pious'. So pious, in fact, that they may have been the last people in Britain to retain the Julian Calendar – celebrating 'Old Christmas' on 6 January – up until the time the island was finally abandoned in 1855. The islanders were given no choice but to depart, coerced into leaving by Augustus Smith, the Scillies' Lord Proprietor. Last to go was Mrs Webber who, it was said,

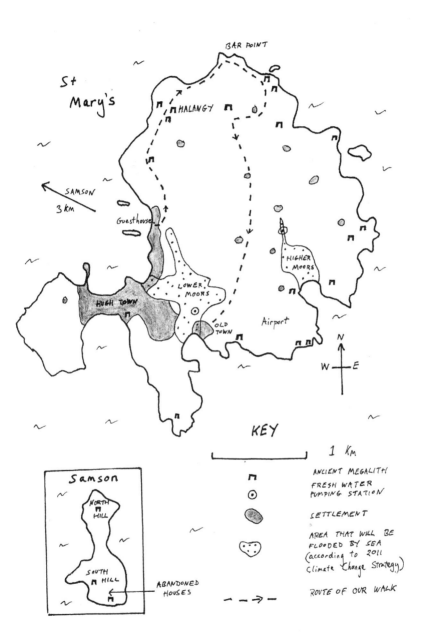

knew magic. As Charles Thomas retells the story, she 'put a spell on' Augustus Smith: 'His legs would not move, he was unable to get back in his boat, and the Tresco boatmen had to persuade the lady to lift the enchantment.' For Thomas, 'among all those strange nuances of atmosphere that Samson still breathes, grief is perhaps the strongest'.

Over its long history, the Isles of Scilly must have seen many abandonments. If it doesn't want more then 'managed retreat' will have to give way to resilience and protection. Easy to say. Especially for fair-weather friends. In a few days I'm scuttling away on a fifteen-minute plane ride, back to Land's End airport. I'm travelling away from a pretty place but I'm not leaving paradise. Like so many islands, fragility and melancholy is threaded through the beauty of the Isles of Scilly.

PART THREE

FUTURE

Future Islands

W HAT ARTIFICIAL ISLANDS will be built over the next fifty years? In order to understand where our age of islands is heading, I want to look at plans for three very different artificial islands: a free-trade utopia (Seasteading); a 6-square-kilometre energy hub (Dogger Bank Power Link Island) and one designed to give homes to over a million people (East Lantau Metropolis).

Will the appetite for new islands ever be sated? It seems we're not going to stop building them anytime soon. The end of the conveyor belt that is dropping islands off the coasts of the Gulf States and China is still not in sight, and many other countries – especially newly aspiring ones that want to attract and keep wealth close to their shores – are keen to get in on the action. They no longer look to places like Britain or the USA as models of development but to Dubai and China, and new islands are part of the package. One of the most ambitious is Lagos's Eko Atlantic, a 10-square-kilometre island of high-end apartments and stores. Designed for 250,000 residents, with a boulevard based on the Champs-Élysées, Eko Atlantic offers a haven for Nigeria's wealthy. They will be safe from the sea (the island is defended by the 8.5-kilometre 'Great Wall of Lagos' flood defence) and from the envious eyes of the rest of Lagos. These are islands of affluence; more specifically, they are examples of what some geographers call 'secessionary affluence': leaving the problems and the people of the ordinary city far behind.

Spin the globe to newly affluent economies further east and we find plenty more islands in the pipeline. One of the most spectacular will be Forest City, set in the Johor Strait between Malaysia and Singapore. It began in 2014 and its four artificial islands are designed to accommodate 700,000 people. As I write this, the first island, Country Garden Island, is already visible on Google Earth as a rather bleak building site, with a striking green patch where turf and tree-lined walkways have been rolled out around a hotel. The sales pitch for Forest City has an ethnic target. In one of the promotional videos a Chinese couple tell us that 'Many ethnic Chinese live here. For us, it's more like we're living in our hometown than a foreign country.' The idea seems to be that well-heeled Chinese, who are fed up with the pollution and crowds of Chinese cities, will want to invest in this cleaner, greener alternative. It almost goes without saying that another striking feature of Forest City is how much forest and other natural habitats have been destroyed to make it. Instead of mangrove forests there are golf courses; instead of seagrass meadows, there are planted road verges and gardens.

The offshoring of wealth and leisure demands both the presence of nature and that nature be ripped apart. These upmarket islands are outposts of a predatory and controlling infatuation: we love nature so much we have to own it, kill it then reproduce it in forms so small, so reduced, that it is graspable. The plans and pictures that sell these planned islands make them look like green fantasy lands. The painterly images produced for Toronto's new Villiers Island, which has the Don River winding through its middle and navigable canals on either side, show acres of flowering meadows and joggers joyously bouncing through canyons of trees. Property agents gush that 'Villiers Island will be roughly 88 acres in size and will be an ecological masterpiece.' However, this is a development that will provide the city with flood defence, as well as new land for houses and parks. At this stage, it does seem genuine in its attempt to strike a balance between environment, infrastructure and housing. It is being built around an urban river and on abandoned city lots. Unlike so many new islands, this is not a pristine habitat about to be wrecked but somewhere that a new island could have real environmental value and serve the city.

Today, environmental damage is one of the key reasons that island-building plans are likely to founder. Island-building projects are big, complex endeavours and there is ample opportunity and time for one partner or another to stall things or pull out. In the late 2010s the island-building market was showing signs of nerves. Plans were shelved, then dusted off again, only to be shelved once more. One plan that caught my eye was in Slovenia. Slovenia has no coastal islands: a point rubbed in by the fact that its southern neighbour, Croatia, has built a tourist economy on the back of having more than 1200. When it comes to tourism, countries with lots of islands are regarded as blessed. It follows that countries without any might want to build one. Slovenia's plan was modest: an island about the size of a large shopping mall, offering beaches, bars, restaurants, a wellness centre and a marina. But the finance for the new island comes and goes and politicians are uncertain. The project is in danger of turning from a grand hope into a national embarrassment. The same can be said, on a much bigger scale, about the Federation Islands, a 330-hectare archipelago in the shape of the Russian Federation planned for the Black Sea. After much fanfare, this great patriotic project stalled in 2012 and seems to have been officially forgotten. Jakarta's Great Garuda, a seventeen-island sea defence built in the shape of a giant eagle that was to be home to 300,000 people, has gone the same way. Once a centrepiece of national pride and not a little hope, its sea-wall – at 40 kilometres long and 24 metres tall – was supposed to bring long-term security and new housing land to the rapidly sinking city. But politicians began to look at it not as an eagle but a white elephant, and in 2018 the funding was pulled.

There are plenty of reasons to get cold feet. It often occurs when someone dares to ask what this shiny new island will look like in fifty or a hundred years' time. The blueprint that developers and politicians were enthusing over a moment ago suddenly seems less attractive. Some bright spark might venture that one solution to sea-level rise is to build floating platforms: they are cheap to construct and highly adaptable. But floating islands are dependent upon links to the mainland. They are also very vulnerable to storms and have a short shelf-life. The leading authority on floating platforms, Professor Wang Chien Ming, points out that platforms can only last fifty to a hundred years and that 'nobody would want to live there after a hundred years'.

In democratic societies, plans for new islands are always the subject of intense debate. Public controversy derailed plans for Belgium's first artificial island in 2018. Its supporters said it would protect the coast; its detractors said it would turn local beaches into rubbish-strewn dead zones. The mayor of the town next to the proposed island said: 'I was in Dubai to see how they handled it there. I passed a sewer full of plastic and oil. I wouldn't want to spend my holiday there.'

Because the role models come from the Gulf States and China, artificial islands come weighed down with certain images: of heedless consumerism, authoritarian government and environmental irresponsibility. In the West, the fame of these high-profile examples is acting as a brake on development. Since islands can protect coasts and create new land not just for people but for trees and wildlife, blanket hostility to them is short-sighted. The proponents of Belgium's island have thrown the question back to the objectors: if not this, then what?

As we have seen, most artificial islands cater for short-term and short-sighted human ambitions. As long as a sea view continues to attract premium property prices, the strange, paradoxical nature of our age of islands will persist. The need for infrastructure islands for dirty and noisy industries is also unlikely to abate, nor the military and territorial value of artificial islands, which has been proved in recent years in the South China Sea. Our age of islands is thrumming with activity: plenty are being built and plenty more are in the pipeline. But whatever they are used for, twenty-first-century islands will require a lot of maintenance: pumping stations will need to be oiled and ready to work round the clock, and sea-walls will need to be high.

SEASTEADING

Plans for the floating, libertarian city of Seasteading are well advanced. With the help of wealthy backers it is good to go; if only it could find a home. For a while it was envisaged Seasteading would land off the coast of

Honduras, then a lagoon in French Polynesia, where high-level conferences and a 'memorandum of understanding' seemed to have cemented the deal, with building to start in 2020. But protesters objected to the environmental impact of their would-be new neighbour, accusing Seasteading of being an elite plaything. In February 2018 the government of French Polynesia declared that the deal was off.

Seasteading is a tenacious project driven by the conviction that a free, mobile and entrepreneurial (or, as Seasteaders say, 'aquapreneurial') utopia is just within reach. Founded in 2008 with the help of a $500,000 donation from the co-founder of PayPal, Peter Thiel, it proposes a new model of citizenship based on 'dynamic geography'. Flexibility and choice are the guiding principles. The Seastead is conceived, as far as possible, to be separable into individual units that can relocate at will. The initial plans envisaged '50-meter-sided square and pentagon platforms with three-story buildings'. The platforms would be made of concrete and 'could be constructed for approximately $500/square foot of usable space'.

Concrete floating platforms, usually held in position by anchored wires, have been in use for thirty years and are a proven technology. The innovation was not in the engineering but in the overall ambition. Seasteading is a way of life, a movement, that wants to reimagine our relationship to government and territory. By preference, its destination is the open sea, since in international waters Seasteaders would not be thwarted by government. Beyond territorial waters, a new beginning can be made. Seasteading was founded by Patri Friedman, the grandson of the famous, Nobel-prize winning advocate of the free market, the economist Milton Friedman. Patri explains that 'When seasteading becomes a viable alternative, switching from one government to another would be a matter of sailing to the other without even leaving your house.' In the project's principal research report, it is explained that 'If modular ocean homes and offices are mobile and can be reassembled according to individual preferences, small groups of entrepreneurs and investors can feasibly build "startup" societies on earth's last unclaimed frontier.'

Although 'movability all the way down to the size of a single autonomous house' is the ideal, the authors of the project's report are aware of the problems that multiple connections between lots of individual units would create and so they propose a variety of configurations. The Seasteaders are not wedded to any one design: 'Seasteading' is a verb rather than a thing, it is a practice that can be adopted and adapted, allowing 'the evolution of new societies and forms of governance'.

Seasteading: How Floating Nations Will Restore the Environment, Enrich the Poor, Cure the Sick, and Liberate Humanity from Politicians is the ambitious title of Seasteading spokesperson Joe Quirk's book-length manifesto. It's worth drilling down into that long subtitle.

"Scenarios of Relocation"

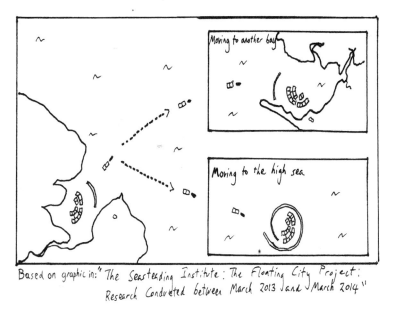

Based on graphic in:" The Seasteading Institute: The Floating City Project: Research Conducted between March 2013 and March 2014"

'Cure the sick'? In a series of web shorts, Quirk explains that 'our parents' regulations are preventing today's innovations, and that today: 'In the United States it takes ten years and a billion dollars to bring a new drug to market'. Free of all that red tape, seasteads will be places where new medicines can be created. 'Enrich the poor'? Seasteading takes inspiration from small island nations that have been rapidly transformed from poor to rich. To a backdrop of glitzy photographs of Singapore and Hong Kong, Quirk's message is that 'every time a new island nation hits restart with new rules based on modern knowledge, the poor create their own wealth'. 'Restore the environment'? This claim is based on a variety of green-tech solutions, most notably the use of the temperature difference between deep ocean water and warm tropical surface waters to produce electricity (ocean thermal energy conversion) and the farming of algae-based biofuels.

There is a bubbling energy to the seasteading movement. I'm not attracted to its ultra-mobile, aquapreneurial, political programme. But then I'm not much of a libertarian: from what I've seen, when we turn our back on government the outcome is an even worse kind of tyranny. Yet I can't help admiring Seasteading: like all the best utopias, it combines big ideas with an obsession with the details.

A willingness to adapt the grand plan in order to get the ball rolling led to the 'memorandum of understanding' with French Polynesia and an agreed site, a sheltered lagoon in French Polynesian waters. The French Polynesians were interested in hosting an innovative 'smart city' that could bring in jobs and money. For their part, the Seasteaders have come to accept that international waters are a tough place to launch their dreams. Big waves and deep waters mean that small-scale floating structures would be tossed about like a cork. A larger city would fare better but as a first step that was never likely and, in any case, there is still much to learn about how any such structure would cope with rough water. A Seasteading feasibility report notes that 'semisubmersibles and breakwaters are the options most suitable for the open ocean' but that 'the costs of a breakwater are prohibitively expensive'. The idea that individual units would be detachable and be able to sail away at any time, adds on even more costs. The favoured plan for the Polynesian site was a decidedly fixed-looking horseshoe of individual floating homes joined by short pontoons to a large multi-storeyed platform with shops and offices. The promotional film made to sell the project doesn't even mention the detachability of units. The emphasis is on convincing the outside world that this is an environmentally sensitive proposal and that it would be self-funded.

So what next for Seasteading? Its relationship to the Pacific has been kept alive by Marc Collins, a Tahiti-based entrepreneur who was instrumental in first getting the Seasteaders to locate their operations to French Polynesia. Collins's company, Blue Frontiers, caused a lot of media interest when its plans for a sustainable floating city were unveiled at the United Nations in New York in 2019. Blue Frontier's focus is on creating self-sufficient, environmentally friendly cities that can survive an era of climate chaos. The libertarian politics is no longer quite so prominent. But Collins is very much a seasteader: it's an idea, an identity, that is proving adaptable and tenacious. A seastead city is still probably a long way off. But this movement has already, in part, succeeded: the idea is out there.

DOGGER BANK POWER LINK ISLAND, NORTH SEA

The North Sea is rough and cold but it boasts the world's largest collection of wind farms. All these turbines need regular maintenance and long cables connecting them, so it's no surprise that a new 'Power Link' island is being planned at the heart of the North Sea, about 100 kilometres off the east coast of England. The proposed island is perfectly round, with a key-shaped harbour running into its centre to allow sheltered anchorage. It will also have workshops, accommodation blocks and a runway. Dogger Bank Power Link Island is designed to be a place staff can live on rather than just endure, so it also has an artificial lake and a cluster of trees and green spaces. The planned island is 6 square kilometres: a little smaller than Gibraltar. It is a major undertaking and, once completed, will transform how we think about the North Sea. At the time of writing, work on the island has not started but the plans are well advanced and backed by serious money. It is estimated it will take seven years to build and is scheduled for completion between 2030 and 2050.

Over 70 per cent of Europe's offshore wind installations are in the North Sea. Rob van der Hage, who works for one of the energy firms investing in the project, explained to the *Guardian*, 'The big challenge we are facing towards 2030 and 2050 is onshore wind is hampered by local opposition and nearshore is nearly full. It's logical we are looking at areas further offshore.' Going that far out to sea also means that turbines can take advantage of the fact that wind speeds are generally faster and more constant in open water. Distance from shore normally means greater water depths, but the North Sea has an unusual underwater topographical feature: a range of underwater sandy hills, called Dogger Bank. In this shallow zone the water is just 15–20 metres deep, which makes it far cheaper and safer to build on.

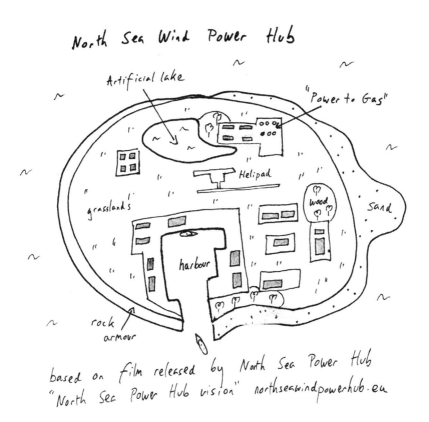

North Sea Wind Power Hub

based on film released by North Sea Power Hub
"North Sea Power Hub vision" northseawindpowerhub.eu

Dogger Bank Power Link Island will sit at the centre of 10,000 wind turbines. It is the brainchild of North Sea Wind Power Hub, a consortium of European power suppliers (TenneT and Gasunie in the Netherlands and Germany and Energinet in Denmark), with additional collaboration from the Port of Rotterdam. Torben Glar Nielsen, Energinet's technical director, told the *Independent*: 'Maybe it sounds a bit crazy and science fiction-like but an island on Dogger Bank could make the wind power of the future a lot cheaper and more effective.' The word 'crazy' was picked up in the newspaper's headline but it's an increasingly old-fashioned perspective. Artificial islands have long since ceased to be outlandish. The Dutch are well used to building islands and, given the growth of turbines in the North Sea, the proposal is long overdue.

The island will be built at the far end of Dutch waters, so it will be within the Dutch Exclusive Economic Zone. If it was moved a bit to the west it would be in British waters, but this is a Dutch-German-Danish initiative rather than a British one and it is Europe-facing. It seeks to create an integrated cross-border network of sustainable energy supply. It's interesting to note that the island would give the Dutch a case to extend their territorial waters westwards into UK waters (since, once built, Dutch waters would extend from the island). This is not a topic that has even been raised, at least not publicly, but it's a reminder of the importance of being involved early on in big schemes on your doorstep. If ever relations between the UK and the rest of Europe were to get even worse than they are at present, and the lines of ownership in the North Sea were to come into dispute, Dogger Bank Power Link Island would quickly come to be seen as more than just an energy hub.

Looking at the plans of the company that has been doing most of the legwork, the Dutch state-owned TenneT, it's clear that Dogger Bank Power Link Island is a long-term destination and that there will be other, smaller hub islands built before it. These will also be in Dutch waters but closer to home, feeding energy back into what the company identifies as European 'load pockets'. Load pockets are zones of high demand, and the companies involved in the Dogger Bank project have identified six: high-demand, densely populated areas of England, the Netherlands, Germany and Belgium, with the North Sea Hub sitting at their centre.

The bottom line for the Dogger Bank island and its smaller forebears is that they will reduce costs. Running off-shore wind farms from the mainland is expensive: constant ferrying of people and equipment over choppy waters adds up and so does having to stretch submarine power cables over such great distances. Having the island on Dogger Bank will shorten all sorts of connections and make it possible to send off energy in different directions, enabling the island's owners to trade power in multiple markets. The involvement of the gas company Gasunie, which is also owned by the

Dutch government, tells us that the island will not just be for electricity; the idea is that it will also enable 'power to gas'. What this means is that some of the electricity generated by wind power will be turned into gas. This can be done by electrolysis: splitting water into hydrogen and oxygen. The hydrogen can then be stored underground in empty oil and gas fields. The point, as always, is cost. Gas is much cheaper to send and store than electricity.

Tens of millions of people pass through infrastructure islands, such as airports, but most are out of sight and out of mind. We are increasingly intolerant of seeing, smelling and hearing the consequences of our industrialized lives – the garbage depots and chemical works we all rely on – and the twenty-first century is likely to see many more planners reach for the neat but expensive solution of offshoring. A lot of people in the crowded nations of north-west Europe don't want huge wind turbines marching over their precious countryside. But that's not the only thing going on here. The North Sea is being reimagined: turned from an empty in-between space into a heartland. It sits at the centre of one of the world's most populous and wealthiest regions. In every one of those nations people are scratching their heads, trying to find new sources of clean energy. Reimagining the North Sea as no longer a zone to hurry over but as a hub – a site of connections and networks, sending out power in all directions – is ambitious, even visionary, but it's also sensible.

EAST LANTAU METROPOLIS, HONG KONG

Housing costs are sky-high in Hong Kong. A lot of people find they don't have much left over once they have paid the rent, and even those with decent jobs can find themselves wedged into apartments not much bigger than a parking space. It's no wonder that the Hong Kong government's 'Lantau Tomorrow Vision' – a plan to provide new housing for 1.1 million people, with 70 per cent promised to be public housing – is attractive. East Lantau Metropolis is due to be constructed over the next thirty years on 1700 hectares of new islands.

Lantau is Hong Kong's largest island. It's a hilly oasis of green, home to the 'Buddhist Five Zen Forests', with the flat expanse of Chek Lap Kok International Airport sprouting off its northern side. The 'new vision' is for three islands on its eastern side. The official plan shows that the first to be built will completely surround the small uninhabited island of Kau Yi Chau, which would be retained as a park sitting at the centre of the new townscape. The second phase will be the Hei Ling Chau artificial islands, which will be squeezed between a number of natural islands, turning the landscape into a hopscotch of urban and green islands.

Everyone agrees that the current scarcity of housing is unacceptable. The Hong Kong government has said that if

East Lantau Metropolis

CHEK LAP KOK AIRPORT

DISNEY LAND

KAU YI CHAU

LANTAU

forest

forest

forest

mountains

mountains

reservoir

SUNSHINE ISLAND

HEI LING CHAU

KEY

4 km

+ + + + + + PLANNED RAIL

PLANNED ROAD

+ + + + + + POSSIBLE RAIL

- - - - - - POSSIBLE ROAD

EAST LANTAU METROPOLIS

Source: based on 'Lantau Tomorrow' (2019)

new homes are not going to be built in open water then Hong Kong will have to sacrifice some of its much-loved countryside. Amy Cheung Yi-mei, a director from the government's Planning Department points out: 'If we are able to develop the East Lantau Metropolis, we would not need to touch the country parks.' With the new islands, the government argues, a balance between nature and development can be struck. The islands will be plugged into road, rail and air transport links, turning Lantau into a major international economic hub. The idea is that, where possible, the new land will be bulked out with local construction waste

(Hong Kong produces about 1500 tonnes of rubble a year) rather than imported sand. There are other green promises. The new islands will have 'eco-shorelines' to nurture biodiversity and will be part of a wider programme of nature conservation across Lantau.

The plans for East Lantau Metropolis have met with serious push-back. A decade or two ago this kind of megaproject would have sailed through – just another incredible feat following in the wake of the new airport and the Hong Kong–Macao bridge. But the mood has shifted. When critics point out that the new islands could be underwater by the end of the century, they are listened to. Creating homes for such a huge number of people on a coastal 'frontline' that is set to be pounded by typhoons and swamped by sea-surges seems a curious way of spending $64 billion (this is the estimated cost, though some say it will be double that). The project is also highlighting Hong Kong's fractious relationship with mainland China. Its advocates think it will help preserve autonomy but many Hongkongers regard it as just another mainland imposition. It's hard to find anyone in favour of the 'Lantau Tomorrow Vision' in the comment pages of Hong Kong newspapers: 'Like all major HK recent projects, this useless idea will take close to 29 years to materialise. By that time HK will be part of Shenzhen with a lot more available land and more beyond'; 'By the time it's finished, it will seem ridiculous to have spent so much time and so much money on making a small piece of land in the sea.'

For others the main issue is the destruction of the green island of Lantau. A Save Lantau Alliance has sprung up, arguing that 'the protection of Lantau Island is not only to defend Hong Kong's back garden and the last piece of pure land, but also to say "no" to the government's violent rape of public opinion and blindly following the Mainland!' Protesters have taken to the streets, and public opinion, which might once have been assumed to be desperate for new homes, seems to have turned. In part this is because the claim that there is nowhere else to build has been disputed by those who point to large areas of undeveloped and 'brownfield' land in the city, especially in the New Territories area. Tom Yam from Save Lantau Alliance says: 'The government wants to take the path of least resistance: the middle of the sea', even though 'brownfield patches remain untouched'.

In the Gulf States and now in China, island-building has started to become a default option for growing coastal cities looking for more land. Island-building is tried, tested and cost-effective. The Hong Kong government says that the cost of creating land on new islands is up to 30 per cent cheaper than building on brownfield sites and that it makes more sense to have housing close to the city centre than in the relatively distant New Territories. It's also true that properties with sea views still sell for more than those staring over urban sprawl so, whatever the promises of social housing, developers can look forward to healthy profits.

But something is missing: a proper appreciation of the climate changes and disappearing shorelines that threaten Hong Kong. The master plan, which goes under the title 'Preliminary Concepts for the East Lantau Metropolis', gives climate change just one cursory sentence: 'The reclamation level and infrastructure at the coastal areas should be resilient to extreme weather conditions.' It's a throwaway line, an afterthought. East Lantau Metropolis may well be home for 1.1 million people but surprisingly little attention has been given to its future.

Not an Ending

ISLANDS ARE RISING and falling. We keep building islands even as natural islands are disappearing. The new ones are not very high and they are vulnerable to storms and sea-surges. Are we crazy?

It's a serious question. In the HQ of a Dubai developer looking at maps of The World and The Universe – or watching the film of China's Ocean Flower, whose leaf-shaped islands jostle with high-rises and enclose a lotus-shaped island of medieval castles and rollercoasters, or entering the gloom of a hut made of palm fronds in Panama, where each winter the water swirls across the sandy floor – it seems an inevitable question. The delirious, abnormal quality of many artificial islands is brazenly celebrated, and any species that wilfully wrecks its habitat can justifiably be accused of losing the plot.

So are we crazy? I guess we must be. But it's an infectious madness. So many yearnings are being concentrated on islands – these little spaces of escape, delight and fear. And as long as people will pay over the odds for the privilege of looking out over water, island-building will continue to be a moneymaker. The story of relocation will continue too – as long as people in places that are disappearing are unable or unwilling to protect themselves. Relocation is a chapter in this story that has barely begun. We are on its first page, perhaps even just its first line. The rises in sea level seen so far are as nothing to what is predicted. Hundreds of millions live on vulnerable coastlines and every year more arrive.

We can't keep away from the sea even though we know it is dangerous. It's a perilous love affair, a deep need that goes beyond the pursuit of wealth, exclusivity or glamour. The central question of *The Drowned World*, J. G. Ballard's 1962 science-fiction novel about an inundated, overheating planet, is why people don't do anything to stop it. Ballard's curious speculative theory is that an 'atavistic' part of the brain has been triggered – a primal urge to *go back* to the place where we first evolved, and to slip, slither and fall away into the amniotic ocean.

Shorn of the idea that all we ever really wanted is to grow back our gills, and rephrased as an evolutionary predisposition to seek out and be close to water, 'aquaphilia' does help explain something of our current dilemma, of our simultaneous running towards and away from the threatening shoreline. At the start of this book I dragged up a memory: of how, as children, my brother, sister and I would scramble across to a tiny island in a patch of woodland called Wintry Wood and then stand there, wondering what to do next. It's an experience I've had many times on my island travels. For each island I've wanted to get to, I've had to plan my trip very carefully, not having the time or the money for a second attempt. The build-up has been long and costly but, once there – once I'm safely ashore – well, what then? There is not much to do on small islands. It's just like back in Wintry Wood. Elation and restlessness. It was the journey that mattered. The heart of any island is the water crossed.

Artificial islands are older than recorded history but the most ancient examples tend to be modest and low-lying affairs even when they required untold generations to build them. By contrast, many twenty-first-century islands are eye candy, whoopingly unnatural. They are deranged. But with that off-kilter ambition comes hope, for all things seem possible. Time and again, from Phoenix Island to Chek Lap Kok and from Ocean Reef to Fiery Cross Reef, I've been startled and – despite everything, despite knowing better – delighted at the audacity and creativity of our age of islands.

The big question is this: is it possible to harness all that boldness and inventiveness for schemes that are sustainable and of value to a threatened planet? We know that islands can be key to coastal protection, that they can act as flood defences. If built wisely they could provide protection, farmland and living space as well as enhance terrestrial biodiversity and increase forest cover. Flevopolder, the oldest of our era's unnatural islands, is still the biggest and – despite its flat, geometric landscape – in many ways the most impressive. Not only does it provide arable crops, flood defence for a swathe of the Netherlands, and houses for people of all incomes, but recent years have seen a determined effort both on Flevopolder and on small, wildlife haven islands off its shores to provide habitats for species other than our own.

Building an island always comes with costs but if they are going to be built, we should insist they add more than they subtract from the environment. There are various international protocols already in place that nudge developers in this direction but they clearly aren't working. A robust evaluation would look at the whole operation – from the energy spent in digging the first spadefuls of sand to the ongoing resources allocated in keeping the lights on and the toilets flushing in 'ultra-star' hotels – and insist that, overall, there is a net benefit to climate change and biodiversity. That might drain the blood from some developers' faces but, as we have seen, the watchwords of modern island-building are boldness and ambition; the impossible is being built in such places every day. That unstoppable energy is just what we need, but channelled towards a greener, long-term future.

Thinking up new islands is a lot of fun. I couldn't leave this journey without coming up with one of my own. Here it is, set in the wide bay in eastern England called The Wash. I've often thought it was odd that, almost within foghorn distance of the industrious Dutch, this large, square-shaped and shallow inlet has been left fallow. It does have a couple of small infrastructure islands, built and then abandoned in the 1970s to test the feasibility of creating a tidal barrage, and much of the surrounding land was reclaimed from the sea centuries ago. Today, a significant portion of eastern England is threatened with flooding. A new island in The Wash wouldn't solve that problem but it could make any inundations more manageable and less disastrous. Guthlac Island is named after St Guthlac, a local island-dwelling hermit who was once much venerated in the region. It would be a wetland, some 1521 square kilometres in size, given over to marsh and river species now extinct or largely diminished elsewhere in the UK. It would be dotted with small

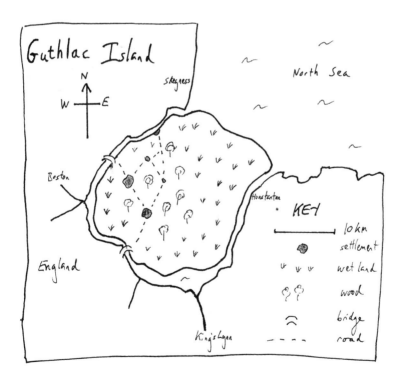

settlements and, to make it financially possible, a couple of towns. It would be spectacular but nothing like Dubai; Guthlac would offer a different type of amazement. It would be an island for geese, herons, otters and eels as much as for people – one designed for today and for tomorrow.

I started this book with a pull of the oars that took me ashore an unnamed crannog, one of many antique artificial islands that sprinkle the lochs of Ireland and Scotland. We've been building islands for a long, long time. They have been disappearing for a long time too. Those two things have now speeded up and changed in scale and meaning. Island-building is not working with the planet anymore; it has been malformed by hubris and greed. The remnants of much older human-made islands are still there, signposts to the brevity of our lives and our era. Unvisited and unnamed like the crannog, little more than a black lump of lifeless stones in a cold Scottish loch. Yet, for all that, it catches the eye and the prow draws closer.

Acknowledgements

Many people have helped me with this book over the past few years, given me their time, shown me hospitality or simply shown me the way. My editors – James Nightingale, Charlotte Atyeo and Mary Laur – have also provided invaluable assistance. Special thanks are due to my Rachel, Louis and Aphra and also my mum, Shirley Bonnett, for diligently reading through the manuscript and trying to sort out my punctuation.

Bibliography

Appleton, Jay, *The Experience of Landscape*, John Wiley: London, 1975

Baldacchino, Godfrey, *A World of Islands: An Island Studies Reader*, Institute of Island Studies, University of Prince Edward Island: Prince Edward Island, 2007

Ballard, J. G., *The Drowned World*, Victor Gollancz: London, 1962

Bauhaus, Eric, *The Panama Cruising Guide*, Sailors Publications: Panama, 2014

Cronin, William, *The Disappearing Islands of the Chesapeake*, Johns Hopkins University Press: Baltimore, 2005

Díaz del Castillo, Bernal, *The True History of the Conquest of New Spain: Volume One*, Routledge: Abingdon, 2016

Displacement Solutions, *One Step at a Time: The Relocation Process of the Gardi Sugdub Community in Gunayala, Panama: Mission Report*, Displacement Solutions, 2015, accessed at: http://displacementsolutions.org/new-report-on-the-planned-relocation-of-the-gardi-sug-dub-community-in-gunayala-panama/

Gutiérrez, Gerardo, 'Mexico-Tenochtitlan: origin and transformations of the last Mesoamerican imperial city', in

Yoffee, Norman (Editor), *The Cambridge World History: Volume 3, Early Cities in Comparative Perspective, 4000 BCE-12000 CE*, Cambridge University Press: Cambridge, 2015

Herodotus, *Histories*, Hackett: Indianapolis, 2014

Hong Kong Government, *Hong Kong 2030: Preliminary Concepts for the East Lantau Metropolis*, Development Bureau and Planning Department: Hong Kong, 2016

Howe, James, *A People Who Would Not Kneel: Panama, the United States and the San Blas Kuna*, Smithsonian Institution: Washington, D.C, 1998

Lawrence, D. H., 'The Man Who Loved Islands' in *D. H. Lawrence: Selected Stories*, Penguin: London, 2007

More, Thomas, *Utopia*, Cambridge University Press: Cambridge, 2016

Quirk, Joe, *Seasteading: How Floating Nations Will Restore the Environment, Enrich the Poor, Cure the Sick, and Liberate Humanity from Politicians*, Free Press: New York, 2017

Records of the Grand Historian: Records of the Grand Historian of China: The Age of Emperor Wu, 140 to circa 100 B.C., Columbia University Press: New York, 1961

The Rough Guide to Dubai, Rough Guides Ltd: London, 2016

The Seasteading Institute, *The Floating City Project: Research Conducted between March 2013 and March 2014*, The Seasteading Institute, accessed at: http://www. seasteading.org/wp-content/uploads/2015/12/Floating-City-Project-Report-4_25_2014.pdf

Thomas, Charles, *Exploration of a Drowned Landscape: Archaeology and History of the Isles of Scilly*, B.T. Batsford: London, 1985

Tuan, Yi-Fu, *Topophilia: A Study of Environmental Perception, Attitudes, and Values*, Prentice Hall: Englewood Cliffs, N.J., 1974

Index